ENLIGHTENED SENTIMENTS

Enlightened Sentiments

JUDGMENT AND AUTONOMY IN THE
AGE OF SENSIBILITY

Hina Nazar

Fordham University Press

NEW YORK ‡ 2012

Fordham University Press has no responsibility for the persistence or
accuracy of URLs for external or third-party Internet websites referred
to in this publication and does not guarantee that any content on such
websites is, or will remain, accurate or appropriate.

Fordham University Press also publishes its books in a variety of
electronic formats. Some content that appears in print may not be
available in electronic books.

Library of Congress Cataloging-in-Publication Data

Nazar, Hina.
  Enlightened sentiments : judgment and autonomy in the
age of sensibility / Hina Nazar. — 1st ed.
    p. cm.
  Includes bibliographical references and index.
  ISBN 978-0-8232-4007-4 (cloth : alk. paper)
  1. English fiction—18th century—History and criticism.
  2. French fiction—18th century—History and criticism.
  3. Sentimentalism in literature. 4. Judgment in literature.
  5. Richardson, Samuel, 1689–1761. Clarissa. 6. Rousseau, Jean-Jacques,
  1712–1778. Nouvelle Héloïse. 7. Austen, Jane, 1775–1817. Sense and
  sensibility. 8. Judgment (Ethics)—
History—18th century. 9. Autonomy (Philosophy)—History—18th
century. 10. Aesthetics, Modern—18th century. I. Title.
II. Title: Judgment and autonomy in the age of sensibility.
  PR830.S45N39 2012
  820.9′005—dc23

                                              2011046354

Printed in the United States of America
14 13 12 5 4 3 2 1
First edition

CONTENTS

ACKNOWLEDGMENTS

It is gratifying that a book about the dialogic entailments of the critical posture should itself have been shaped by sustained conversation and debate. I am especially indebted to many long discussions with Amanda Anderson and Frances Ferguson, whose encouragement and insights I have found consistently enabling. Thanks are due also to my other teachers at Johns Hopkins University—Neil Hertz, Walter Benn Michaels, Jerome Christensen, and Alan Grossman—all of whom encouraged their students to defy conventional wisdom with courage and *éclat* whenever possible. My postdoctoral fellowship at Cornell University brought me in contact with Harry E. Shaw and James Eli Adams, both of whom exemplify that rare combination of scrupulous intellect and affability which Enlightenment thinkers like David Hume valued so greatly. At the University of Illinois I have been lucky to count as colleagues Peter K. Garrett, Lauren M. E. Goodlad, Anthony Pollock, Robert Markley, Vicki Mahaffey, Curtis Perry, Jed Esty, Julia Saville, Ted Underwood, Eleanor Courtemanche, and Gillen d'Arcy Wood, all of whom have generously read and commented upon my work at various points. Conversations with scholars at other institutions, including David Wayne Thomas, Andrew H. Miller, Amy Hungerford, and Kantik Ghosh, have fundamentally shaped my thinking about professional and intellectual matters alike.

Helen Tartar and Tom Lay at Fordham University Press have been remarkably generous guides through the impersonal publication process. I thank them for their support and their attentiveness to the imperatives of first-book publishing.

On a more personal note, I want to acknowledge the unstinting encouragement of my family in Pakistan, England, and Italy—especially my father, Nazar Abbas Siddiqui, and my sisters, Saba Nazar and Bina Qasim—and of friends like Vanessa de l'Or and Marianne Camerer. Above all, I thank my husband, Gian Casartelli, who read every word of this book multiple times, talked about reflective judgment with anyone who would listen, and lifted me from the doldrums on many an occasion with the most amazing cooking from Emilia Romagna.

Institutional support from the University of Illinois at Urbana-Champaign and a Mellon postdoctoral fellowship at Cornell University enabled research on this book. Portions of chapter 5 appeared in an early form as "The Imagination Goes Visiting: Jane Austen, Judgment, and the Social," *Nineteenth-Century Literature* 59, no. 2 (September 2004): 145–78, © 2004 by the Regents of the University of California. An article version of chapter 3 was published as "Judging Clarissa's Heart" in *ELH* 79, no. 1 (March 2012), © Johns Hopkins University Press. I thank the University of California Press and Johns Hopkins University Press for permission to reprint this material.

This book is dedicated with the greatest affection to my mother, Suraiya Nazar (1943–1995), who first introduced me to the provocations of literature.

ENLIGHTENED SENTIMENTS

Introduction

A REVALUATION OF THE ENLIGHTENMENT is currently under-
way in literary studies and critical theory. Blanket suspicion of
the eighteenth century's liberal legacies, of the sort instantiated by
poststructuralism and related critical developments of the past few
decades, no longer appears as critical as it once did. Several scholars
have argued that a wholesale rejection of Enlightenment values
produces a damaging gap between our theories and practices, since
intellectual work is far more indebted to the Enlightenment norms of
critical distance and reflective individuality than our theoretical
hostility toward them implies.[1] Others have pointed to the diversity
and internal complexity of the liberal tradition emanating from the
eighteenth century, which discourage sweeping generalizations about
the Enlightenment or *the* project of modernity.[2] On these readings, we
risk questioning the interest of our own engagement with the period
when we reduce its normative claims to a set of obviously problematic
theses about infallible reason and sovereign selfhood.[3] And finally,
some of the most intriguing trends in recent theory, such as the turns
to ethics and aesthetics, have sympathetically reassessed the subject-
centered perspectives dominating eighteenth-century literature and
philosophy.[4]

Enlightened Sentiments builds on these reassessments but directs
attention to a chapter of Enlightenment history and modern liberal
culture that has remained in the shadows of recent discussions: the
wide-ranging development of eighteenth-century letters known as
sentimentalism.[5] Often interpreted as an affective outlier vis-à-vis a
predominantly rationalist Enlightenment, sentimentalism, I argue,
importantly shaped one of the Enlightenment's principal legacies to
the modern world: the ideal of autonomy or moral self-direction,

which began to compete with an older morality of obedience in the eighteenth century.[6] Highly controversial in recent times—owing to its supposed neglect of the social and material contexts of subjectivity—autonomy, I contend, takes on a flexible and postmetaphysical character when viewed through the lens of such key works of the long eighteenth century as David Hume's *A Treatise of Human Nature* (1739–40) and "Of the Standard of Taste" (1757); Samuel Richardson's *Clarissa; or, The History of a Young Lady* (1747–48); Adam Smith's *Theory of Moral Sentiments* (1759, 1790); Jean-Jacques Rousseau's *Julie; or, The New Heloise* (1761); Henry Mackenzie's *Julia de Roubigné* (1777); William Godwin's *Fleetwood; or, The New Man of Feeling* (1805); and Jane Austen's *Sense and Sensibility* (1811).

In making this argument, I follow especially closely the sentimental rhetoric of *judgment*, a principle connotation of the word sentiment in the eighteenth century.[7] By contrast with the a priori character it develops in many Enlightenment paradigms, judgment emerges under sentimentalism as a worldly and contingent process, one that is inextricably tied to feelings and sociability. The sentimental judge I reconstruct in this study is unlike, for example, the moral judge described by Immanuel Kant in such influential expositions of autonomy as the *Groundwork of the Metaphysics of Morals* (1785) and the *Critique of Practical Reason* (1788). While Kant's judge assumes the persona of a radically detached noumenal self, the judge of sentimental fiction and philosophy finds her reasoned standards in dialogue with other people. In this context, I highlight the extensive parallelism of ethics and aesthetics established by sentimental writers such as David Hume, Adam Smith, and Henry Mackenzie, as well as by seemingly unsentimental authors such as William Godwin and Jane Austen. In *A Treatise of Human Nature*, Hume contends, for example, that goodness is like beauty in that it does not inhere in the objects or actions that we deem beautiful or good. Instead, aesthetic and moral judgments have an ineluctable subjective quality—they are subjective perceptions—and the only standard we can bring to bear in ascribing goodness or beauty to things in the world is intersubjectively enabled.[8] Taste, Hume argues in "Of the Standard of Taste," finds its (always contingent) standards in "a considerable uniformity of sentiment among men."[9] The eponymous heroine of Samuel Richardson's *Clarissa* concurs when she asks her friend Anna Howe whether it should "not be our aim to judge of ourselves, and of everything that affects us, as we may reasonably imagine other people would judge of us and our actions?"[10] As I explain in chapter 3 below, Clarissa Harlowe's point is not that young women should accept the judgments of others but rather that they should engage the judgments of as many others as possible in order to cultivate critical distance from their own personal biases—that is, in order to cultivate the standpoint of impartiality, a pivotal standard of judgment in Richardson's narrative. The interest of Clarissa's curiously sociable quest for impartiality is reinforced by the epistolary form of the novel in which she appears, which depicts judgment as a development of written exchange between peers rather than as a lonely monologue in the head of its heroine.

The sentimentalists' accounts of impartiality and the standards of judgment have resonance, moreover, well beyond the British Enlightenment, and I track, in particular, how the motif of judgment produces a still understudied line of connection between the British and the German Enlightenments. What the political theorist Michael Frazer has recently described as the myth of the two Enlightenments—a British Enlightenment that was empiricist and sentimental, and a German Enlightenment that was rationalist—has long diminished our understandings of each national Enlightenment, as well as of the larger tradition of liberal ethics and politics to which both contributed.[11] Rather than interpreting sentimentalists like Hume as the natural antagonists of rationalists like Kant, I treat them as mutually engaged in an ongoing liberal project that seeks normative underpinnings for a postmetaphysical age. The British sentimentalists' understanding of moral and aesthetic judgment shows remarkable affinity, for example, to aesthetic judgment as theorized by Kant in the *Critique of Judgment* (1790).[12] Like the British sentimentalists, Kant, and still more force-fully, recent interpreters of his work such as Hannah Arendt, suggest that aesthetic judgment finds its rules not in a supersensible Reason but in an interactive procedure of dialogue and deliberation. "The power of judgment," Arendt contends, "rests on a potential agreement with others, and the thinking process which is active in judging something is not, like the thought process of pure reasoning, a dialogue between me and myself, but finds itself always and primarily, even if I am quite alone in making up my mind, in an anticipated communication with others with whom I know I must finally come to an agreement."[13] Elsewhere she observes that "the only nonsubjective element in the nonobjective senses [aesthetic taste] is intersubjectivity."[14]

The picture of autonomy that accompanies aesthetic and sentimental delineations of judgment situates the self in a social space, as exemplified by the epistolary space of innumerable eighteenth-century sentimental novels, as well as by the drawing rooms of Jane Austen's nineteenth-century novels of manners. I suggest that British sentimentalism's and Kantian aesthetics' pointed invocations of sociability as the grounds of impartiality produce a valuable intervention also in recent debates about the socially constituted subject, a near-universal premise of the contemporary humanities. As interpreted by poststructuralist theorists such as Michel Foucault and Judith Butler, the premise of constitution invokes a social order in which hegemonic norms identify individual claims to critical distance and autonomy as yet another instantiation of the power–knowledge matrix of modern disciplinary societies.[15] By contrast, the writers on judgment I consider specify a social domain of competing perspectives that can be brought into productive interplay. Nothing in this broadly liberal alternative to poststructuralist understandings denies the existence of power asymmetries or the possibility that individual standpoints are shaped and circumscribed by particular historical and material circumstances. Indeed, it is because they are so shaped and circumscribed that it becomes interesting and important to bring them into conversation. The sentimentalists and Kantians I summon depart from their poststructuralist interlocutors not because they ignore the social constituents of subjectivity but because they are interested in how differently constituted standpoints can be engaged to complicate—rather than transcend—bias. As I explain in chapter 1, they thereby maintain a perspectivism that Foucauldian and queer theories obscure through their representation of all points of view as the point of view of a univocal power.

In the next chapter, "Reconstructing Sentimentalism," I situate my study in the contexts of recent scholarship on sentimentalism and recent debates about the pros and cons of Enlightenment modernity. New Historicist rehabilitations of an eighteenth-century "culture of sensibility" have productively complicated traditional literary history's dismissal of sentimentalism as a cultural embarrassment and have significantly enhanced our understanding of noncanonical fiction between Richardson and Austen.[16] Nonetheless, the excision of intellectual history from many such readings has oftentimes obscured the ideological diversity of sentimental writings and even reinforced traditional literary history's argument that sentimentalism was grounded in dubious claims about an essentially good human nature and innately good feelings. I challenge this simplification by foregrounding the rhetoric of detachment and judgment permeating such key works of the sentimental tradition as Henry Mackenzie's *Julia de Roubigné*, David Hume's *A Treatise of Human Nature* and *An Enquiry Concerning the Principles of Morals* (1751), and Adam Smith's *Theory of Moral Sentiments*. By highlighting the ways in which the sentiments must themselves be reflectively endorsed in a process of judgment that is not reducible to sentiment as such, writers like Hume, Smith, and Mackenzie complicate the perception that sentimentalism was an unselfconscious outlier vis-à-vis the mainstream Enlightenment.

In chapter 2, "Sentimentalism and the Discourses of Freedom: The Aesthetic Analogy from Hume to Arendt," I explore sentimental moral philosophy's engagement of the modern norm of autonomy by bringing into focus a hallmark of sentimental ethics from its beginnings in the writings of Anthony Ashley Cooper, the third Earl of Shaftesbury, to Smith's *Theory*: its representation of moral experience as broadly analogous to aesthetic experience. The sentimentalists' use of an aesthetic analogy for moral judgment produces an unexpected connection to the Kantian liberal tradition, and especially to Hannah Arendt's interpretation of Kant's *Critique of Judgment*, developed in essays and lectures culminating in the posthumously published *Lectures on Kant's Political Philosophy*. Like the sentimentalists, Arendt perceives aesthetic experience to be a paradigmatic kind of experience, with implications that extend well beyond the aesthetic domain itself. While the sentimental moral philosophers foreground the parallelism of aesthetic and moral judgment, and Arendt is concerned with the links between aesthetic and political judgment, together they enable a revisionist reading of autonomy under which independence of judgment is not perceived to mobilize transcendental standards or a denial of the subject's social inscription. As such, they move the conception of autonomy developed in Kant's moral writings in a context-sensitive, this-worldly direction.

Autonomy was a concern not only of sentimental moral philosophy but also of the sentimental novel, as is highlighted by the battle of wills between a father and a daughter at the center of Samuel Richardson's *Clarissa; or, The History of a Young Lady*. In chapter 3, "Judging Clarissa's Heart," I consider the famous "inward turn" *Clarissa* instantiates at the level of both form and moral theme. The story of a virtuous young woman who finds that virtue can no be longer realized in obedience to her elders, Richardson's second novel locates itself at the heart of the liberal Enlightenment through the importance it attaches to its heroine's independence of judgment. But it posits an ambiguous relationship between judgment and feeling. On the one hand, Clarissa portrays her judgments as instinctive responses, the work of her judging heart, which mysteriously reveals to her God's standards of right and wrong. On the other hand, she understands the heart to be itself an object of judgment, which must be approached from a standpoint of relative impartiality. This latter account is "sentimental" because it takes impartiality to be a contingency of Clarissa's epistolary friendship with Anna Howe. Becoming a co-spectator of Clarissa's heart's promptings, Anna helps her friend gain distance from them.

I suggest that the first, and broadly religious, paradigm of judgment identifies Clarissa only ambiguously as an independent moral agent: While she is justified by the highest principles to defy worldly authority, she nonetheless remains God's obedient servant, not unlike the Job of the Old Testament, whose "trials" are repeatedly summoned as prototypical of her story. By contrast, the second, secularizing paradigm mobilizes a more compelling understanding of autonomy as moral independence nurtured by friendship and strengthened by debate. While the epistolary form of Richardson's novel supports this second understanding, its tragic ending reinforces the religious paradigm of the judging heart by minimizing the significance of virtue in the sublunary order and "rewarding" Clarissa instead with premature death and a fast-tracked entry into her heavenly Father's mansion.

The otherworldliness of Richardson's ending militates not only against the worldliness of his heroine as a judge of her heart but also against his own commitment to education. Education, in the broad eighteenth-century sense of the development of the moral person, seems beside the point in the post-rape narrative of *Clarissa*, when its heroine turns her eyes heavenward, assured of the rewards due to her essentially good heart. In chapter 4, "A Sentimental Education: Rousseau to Godwin," I consider how Richardson's partial foreclosure of education in *Clarissa* propels three closely connected works that follow in its wake: Jean-Jacques Rousseau's *Julie; or, The New Heloise* (1761); Henry Mackenzie's *Julia de Roubigné* (1777); and William Godwin's *Fleetwood; or, The New Man of Feeling* (1805). While he was one of Richardson's greatest admirers on the continent, Rousseau believed that the novelist failed to give the passions their due in *Clarissa* by treating its heroine's attraction to its libertine hero, Lovelace, as a fatal flaw. In *Julie*, Rousseau seeks to show that love is a natural passion, susceptible to a "natural education" of self-correction and some fortuitous shaping by others. But Rousseau's nebulous norm of nature, as is highlighted also by *Emile* (1762), turns out to be a double standard, splitting along gender lines and enjoining different virtues and educations for men and women, respectively. Only Julie's lover's *Bildung* entails the development of judgment and the capacity of self-direction. By contrast, Julie develops not judgment but the kind of taste that renders her desirable to her husband. According to Rousseau, man is educated into the freedom of using his own judgment; woman, into the relative "freedom" of pleasing men.

Mackenzie and Godwin challenge Rousseau's opposition of male and female virtues by dramatizing the tragic consequences of treating wives and daughters as second-class citizens in the republic of virtue. In *Julia de Roubigné*, Mackenzie takes the sentimental novel's paradigmatic father–daughter plot and appends to it the plot of misguided passions of Shakespeare's *Othello*. Theatrical metaphors abound in Mackenzie's novel, identifying individuals as spectators of a play who are capable—unlike the actors on the stage—of bringing their passions under reflective scrutiny. While Mackenzie's Julia, like Rousseau's Julie, has a "too tender" heart, she is shown to be far more invested than her prototype in judgment as a prerogative of women.

Taking Mackenzie's plot of misguided passions and Rousseau's paradigm of a natural education as its points of departure, Godwin's *Fleetwood* imagines a future for the sentimental novel in which the Montaubans (those like Julia's husband) and Emiles of the world change their minds about women. A formal departure from the dialogic epistolary novel, *Fleetwood* nonetheless upholds the interest of an education that yields openness about the points of view of others and the flexibility of first-person retrospective narration. Commenting on the two dominant traditions of eighteenth-century sentimentalism, the Rousseauvian and the British, *Fleetwood* aligns itself with the latter through its critique of nature as a norm in the education of persons. Godwin builds in this context on his wife Mary Wollstonecraft's writings about education, especially her novel *Mary* (1788), which highlights the problems inherent in an education structured on Rousseauvian principles. Fleetwood is a "new man of feeling" because his feelings do not destroy others (as do those of Rousseau's natural men); nor are they self-destructive, as were the feelings of Mackenzie's Montauban and his Harley, the most famous—along with Goethe's Werther—of eighteenth-century men of feeling. While Harley swoons his way out of existence, Fleetwood lives to marry his Miss Walton—not once but twice (the second time, after he has learned to respect her individuality and different point of view).

Godwin's "new man of feeling" becomes Jane Austen's new women of feeling in *Sense and Sensibility* (1811), the novel that marks Austen's debut on the literary scene. Like their sentimental precursors, the sisters at the center of Austen's novel are essentially fatherless daughters—in their case, not because their father's authority is corrupted but because he is dead. Unlike their sentimental precursors, however, Elinor and Marianne Dashwood do not die in a fatherless world but live to love and prosper by exercising discriminating judgment. In chapter 5, "Judgment, Propriety, and the Critique of Sensibility: The 'Sentimental' Jane Austen," I interrogate a persistent premise of the dynamic critical industry that has flourished around Jane Austen's fiction in recent decades: the argument that Austen was an antisentimental conservative who opposed the new individualisms exemplified by late-century sensibility and romanticism. I suggest that Austen's career-long critique of the cult of sensibility should not be confused with an antisentimental posture since the terms of her critique come from within the sentimental tradition itself. The most important of these are *judgment*, *taste*, and *propriety*, all of which stand at the center of *Sense and Sensibility*, the novel most indicative of her stance toward eighteenth-century sentimentalism. While the plot-propelling conflict between the Dashwood sisters has been interpreted by many readers as a clash between a traditionalist heroine of propriety and an individualistic heroine of sensibility, I suggest that it is best read as family quarrel within sentimentalism. Both Dashwood sisters value independent judgment, but Marianne, the novel's chief representative of sensibility, simplifies the independence judgment entails when she conflates judgment and subjective preference—and relatedly, taste and instinct. By contrast, Elinor is committed to a reflective and deliberative understanding of judgment. I suggest that Austen, like feminist thinkers of her time such as Mary Wollstonecraft, understands the cultivation of judgment, and hence of autonomy, to be the goal of all education, for men and for women. The control permitted by third-person narration enables Austen to transform the sentimental epistolary novel's commitment to women's independence into the reality of a female Bildungsroman.

I believe that my broadly history-of-ideas approach to sentimental culture, which explores the interface between literature and philosophy, is justified not least by my topic. Sentimental fiction, moral philosophy, and aesthetics, are particularly closely bound together. Like the philosophers, sentimental novelists are pointedly concerned with questions of judgment and a morality of autonomy or self-direction. Correspondingly, sentimental philosophers like Hume and Smith often sound like novelists, interspersing argument with anecdote, and discourse with story.

In taking a history-of-ideas approach to sentimentalism and the Enlightenment, I seek also to challenge the hold on scholarship about eighteenth- and nineteenth-century British literature enjoyed by *one* admittedly powerful, but nonetheless selective, history of ideas about subjectivity and morality: Michel Foucault's "genealogies" of the liberal subject and Enlightenment modernity.[17] While Foucault is sometimes interpreted as rendering the very project of a history of ideas suspect, his highly philosophical interpretations of eighteenth-century social and legal arrangements interweave philosophical and social-historical arguments in the best tradition of intellectual history. Critical applications of genealogy—a method that, as Foucault describes it, reverses the long gaze of traditional history to focus on that which is near, "the body, the nervous system, nutrition, digestion, and energies"—have been especially influential in rehabilitating sentimentalism in recent times.[18] Insofar, however, as they replace a long with a short view, they obscure some of sentimentalism's most challenging claims—and especially the claim of the sentimental judge that that which is near (for example, one's own feelings) can be moved afar, and that which is distant (the feelings of others), can be brought near. It is to a fuller consideration of these claims that I now turn.

1. Reconstructing Sentimentalism

"Had you seen him, Julia, when he pronounced this *for ever*! great as his
soul is, he wept! By Heaven, he wept, at pronouncing it!—These tears,
Julia, these tears of my friend!—Would I had met my dungeon
in silence;—they had not torn my heart thus!"

Maria, mine was swelled to a sort of enthusiastic madness—

I fell at his feet.—[1]

IN THE EPIGRAPH TO THIS CHAPTER, the eponymous heroine of
Henry Mackenzie's *Julia de Roubigné* (1777) writes to a friend about an
emotionally charged interview with her father that will change her life
forever. The meeting she reconstructs pivots around her father's reconstruction of another turbulent encounter, one between his esteemed
friend, the Count Louis de Montauban, and him. In that embedded
narrative, Roubigné describes the proud Montauban weeping as he
renounces his suit for Julia's hand: Having saved Roubigné from debt-
ors' prison, Montauban is anxious that his friend's daughter not feel
pressured into marrying him. Wishing that Julia had witnessed the
scene, Roubigné conjures a tableau of the sublimely principled man
reduced to tears—a sentimental revision, perhaps, of Joseph Addison's
Cato (1713), with the Cato in Roubigné's retelling sacrificing Stoic
self-command to weep for a personal loss.[2] And as if this tableau
were not sufficiently moving in itself, Roubigné also recreates for his
tenderhearted daughter the spectacle of himself as a spectator of
Montauban's tears. He *shows* her "*these* tears of my friend," as though
Montauban were crying right in front of them, entering his own heart

like instruments of torture and tearing it to shreds. To this double spectacle of heartbroken men, Julia responds as her father undoubtedly knew she would: with utmost distress. But in a marked departure from the classical paradigm of tragic spectatorship—in which the spectator's heart is cleansed by the experience of pity and fear—Julia's heart swells to "enthusiastic madness" at the spectacle her father stages, prompting her to step on to the stage and cause a production change.[3] Throwing herself at her father's feet in mute accession to his (but not her) wish that she marry Montauban, Julia takes on the role of a willing human sacrifice. In her letter to Maria de Roncilles, she identifies the "play" that she herself is staging as one of her own favorite dramas, Racine's *Iphigénie* (1674) rather than Addison's *Cato*.

The final images we are left with here, of a young woman's swollen heart and a daughter's abjection, are omnipresent in the sentimental novel. Mackenzie's immediate precursor in this context is Jean-Jacques Rousseau, whose *Julie; or, The New Heloise* (1761) he revises in *Julia de Roubigné*. And Rousseau's *Julie* in turn revises another novel about fathers and daughters, Samuel Richardson's *Clarissa; or, The History of a Young Lady* (1747–48)—the novel that began the entire trend of sentimental fiction. In all three works, autocratic fathers manipulate or try to manipulate dutiful and sensitive daughters into doing things that neither morality nor religion demands. Clarissa's father tries to make her marry a man she dislikes with the unwholesome goal of advancing his family's pecuniary and class ambitions. Julie's father wheedles her into marrying a friend to whom he owes a debt, as does Julia's father. In all three works, the interest of the narrative is given by sentiment more than by story—to borrow Samuel Johnson's distinction, developed with reference to Richardson's *Clarissa*—and in each the heroine's heart is given a starring role in the narrative of sentiment. But, as Mackenzie's *theatrum mundi* metaphor above begins to suggest, the language of the heart appears in this fiction as a framed language, framed by a larger rhetoric of spectatorship. Hence, letter XIX of *Julia de Roubigné* invites interest not in Julia's heart as such but in a spectator's heart. The passage above depicts Julia's heart roused to madness by the spectacle of her father's heart in shreds, which is torn by the spectacle of Montauban's sad heart, which is saddened by a narrative just ended, in which "for ever" signifies not the happily ever after of comedy but the tragic eternity of life without Julia. Put slightly differently, it is less his heroine's feelings that Mackenzie asks us to care about in his epistolary novel than her feelings as a spectator, of the feelings of other spectators.

This study interprets sentimentalism as centrally concerned with the feelings of spectators.[4] To talk about such feelings is to talk not only about certain kinds of experiences—for example, the aesthetic experience of watching a play invoked by my epigraph—but also about the ever-present possibility that one can become a spectator of one's own feelings. According to sentimental novelists like Mackenzie and Richardson, and philosophers like David Hume and Adam Smith, this possibility stands at the epicenter of moral and social life. By becoming spectators of the passions or feelings that motivate our actions, and that comprise our reactions to the actions of others—as well as to paintings, roses, and poems—we become capable of judging the validity of those actions and reactions. As such, we become capable of autonomy or the independence that derives from using one's own judgment.

Judgment and autonomy are controversial concepts in contemporary literary studies and critical theory. To many, judgment signals an unsavory judgmentalism or a rush to ascribe culpability on the basis of inflexible standards. This connotation has one influential origin in Michel Foucault's critical genealogies of Enlightenment modernity and the liberal subject, as developed in works like *Discipline and Punish*. Described by Foucault himself as a "correlative history of the modern soul and of a new power to judge," *Discipline and Punish* recalls one of the Enlightenment's pivotal treatises on judgment: Immanuel Kant's *The Critique Judgment*, the full German title of which translates as *The Critique of the Power of Judgment*.[5] But whereas Kant takes the power of judgment to be an enabling capacity of individuals, Foucault's "new power to judge" connotes one of the darkest legacies of the eighteenth century. Described as a development of the new sciences of the human emergent in the period, judgment, as Foucault understands it, presupposes a normative and "normalizing" conception of the human, and makes insidious distinctions between the sane and the insane, the heterosexual and the homosexual, the adult and the child. For Foucault, as for other recent theorists of judgment like Pierre Bourdieu, to judge is to reinforce the hegemonic regimes of modern disciplinary power.[6]

Liberal autonomy is also viewed by Foucault and his many followers among New Historicists and queer theorists as a deeply troubling
legacy of the Enlightenment. Their readings affiliate it with a paradigm of atomistic and sovereign selfhood that signals an illusory—or,
alternatively, an imperialistic—elision of difference and of the social
and material contexts of subjectivity. For Foucault, for example,
autonomy entails a mode of objectification—the autonomous subject
objectifies itself as a self whose actions, desires, and motives can be
reflected upon—that is also always a form of subjection. As he explains
in "The Subject and Power," "There are two meanings of the word
'subject'; subject to someone else by control and dependence, and tied
to his own identity by a conscience or self-knowledge. Both meanings
suggest a form of power that subjugates and makes subject to."[7] On
this interpretation, the critical self-reflection autonomy enjoins designates yet another instantiation of the normalizing knowledge claims
of the human sciences that are codified in the legal and institutional
arrangements of modern liberal societies. Judith Butler, arguably the
most influential disseminator of Foucault's ideas within the Anglo-
American academy, paraphrases this Foucauldian insight in *Gender
Trouble* as follows: "Juridical notions of power appear to regulate political life in purely negative terms—that is, through the limitation,
prohibition, regulation, control and even 'protection' of individuals
related to that political structure through the contingent and retract-
able operation of choice. But the subjects regulated by such structures
are, by virtue of being subjected to them, formed, defined, and repro-
duced in accordance with the requirements of those structures."[8] More
recently, in *Precarious Life* and *Giving an Account of Oneself*, Butler
incorporates this insight into a vision of ethical relatedness that ascribes
special value to emotions such as grief because they interrupt feelings
of autonomous control and self-sufficiency. The subject's interdepen-
dence with other subjects, Butler argues, is so all-encompassing that
the "I" of the autonomous subject can be invoked only by rejecting the
ethos of relatedness.[9] Intersubjective relations, she suggests in *Giving
an Account of Oneself*, engender a fundamental self-opacity that jars
with the pretensions of autonomy: "Indeed, if it is precisely by virtue
of one's relations to others that one is opaque to oneself, and if those
relations are the venue for one's ethical responsibility, then it may well

follow that it is precisely by virtue of the subject's opacity to itself that it incurs and sustains some of its most important ethical bonds."[10]

Poststructuralist and postmodernist theorists are by no means alone in their skepticism about the claims of the autonomous subject. Objections to this core legacy of the Enlightenment, which is closely associated with Kant's moral philosophy, have proliferated in the postwar period. The philosophers John Christman and Joel Anderson succinctly indicate the principal lines of critique:

> The conception of the person as an autonomous, self-determining, and independent agent has come under fire from various sources. Communitarians and defenders of identity politics point to the hyper-individualism of such a view—the manner in which the autonomous person is seen as existing prior to the formulation of ends and identities that constitute her value orientation and identity. Feminists point up the gender bias implicit in the valorizing of the independent "man" devoid of family ties and caring relations; communitarians note the inability of such a view to make full sense of the social embeddedness of persons; and various postmodernists decry assumptions of a stable and transparent "self" whose rational choices, guided by objective principles of morality, define autonomous agency.[11]

The arguments of feminists, communitarians, postmodernists, and poststructuralists have had an enormous impact on the contemporary humanities, and have contributed valuably to the postmetaphysical turn that is characteristic of recent ethics and social theory. Opinion remains sharply divided, however, about the precise entailments of a key premise of many such critiques of autonomy: the understanding that subjectivity is a social, linguistically mediated development. For some, the assumption of social constitution irreparably damages the claims of autonomy. For others, it serves as a call to reformulate these claims in ways that respect the contingency of selfhood and agency. The stakes of these differences have emerged especially forcefully in recent debates within feminist and gender theory. For example, in the landmark debate among feminists that subsequently appeared in book form as *Feminist Contentions: A Philosophical Exchange*, Butler and Seyla Benhabib take the subject's social constitution to have widely divergent consequences for the future of feminist theory and practice.[12] Butler contends that the assumption of woman as the subject of feminism mobilizes a norm of autonomy that militates against the women's movement's best intuitions about difference and the social constitution of gendered identities. On this understanding, we can tinker all we like with the category of the subject but a subject-centered politics remains, in the last analysis, a politics of metaphysical selfhood. By contrast, Benhabib suggests that feminism is a normative political project, grounded in the principles of universal moral respect and individual rights, and as such it maintains a vital connection to the ideal of autonomy. On this interpretation, subjects are indeed socialized through language and the conventions of their communities but language is an instrument *we* use, even though our usage is shaped by rules that are not of our own making. "The situated and gendered subject," Benhabib argues, is "heteronomously determined but still strives for autonomy."[13]

This study brings the eighteenth century's literature and philosophy of sentiment to bear upon these and related debates. I suggest that sentimentalism and its close cousin, a Kantian tradition of aesthetics extending from Kant's *Critique of Judgment* to Hannah Arendt's *Lectures on Kant's Political Philosophy*, mobilize a conception of autonomy that is premised on an understanding of individuals as socially embedded subjects, whose ability to question the norms of their societies and to constitute alternative principles of action requires active social engagement in the form of critical debate. For the writers I summon below, the moral point of view or standpoint from which judgments are made does not denote a view from nowhere but specifies instead what Kant calls the enlarged mentality of the aesthetic judge—enlarged not because it subsumes the judgments of others, or because it transcends the world, but because it is shaped in communication with other judges. "To think with an enlarged mentality," as Hannah Arendt succinctly indicates in the Kant lectures, "is to train the imagination to go visiting" (43).

Exploring at once the slippery concept of autonomy, which has gathered several meanings in philosophical discussions, and the equally slippery social constitution thesis—which, as the example of the Benhabib–Butler debate indicates, can also be interpreted variably—I argue that the two become incompatible only if we take autonomy to signal a very radical form of independence, as opposed to what Christman and Anderson designate as its core sense of being "directed by considerations, desires, conditions, and characteristic that are not simply imposed externally on one."[14] As the philosopher Alisa L. Carse indicates, "We do not need a Kantian dualistic metaphysics to accept the independence of the self; we need only to be able coherently to claim that an individual, even the socially-constituted one, can stand back reflectively from some particular ends, roles and attachments, and deliberate in such a way as to withstand appealing to them in choosing."[15] Carse's further suggestion that the social constitution thesis is a description and autonomous individuality is a prescription, and that we need to distinguish between descriptions and prescriptions, is also helpful in this regard. Identifying the conflation of descriptions and prescriptions as a genetic fallacy, she argues that "we must distinguish the genetic question of how one comes to be the distinctive individual one is with the preferences, values and capacities one has, from the normative question of how as an individual one ought to invoke those preferences or exercise those capacities in moral judgment."[16] This is not of course to deny that descriptions and prescriptions are, or should be, mutually reinforcing, but it is to maintain their difference of form and address.

My turn to sentimentalism as an important interlocutor in the context of ongoing debates about autonomy is by no means uncontroversial. As the political theorist Michael Frazer has argued, most contemporary philosophers writing about a concept that remains firmly anchored to Kant's moral philosophy have shown little interest in sentimentalism's contributions to it.[17] More pertinent still to this study is the reception of sentimentalism among literary scholars, who have, for the most part, interpreted the movement as instituting a culture of feeling and fellow-feeling with marginal implications for Enlightenment conceptions of autonomous individuality. The "sentimental feeling self," Lynn Festa argues in *Sentimental Figures of Empire*, is best understood as "the Janus face of the Enlightenment rational subject," a point reinforced by Markman Ellis's *Politics of Sensibility: Gender, Race, and Commerce in The Sentimental Novel*; this describes sentimentalism as the other of Enlightenment rationalism—indeed as "a philosophical nightmare of muddled ideas, weak logic and bad writing."[18] For these critics, sentimentalism's principal contribution to modernity lies not in its claims about moral independence but rather in the humanitarian ethos it instituted, an ethos that ascribes special value to affective community and relatedness. Janet Todd reinforces this point in her much-cited study *Sensibility: An Introduction* when she suggests that sentimentalism was an historical "movement discerned in philosophy, politics and art, based on the belief in or hope of the natural goodness of humanity and manifested in a humanitarian concern for the unfortunate and helpless."[19] Todd is especially interested in the essentialist implications of the thesis of natural benevolence and her interpretation of sentimentalism as committed to metaphysical selfhood resonates with poststructuralist arguments that the Enlightenment naturalized a humanist subject constituted by innate qualities. More explicitly engaging poststructuralist arguments, John Mullan suggests in *Sentiment and Sociability: The Language of Feeling in Eighteenth-Century Britain* that sentimentalism sought to naturalize sympathetic sociability as an essential human fact that would magically mitigate the economic and social injustice of a greedy commercial age. While the epigraph to this chapter highlights the aesthetic and other distancing frames through which the sentimental language of the heart emerges, Mullan takes the heart alone to be the principal symbol of sentimental values. The heart, he contends, is figured by novelists like Samuel Richardson, for example, as "guarantee of [a protagonist's] truthfulness" and as a "general principle" prohibiting "introspective ambivalence."[20]

In this chapter I complicate these interpretations by attending to the extensive rhetoric of detachment mobilized by influential sentimentalists such as Mackenzie, Hume, and Adam Smith. Summoned through the figure of the spectator, the detachment at play in works like Hume's *Treatise of Human Nature*, Smith's *Theory of Moral Sentiments*, and Mackenzie's *Julia de Roubigné* is closely affiliated with the motif of judgment and, more particularly, with an understanding of judgment in which more than one spectator becomes important. Offering a sketch of sentimentalism that will gain texture and contour in the chapters to follow, I consider the implications of sentimental spectatorship both for influential recent critiques of autonomy and for the argument that the eighteenth century's belief in sentiment signaled a belief in natural benevolence and an essential human nature.

JUDGMENT AND FEELING

Intellectual and cultural histories of the eighteenth century identify sentimentalism as, in important ways, a response to early social contract theory and its psychological premise of self-interest.[21] In *Leviathan* (1651), a foundational text of modern contractarianism, Thomas Hobbes had argued that the social contract is a construct of self-interested individuals who agree to curb their passions and submit to a sovereign because it is in their interest to do so—because the alternative to civil society is a state of nature in which life would be "solitary, poor, nasty, brutish, and short."[22] Building on Hobbes's assumption of egoism and extending his thesis about the artifice of modern social arrangements, Bernard de Mandeville described morality in his provocative *Fable of the Bees* (1714–28) as a sham or a fabrication of the ultimate con artists, wily law-givers and moralists who flattered men into forms of self-denial wholly unnatural to them. Left to their own devices, individuals, Mandeville contends, "are only Sollicitous of pleasing themselves, and naturally follow the bent of their own Inclinations, without considering the good or harm that from their being pleased will accrue to others."[23] Those responsible for order in society, greedier than all the rest, trick the masses into curbing their passions by representing virtue itself as the highest object of desire. As Mandeville explains:

> They thoroughly examin'd all the Strength and Frailities of our Nature, and observing that none were either so savage as not to be charm'd with Praise, or so despicable as patiently to bear Contempt, justly concluded, that Flattery must be the most powerful Argument that cou'd be used to Human Creatures. Making use of this bewitching Engine, they extoll'd the Excellency of our Nature above other Animals, and setting forth with unbounded Praises the Wonders of our Sagacity and vastness of Understanding, bestow'd a thousand Encomiums on the Rationality of our Souls, by the help of which we were capable of performing the most noble Achievements.

Having by this artful way of Flattery insinuated themselves into the Hearts of Men, they began to instruct them in the Notions of Honour and Shame; representing the one as the worst of all Evils, and the other as the highest good to which Mortals could aspire: Which being done, they laid before them how unbecoming it was the Dignity of such sublime Creatures to be sollicitous about gratifying those Appetites, which they had in common with Brutes, and at the same time unmindful of those higher qualities that gave them pre-eminence over all visible Beings. (82)

In this early instantiation of a hermeneutics of suspicion, ethics is quintessentially a ruse of power. In affirming their capacity for moral choice, individuals, Mandeville argues, merely reproduce existing power asymmetries and confirm their own appetitive nature. Moral virtues, on this reading, are "the Political Offspring which Flattery begot upon Pride" (88).

As developed by philosophers such as David Hume and Adam Smith, the sentimentalists' response to the philosophers of egoism pivots around the thesis that human beings are a mixed bag, driven by self-regarding passions but also capable of sympathy and compassion. Morality, as portrayed by these authors, is not a cunning deception but can be traced to the capacity for judgment or ability to establish moral and aesthetic distinctions. This capacity, in turn, relies upon feelings, including the ability to sympathize with others. Judgments, as described in Hume's *Treatise of Human Nature* and Smith's *Theory of Moral Sentiments*, are registered as the feelings or sentiments of approval and disapproval. But not all sentiments, the sentimentalists caution, are "moral sentiments" or judgments. Only those sentiments of approval and disapproval that have themselves been approved or disapproved when brought under the scrutiny of an impartial observer count as moral judgments. Only the "sentiments of the cool and impartial spectator" (38), as Smith puts it, have normative significance.

The motif of judgment becomes obscured in recent accounts of sentimentalism that focus on its language of feeling alone.[24] In an influential reading of Hume's *Treatise of Human Nature*, John Mullan argues, for example, that Hume's response to a bracing philosophy of egoism entails an idealistic redefinition of the passions as "the very currency of sociability" (24). Whereas for Mandeville, the passions represent "the divisive forces of private desires," for Hume, as interpreted by Mullan, "passion is not appetite but sentiment; the proximity of feeling and judgement, impression and idea" (24). On this reading, Hume elides the growing inequities of a modern commercial era by positing sympathy as a natural principle that enables an instantaneous sharing of the passions. Upholding sympathetic sociability and affective community as counters to self-interest, Hume, Mullan argues, ignores "the potential disparity between the immediate experience of sociability (conversation, the flow of affections, the communication of sentiments) and the implications of belonging to a political society." He conflates two kinds of society in his account of sympathy: "Two distinct meanings of 'society' (the experience of particular contacts and the consistency of a political structure) are elided. Sympathy with 'another' is made congruent with sympathy with 'the interest of society'" (34).[25]

Humean sympathy, as Mullan observes, is indeed a slippery concept, which Hume downplays in the later *Enquiry Concerning the Principles of Morals* (1751)—a work that distils the most important findings of Book III of the *Treatise* (the book on morals) and that Hume himself regarded as his best work. But Mullan's suggestion that Hume upholds sympathetic sociability as a natural neutralizer of self-interest in the *Treatise* elides Hume's nuanced account of self-interest as a motivator of human action. It is owing to the importance he attaches to self-interest that Hume, and following him, Smith, render justice the paramount virtue in their ethical understandings. Individuals, Smith explains, "though naturally sympathetic, feel so little for another, with whom they have no particular connexion" that they must find principles of justice to prevent self-interest from destroying "the great, the immense fabric of society" (86). Justice, he affirms, is the pillar that holds up "the whole edifice of society," while benevolence is merely "the ornament which embellishes, not the foundation which supports the building" (86). Likewise, in the *Treatise* Hume observes that "without justice, society must immediately dissolve and every one must fall into that savage and solitary state which is infinitely worse than the worst situation that can possibly be suppos'd in society" (497).

Mullan's argument that sympathy serves as Hume's structuring principle of sociability understates the role of justice in Hume's

writings and also the dynamics of judgment. Sympathy itself is important to Hume principally owing to the role it plays in a larger process
of judging. In the *Treatise* he suggests that actions are judged to be
appropriate or inappropriate when a spectator deems them to be so
and the spectator's deliberations will be guided, at least in part, by
sympathy with the (real or imagined) recipients of that action. Indeed,
sympathy, as Hume describes it, is always the sympathy of a spectator.
As he puts it, "When I see the effects of passion in the voice and gesture
of any person, my mind immediately passes from these effects to their
causes, and forms such a lively idea of the passion, as is presently con-
verted into the passion itself . . . No passion of another discovers itself
immediately to the mind. We are only sensible of its causes or effects.
From *these* we infer the passion: And consequently these give rise to
our sympathy" (576).[26]

Mullan believes that Hume only turned to the trope of the spectator
and the detachment it signaled in the *Enquiry*, and that such a turn
was atypical of sentimentalism and disabled Hume's theory of
sympathy. As Mullan puts it, "The metaphor of spectatorial scrutiny
is simply at odds with a version of sympathy which allows for the natural mutuality of passions and sentiments" (45). But it is not at odds
with judgment, Hume's primary theme in Book III of the *Treatise*.
Hence:

> An action, or sentiment, or character is virtuous or vicious;
> why? because its view causes a pleasure or uneasiness of a particular
> kind . . . To have the sense of virtue, is nothing but to *feel* a satisfac-
> tion of a particular kind from the contemplation of a character.
> The very *feeling* constitutes our praise or admiration . . . The case
> is the same as in our judgments concerning all kinds of beauty, and
> tastes, and sensations. (471)

Hume's suggestion here is that judgments of vice and virtue are made
by someone who "views" or "contemplates" a character or action.
Elsewhere in the *Treatise*, he refers to the responses of "every spectator"
(591) and the "judicious spectator" (581). In the *Enquiry*, he is still
more explicit: His philosophy, he argues, "defines virtue to be *whatever
mental action or quality gives to a spectator the pleasing sentiment of
approbation*; and vice the contrary" (289).

The spectator garners importance in Hume's writings owing to his understanding that not all sentiments are "moral sentiments" or have normative significance. As already noted, for sentimentalists like Hume and Smith, only the sentiments of approval or disapproval that have been reflectively endorsed from a standpoint of relative impartiality, or a "general of point of view," have such significance. Hence, shortly after describing virtue as that which pleases upon a "mere" viewing, Hume adds:

> Nor is every sentiment of pleasure or pain, which arises from characters and actions, of that *peculiar* kind, which makes us praise or condemn. The good qualities of an enemy are hurtful to us; but may still command our esteem and respect. 'Tis only when a character is considered in general, without reference to our particular interest, that it causes such a feeling or sentiment, as denominates it morally good or evil. 'Tis true, those sentiments, from interest and morals, are apt to be confounded, and naturally run into one another. It seldom happens, that we do not think an enemy vicious, and can distinguish betwixt his opposition to our interest and real villainy or baseness. But this hinders not, but that the sentiments are, in themselves, distinct; and a man of temper and judgment may preserve himself from these illusions. (472)

D. D. Raphael has argued that what distinguishes the contributions to moral philosophy of the Scottish Enlightenment's three key philosophers—Francis Hutcheson, Hume, and Smith—is that they offer a "theory of moral judgment based upon the feelings of spectators."[27] Nonetheless, Raphael underscores that Hume and Smith can be distinguished from earlier sentimentalists like Hutcheson in that they deny the presence of an internal moral sense that works like the external senses, making the perception of goodness or beauty like the perception of the color yellow. Hume and Smith take moral judgments to be *deliberative* processes that mobilize both feeling and reason.

Mullan's identification of Hume as a theorist predominantly of the passions and sympathy is only partially justified by the opening provocation of the *Treatise*'s Book III, in which Hume declares that "Morality . . . is more properly felt than judg'd of" (470). This bold thesis is preceded, however, by the claim that morality requires assessing the passions: The "moral deformity" of an action is determined by "means of *some sentiment, which the reflecting on such an action naturally occasions*" (466; my emphasis). In the *Enquiry*, Hume further clarifies the role of reason and reflection in judgment:

> I am apt to suspect . . . that reason and sentiment concur in almost all moral determinations and conclusions. The final sentence, it is probable, which pronounces characters and actions amiable or odious, praise-worthy or blameable . . . it is probable, I say, that this final sentence depends on some internal sense or feeling, which nature has made universal in the whole species . . . But in order to pave the way for such a sentiment, and give a proper discernment of its object, it is often necessary, we find, that much reasoning should precede, that nice distinctions be made, just conclusions drawn, distant comparisons formed, complicated relations examined, and general facts fixed and ascertained. (172–73)

In *The Theory of Moral Sentiments*, Smith also highlights the interplay of feeling and reasoning in moral judgment, even arguing at one point that "virtue may very properly be said to consist in a conformity to reason" (320). It is through reason, he suggests, that "we discover those general rules of justice by which we ought to regulate our actions: and it is by the same faculty that we form those more vague and indeterminate ideas of what is prudent, of what is decent, of what is generous or noble, which we carry constantly about with us, and according to which we endeavour, as well as we can, to model the tenor of our conduct" (319). On Smith's interpretation, moreover, to accord value to reason is by no means to detract from the claims of feeling. Reason, he affirms, "cannot render any particular object either agreeable or disagreeable to the mind for its own sake" (320). This is instead the role of feeling. We feel an action to be good before we develop the standards of goodness. But we do not call an action good just because we feel it to be so. That is the work of critical reflection.

Mullan is not alone in downplaying the interest of the sentimentalists' rhetoric of detachment and judgment. His reading harks back in important respects to R. F. Brissenden's pioneering book-length study on sentimentalism, *Virtue in Distress: Studies in the Novel of Sentiment from Richardson to Sade* (1974). Brissenden takes his title from the many spectacles of distressed virtue represented by eighteenth-century fiction: representations that, he argues, enjoin the reader to attend to the suffering not only of the various victims of social injustice but also of the observers of their suffering. On Brissenden's account, sentimentalism produced a cultural shift away from an active, practical conception of virtue to a privileging of sympathetic (and passive) absorption in the suffering of others. His reading of Smith's *Theory of Moral Sentiments* is revealing in this context. While Brissenden characterizes the *Theory* as a seminal work of social theory that "opened the way for what were to become central lines of development in modern sociological and psychological theory" (36), he attributes to it an endorsement also of "some of the deepest fantasies of the age":

> And the deepest fantasy of all is the notion that the spontaneous moral responses of the individual, despite their basic subjectivity, possess some special and general authority, that one's *better* feelings are necessarily reasonable. This is what "sentiment" comes ultimately to mean—a *reasonable feeling*—not merely in the language of ordinary educated people but also in the language of the philosophers. It is highly suggestive that, despite their thoroughgoing empiricism, none of the English Moral Sense philosophers ever seriously considers the notion that the right feelings for some people may in fact not be aroused by the social virtues; that the good of the individual may not coincide with the good of society. (54)

Anticipating Mullan, Brissenden suggests that the sentimental moral philosophers were unable to rise to the challenge of philosophical egoism because of their untenable idealization of spontaneous feelings and social relations. However, his claim that the sentimentalists failed to acknowledge the gap between private desire and public good sidesteps their argument that justice is the main pillar of society precisely because society is comprised of self-interested individuals (who are, nonetheless, also endowed with other-regarding sentiments).

Brissenden's suggestion that the sentimentalists ascribed normative significance to "spontaneous moral responses" jars, moreover, with another important, though underdeveloped, argument of *Virtue in Distress*: that sentimentalism was an integral part of a liberal culture grounded in the right of private judgment, the right upon which, according to William Godwin, all others are predicated.[28] Sentimentalism, Brissenden contends, distinguished itself from the other strands of Enlightenment liberalism by its innovative entwinement of judgment and feeling:

> The role of the feelings, especially in the formation of moral judgments, was particularly emphasized. As David Hume put it in a striking and widely misunderstood phrase, the reason was now seen to be "the slave of the passions." This did not mean—especially in Hume's own moral theory—that reasoned and reasonable opinions and judgments were necessarily subordinate or inferior to the feelings or the emotions, but merely that feeling was necessarily the primary element in the process which led to the formation of a moral sentiment. And the feelings, the passions and the rational considerations which went into the making of moral judgments were, of course, one's own. Disproportionate weight eventually came to be placed on the feelings—on sensibility at the expense of sense. But this is not so significant as the fact that the process of moral judgment was held to be essentially private and subjective. (24)

Brissenden goes on to describe the eighteenth century as the "Age of Reasoning" rather than the "Age of Reason" because of its preoccupation with the reasoning and judging processes, which, he suggests, sentimentalism securely anchored to the feelings. And in one of the most engaging formulations of his study, he describes the French revolutionaries' *Declaration of the Rights of Man and the Citizen* (1789), a foundational text of modern liberalism, as a quintessentially sentimental document because sentimentalism had a great deal to say about rights and freedoms (in addition to the passions).

The internal complexity that Brissenden introduces into his own reading of sentimentalism by invoking its motif of judgment finds support in recent studies by Michael Bell, Chris Jones, and Patricia Meyer Spacks.[29] All of these critics highlight the multivalent implications of feeling, as invoked by sentimental literature and philosophy, and attend to the mediating work performed by reason and imagination in sentimental arguments about feeling's role in ethics and politics. Also broadly sympathetic to sentimentalism's ambitions is David Marshall's recent study *The Frame of Art: Fictions of Aesthetic*

Experience, 1750–1815. While Marshall's primary focus is aesthetics rather than sentimentalism per se, virtually all of the writers he discusses are sentimentalists, and I therefore take *The Frame of Art* to constitute an important intervention also in debates about sentimentalism. Marshall's reading pivots around the question, posed by eighteenth-century aesthetic and novelistic discourses, of what it means to view everyday life as though through the frame of art. Writers like Hume, Mackenzie, and Rousseau, he argues, delineate a novel conception of critical distance, very different from the distance enjoined by a museum experience of art, when they aestheticize the world, so to speak. The experiences they describe are "neither disinterested (indeed they are often related to appetites, such as sexual desire) nor removed from everyday life."[30] Suggesting a new way of looking, eighteenth-century aesthetic and sentimental writings, Marshall contends, direct attention, above all, to perspective itself: "The focus is not on the object of art, the work of art, but rather the experience of art, the perspective or point of view that frames aesthetic experience."[31]

What Marshall characterizes as the perspectivism of eighteenth-century aesthetics has another dimension too, which remains mostly implicit in his book. This is what Hannah Arendt, building on Kant's aesthetics, describes as "the basic other-directedness of taste and judgment" (68). If, as Marshall suggests, aesthetic discourse enables a shift from the question of what one sees to that of how one looks, then the question of how others might view the same object also becomes important. As soon as the quality of one's looking becomes important and we acknowledge that there are better and worse ways of looking at the object at hand then we also acknowledge that there are other standpoints—including the standpoints of *others*—that can be brought to bear in assessing its beauty or significance. The sentimental novel is productively engaged to further unpack this key claim of Enlightenment writings.

PEER-REVIEWING WOMEN

Why does the heroine of *Julia de Roubigné* write about a meeting with her father as though she were describing an evening at the theater?

Julia's invocation of the *theatrum mundi* metaphor in letter XIX of Mackenzie's novel sustains an extensive pattern of such images in her narrative, as in her representation of herself at one point as a spectator of the domestic theater of her parents' strained marriage, put to the test by their loss of fortune and social status. Julia worries that her "heart is too much interested in the scene, to allow me that command over myself, which would make me useful" (8). In another letter to Maria, she is saddened by the need to erase the memory of a childhood and adolescence spent with her beloved Savillon, which she conjures as a play or a series of tableaus: "Must I forget the scenes of our early days, the opinions we formed, the authors we read, the music we played together?" (43). Julia's letter-writing maid Lisette—a Pamela Andrews in the making—writes to Maria after Madame de Roubigné's death that her head is "full of the melancholy scenes I have seen" (50). In another epistolary stream, Savillon congratulates his friend Beauvaris on the vividness of his epistolary style: "your scene-painting is delightful" (96). Elsewhere he writes of the West Indian colonies where he is transplanted as "a theatre of rapine, of slavery, and of murder" (101). And finally, Montauban's relative's concluding letter to Maria, describing Julia and Montauban's deaths, refers to the "the fatal scenes . . . lately witnessed" (159).

All the world's a stage and all men and women are spectators: This appears to be the crux of Mackenzie's sentimental revision of Shakespeare's melancholy Jacques, whose monologue on the seven ages of man fails to acknowledge what it enacts, that men and women are not "merely players" on the stage of the world but are also always spectators, of themselves and others. In approaching domestic and social life as a beholder of various dramatic scenes, Julia identifies herself as precisely such a spectator—not only of the feelings and actions of others but also of her own feelings, motives, and actions. Consider now the beginning of letter XIX of Mackenzie's novel:

> In the intricacies of my fate, or of my conduct, I have long been accustomed to consider you [Maria] my support and my judge. For some days past these have come thick upon me; but I could not find composure enough to state them coolly even to myself. At this hour of midnight, I have summoned up a still recollection of the past; and with you, as my other conscience, I will unfold and examine it. (66)

The owl of Minerva flies only at night, writes Julia, anticipating Hegel.[32] In the quiet of the night, Julia can freeze the events of the day into a "still recollection"—a still life rather than a moving picture. Here she can behold with the requisite distance the pity that led her to accept Montauban's offer of marriage. Was "enthusiastic madness" the right response to her father's staging of Montauban's tears? Must a daughter always accede to her father's wishes? What are the relative claims of pity for others and justice to oneself? These are the kinds of questions that Julia persistently poses in her letters to Maria. And just as persistently she enjoins her friend to become a co-spectator of the still life Julia presents and beholds, addressing Maria as "my support and my judge" and as "my other conscience."

By the time Mackenzie came to write *Julia de Roubigné*, this mode of address—whereby a heroine calls upon a close female friend or relative, who is also the principal recipient of her letters, to become a co-judge and co-spectator of her actions—had become a fictional convention. The mistress of this form of address is the eponymous heroine of Richardson's *Clarissa*, who also begins the trend, calling upon her witty and acerbic friend Anna Howe to help her navigate the murky moral world in which she finds herself—a world in which the once secure connection between virtue and filial obedience has been irrevocably dissevered. Anticipating Julia's trope of judicious co-spectatorship, Clarissa enjoins Anna at one point to "lay [my heart] open . . . and [to] spare me not, if you find or think me culpable" (596), representing her heart as though it were a book on a lectern that could be read by both friends. The epistolary address of *Clarissa* and *Julia de Roubigné* opens up a pluralized paradigm of judgment and spectatorship in which one person's perceptions of motives and actions gain legitimacy by engaging at least one other person's interpretation of the same.

The idea that judgment requires such joint looking is a crucial theme also of the sentimental moral philosophers, as is implicit in Hume's call in the *Treatise* to think as "a man in general." It has its origins in the fact–value distinction, subsequently codified as Hume's law, that sentimentalism instituted. Hence, Hume maintains that moral and aesthetic judgments, as evaluative judgments, are unlike the knowledge claims of the empirical sciences because differences of judgment in the first case cannot be settled by reference to an empirical existent. We do not judge the beauty of a landscape in the same manner as we judge the land's utility for farming. The second judgment is shaped by measures such as the quality of the soil whereas the first is, at least to begin with, a subjective perception or matter of feeling. According to Hume, insofar as this feeling lends itself to some standard it does so not by invoking objective truths but by engaging other subjective perceptions of the object at hand. The only standard belonging to taste and judgment, he affirms, is the regulative ideal of a "common point of view" that individuals can cultivate by engaging points of view other than their own. Hence, "'tis impossible men cou'd ever agree in their sentiments and judgements, unless they chose some common point of view, from which they might survey their object, and which might cause it to appear the same to all of them" (591). In the *Enquiry Concerning the Principles of Morals* he further expands on the viability and desirability of such a standpoint when he observes that "we every day meet with persons who are in a situation different from us, and who could never converse with us were we to remain constantly in that position and point of view, which is peculiar to ourselves. The intercourse of sentiments, therefore, in society and conversation, makes us form some general unalterable standard, by which we may approve or disapprove of characters and manners" (229).

Such a standard–standpoint stands at the center too of the Kantian tradition of aesthetics. For example, in the *Lectures on Kant's Political Philosophy*, Arendt suggests that that the only objectivity belonging to aesthetic judgment comes from inserting the judge into a community of judgment and opinion sharing: "the nonsubjective element in the nonobjective senses [taste] is intersubjectivity" (67). "Judgment," she argues, "always reflects upon others and their taste, takes their possible judgments into account. . . . I judge as a member of this community and not as a member of a supersensible realm, perhaps inhabited with beings endowed with reason but not with the same sense apparatus" (67–68). As I will explain at greater length in the next chapter, Arendt upholds the norm of an enlarged mentality or a general standpoint that is strikingly like Hume's general or common point of view because it enjoins complicating bias through dialogue and debate.

Anticipating that discussion, I would like to hone in briefly on Arendt's treatment, in the Kant lectures, of the figure of the aesthetic

spectator. The spectator, she observes, is a favorite trope of all philosophers going back to Pythagoras, who had represented the philosopher
as a spectator at the games in the festival that is human life.[33] Kant,
Arendt suggests, shares philosophy's fascination with this figure: Kant
is "convinced that the world without man would be a desert, and a
world without man means for him: without spectators" (62). Yet there
is a profound difference, on Arendt's reading, between the spectator of
the philosophers and the Kantian spectator of the *Critique of Judgment*.
The difference, she contends, resides in the two very different conceptions of withdrawal—that is, the distance required to properly view
the games—delineated by Kant and the philosophers:

> Translating this [Pythagoras's metaphor of the festival] into the terms
> of the philosophers, one arrives at the supremacy of the spectator's
> way of life, the *bios theoretikos* (from *theorein*, "to look at"). Here one
> escapes from the cave of opinions altogether and goes hunting for
> truth—no longer the truth of the games in the festival but the truth
> of things that are everlasting, that cannot be different from what they
> are (all human affairs can be different from what they actually are)
> and therefore are necessary. To the extent that one can actualize this
> withdrawal, one does what Aristotle called *athanatazein*, "to immor-
> talize" (understood as an activity), and this one does with the divine
> part of one's soul. Kant's view is different: one withdraws also to the
> "theoretical", the onlooking, standpoint of the spectator, but this
> position is the position of the Judge. The whole terminology of Kant's
> philosophy is shot through with legal metaphors: it is the Tribunal of
> Reason before which the occurrences of the world appear. (55–56)

At some level, the philosophers' spectator, as represented by Arendt,
is no spectator at all because what matters to him ultimately is not
the place from which he looks, or how he looks, but rather the unchang-
ing truths he (thinks he) beholds. The Kantian judge-spectator is
distinguished from this figure because she does not seek to penetrate
a phenomenal realm of appearances to reach an ideal world of self-
evident truths. She respects appearances qua appearances, even as
she too "withdraws." She withdraws in the sense that she does not
participate directly in the games: "withdrawal from direct involvement to a standpoint outside the game is a condition sine qua non of

all judgment" (55). She withdraws also in the sense that judgment is less a matter of perception than of representation: "It is not important whether it [the beautiful object] pleases in perception; what pleases merely in perception is gratifying but not beautiful. It pleases in representation, for now the imagination has prepared it so that I can reflect on it" (67). Both kinds of withdrawal, however, are framed by participation—not participation in the games themselves but engagement with other spectators. Whereas in Plato's allegory of the cave—the "cave of opinions" to which Arendt refers in the passage cited above— the spectators or inhabitants of the cave are chained not only by the legs but also by the neck and cannot turn to one another—cannot, as Arendt puts it, "communicate about what they see" (59)—the Kantian spectator engages other spectators. For Kant, as Arendt puts it, "Spectators exist only in the plural. The spectator is not involved in the act, but he is always involved with his fellow spectators" (63). Spectatorship, in other words, only qualifies as such, only matters, when there is more than one way of looking.

I am arguing that a related pluralism or perspectivism can be gleaned from sentimental novels like *Julia de Roubigné* and philosophical texts like Hume's *Treatise*. As such, the sentimentalists' claims about judgment can be distinguished from the paradigm of spectatorial distance delineated in Joseph Addison and Richard Steele's influential *Spectator* periodical (1711–14)—a paper that is often accorded a catalytic role in the emergence of the bourgeois public sphere.[34] The differences between the sentimental spectator and Mr. Spectator derive from the degree and kind of participation that spectatorship presupposes and enjoins. Addison and Steele's taciturn Mr. Spectator is closer to the observer of ideal observer theories than to the impartial spectator of the sentimentalists because his judgments lack the dialogic element that accounts for the distinctiveness of sentimental judgment.[35] They presuppose a far higher degree of detachment than anywhere in sentimental writings. Hence, Mr. Spectator is a bachelor of independent means, beholden to no one else, and his affiliation with "the Fraternity of Spectators who live in the World without having any thing to do in it" doesn't entail the kind of critical exchange in which differences of opinion are fed by actual social participation.[36] While Mr. Spectator has the egalitarian intent of bringing philosophy down from the heavens into the world, he himself seems not to be of the world at all.[37] While the sentimentalists' metaphor of eyes readily affiliates with metaphors of voice, Mr. Spectator's solitary surveillance of the modern commercial city stands at some distance from a conversational ideal.

Contemporary critiques of detachment, and hence, of judgment and autonomy, appear more pertinent to Addisonian and ideal observer theories of spectatorship than to sentimentalism. Influential recent critiques like Foucault's, moreover, deserve further unpacking not least because, as I will now suggest, they risk minimizing the interest of perspective altogether in their distrust of spectatorial paradigms.

THE SUBJECT OF MODERNITY

Like Arendt and the sentimentalists, Foucault also figures judgment as the work of a spectator. The "new power to judge" delineated in *Discipline and Punish*, and embodied in a paradigmatic form by the modern human sciences, is represented by Foucault as a scopic regime. Foucault argues that whereas in traditional societies, only a powerful elite was visible, in modernity everyone becomes visible. The human sciences transform "the whole social body into a field of perception" (214). As is well known, *Discipline and Punish* invokes Jeremy Bentham's Panopticon prison model to elaborate the workings of modern power. As Foucault describes it, under this system of prisoner surveillance:

> All that is needed . . . is to place a supervisor in a central tower and to shut up in each cell a madman, a patient, a condemned man, a worker or a schoolboy. By the effect of backlighting, one can observe from the tower, standing out precisely against the light, the small captive shadows in the cells of the periphery. They are like so many cages, so many small theatres, in which each actor is alone, perfectly individualized and constantly visible. The panoptic mechanism arranges spatial unities that make it possible to see constantly and to recognize immediately. In short, it reverses the principle of the dungeon; or rather of its three functions—to enclose, to deprive of light and to hide—it preserves only the first and eliminates the other two. Full lighting and the eye of a supervisor capture better than darkness, which ultimately protected. Visibility is a trap.[38]

We are each of us constantly exposed, constantly lit up, so to speak, by the normalizing judgments of the human sciences. Under panopticism, self-reflection becomes self-surveillance because those exposed continuously to the eyes of power internalize them as one's own eyes. Hence, "He who is subjected to a field of visibility, and who knows it, assumes responsibility for the constraints of power; he makes them play spontaneously upon himself; he inscribes in himself the power relation in which he plays both roles; he becomes the principle of his own subjection" (202–3).

Tellingly, however, Foucault's prisoner or modern subject never encounters others in a reciprocal exchange: He knows that he is being watched by the supervisor but he cannot look back at him. Nor can he engage the other prisoners, who, like him, are placed under solitary confinement. In this atomistic picture of modern liberal society, each individual or prisoner is absolutely alone, "perfectly individualized," in an endless soliloquy on a small stage. As such, Foucault's modern subjects are reminiscent of the inhabitants of Plato's cave of opinions, who, as Arendt describes them, cannot engage one another, "cannot communicate about what they see." Indeed, communication becomes irrelevant under panopticism since everyone's experience or relation to power is fundamentally identical: All points of view are the point of view of power.

In later writings including "The Subject and Power" (1982), "On the Genealogy of Ethics" (1983), and "The Ethics of the Concern for the Self as a Practice of Freedom" (1984), Foucault attempts to complicate the monolithic picture of power delineated in *Discipline and Punish*.[39] Power, he indicates, is not merely repressive but also productive, and a certain freedom is presupposed by power. But the figure of the spectator and the reflective posture it symbolizes remain enduring objects of suspicion throughout Foucault's work.[40] They remain closely bound to a scientistic paradigm of truth and knowledge construction. Hence, in developing his alternative to Enlightenment ethics in an ethics of a care for the self, Foucault's emphasis falls not on reflection but on action, with ethics finding embodiment in certain valued performances of prescribed roles, as in ancient ethics. As Foucault indicates, "If I am now interested in how the subject constitutes itself in an active fashion through practices of the self, these practices are nevertheless not something invented by the individual himself. They are models that he finds in his culture and are proposed, suggested, imposed upon him by his culture, his society, and his social group."⁴¹ The individual's relation to these practices, he adds, is not a scrutinizing one but entails "listening to the lessons of a master" (287).

Foucault's "ocularphobia" is a widely shared feature of postwar French theory, as the intellectual historian Martin Jay notes in his wide-ranging study, *Downcast Eyes: The Denigration of Vision in Twentieth-Century French Thought*.⁴² Looking is something to be feared in the writings also of other thinkers, including Jacques Lacan, Guy Debord, Jacques Derrida, Luce Irigaray, Louis Althusser, and Emmanuel Levinas. It is associated with practices of reification, objectification, and the denigration of difference. Levinas, for example, figures spectatorial reflection, as privileged by Enlightenment ethics, as a mode of colonizing the object world (including the world of other subjects). On his interpretation, reflection denotes "a search for adequation; it is what par excellence absorbs being."⁴³ Against ethical universalism, which enjoins respecting others as ends in themselves rather than as means to one's own ends, Levinas contends that a truly ethical relation to the other is unmediated by representational imperatives: "being in direct [ethical] relation to the Other is not to thematize the Other and consider him in the same manner one considers a known object, nor to communicate a knowledge to him" (57–58).

But does a liberal conception of ethics make knowledge claims about the self or the other? Is the standpoint of the spectator always and only the standpoint of a knower? Do judgment and evaluation seek some truth about the world? The sentimentalists, as is highlighted by their fact–value distinction, didn't think so. Neither did Kant. Paraphrasing Kant, Arendt argues: *"The need of reason is not inspired by the quest for truth but by the quest for meaning. And truth and meaning are not the same. The basic fallacy, taking precedence over all specific metaphysical fallacies, is to interpret meaning on the model of truth."*⁴⁴ Relatedly, the philosopher Christine Korsgaard suggests, "the normative question is not a request for knowledge."⁴⁵ Values are not entities in the world or Platonic Ideas that we can access by embarking upon a fact-finding mission. As Korsgaard indicates, "It is not because we notice normative entities in the course of our experience, but because we are normative animals who can question our experiences, that normative concepts exist."

Such an understanding of normativity stands at the center also of sentimentalism and renders the spectator a figure of particular interest to the sentimental imagination. And significantly, the sentimental spectator is anyone. Judgment, as the father–daughter plot of the sentimental novel suggests, is a right of all adults. The sentimental moral philosophers imply this in the many vignettes that serve as evidence and example in Hume's *Treatise of Human Nature* and *Enquiry Concerning the Principles of Morals* and in Adam Smith's *Theory of Moral Sentiments*—vignettes that take as their protagonists every man, "every spectator," "any person," or "the judge." Sentimental novelists such as Richardson and Mackenzie transform every man into marriageable young women and dramatize the tragic consequences of trampling on their rights to judge and choose for themselves. The worldviews of both the novelists and the philosophers are circumscribed and limited by various factors—as all worldviews are. The novelists, for example, focus on the marital choices of women of a certain class, race, and sexuality; the philosophers' anecdotes spotlight mostly the lives of privileged men of a certain class, race, and sexuality. But the idea they present to us through the intertwined forms of fiction and philosophy—which address the reader differently but respond to shared cultural concerns—remains a powerful one. This is the assumption that individuals are capable of reflecting on their commitments and attachments, on past and projected actions, and on representations of all kinds. It underwrites not only the institutional design of modern liberal democracies but the critical posture itself—that is, our own status as critics and interpreters of literature and culture.

2. Sentimentalism and the Discourses of Freedom: The Aesthetic Analogy from Hume to Arendt

SENTIMENTALISM'S IMPORTANCE within the history of moral thought is often said to rest upon its innovative moral psychology rather than its claims about moral obligation or freedom.[1] This perception has begun to change in recent times, as several commentators have highlighted previously underremarked affinities between the Scottish Enlightenment and the Kantian tradition of liberal ethics, with which the concept of autonomy is most closely associated. Christine Korsgaard argues, for example, that sentimentalists like David Hume anticipate Immanuel Kant in the challenge they pose to the realism of the ancients. Whereas for the latter "being guided by value is a matter of being guided by the way things ultimately are," for the modern theorists of ethics value is perforce subjective, a subjective perception rather than an empirical existent.[2] Likewise, Michael Frazer attributes to Hume and Adam Smith an understanding of ethical reflection that looks forward to the one developed by twentieth-century rehabilitators of Kant such as John Rawls.[3] And in *A Third Concept of Liberty*, Samuel Fleischacker suggests that Smith's *Theory of Moral Sentiments* can be productively brought into dialogue with Kant's *Critique of Judgment* to yield a less legalistic and rationalist account of autonomy than the one proffered by Kant in his moral philosophy.[4]

In this chapter I too seek to vivify sentimentalism's contributions to the modern ideal of autonomy by staging a conversation between its moral philosophers and the Kantians. But I bring into focus a connection that has garnered little attention in recent discussions, one that is produced by the parallelism of judgment, as theorized by sentimentalists like Hume and Smith, and by one of Kant's foremost interpreters in the twentieth century, Hannah Arendt.[5] The key here is a shared interest in aesthetics and comparable assumptions about aesthetic objectivity and the standards of judgment. My contention below is that together Arendt and the sentimentalists mobilize an understanding of judgment, and hence of autonomy, that can be made to challenge the poststructuralist critique of autonomy as perniciously abstractive from the social and material contexts of subjectivity. I have argued that a too unquestioning acceptance of this criticism discourages critical encounters with sentimentalism and the Enlightenment that enable the past to challenge present assumptions in a more reciprocal dialogue. I have also argued that insofar as critical theory is here to stay in literary and cultural studies, we need to bring more diverse voices to bear upon our judgments of the Enlightenment.[6] More particularly, as Amanda Anderson and David Wayne Thomas have suggested, we need to bring more Enlightenment-friendly voices into the mix.[7] This is what I seek to do in this chapter.

This goal should justify an argument that has the inevitable and ironic selectivity characteristic of all interdisciplinary arguments. Bringing together moral philosophers, political theorists, and cultural critics who are not often in dialogue, I risk framing the conversation in ways that obscure crucial intradisciplinary conversations. The scope of this chapter prohibits extended engagement with, for example, Kant's moral philosophy and the British aesthetic tradition (to which sentimentalism was a major contributor), both of which have large bodies of scholarship dedicated to them. I believe, however, that the risk of selectivity will be offset by the reward of engaging sentimentalism *on its own terms*, since sentimentalism itself produced the interface of aesthetics, politics, and morals that I foreground—or so I am arguing in this study.

I begin with a reconstruction of Arendtian judgment, as this emerges in lectures and essays that Arendt did not live to condense into a systematic theory of judgment.[8] To provide one was certainly her intention, since the unwritten final section of her last book, *The Life of the Mind*, was entitled "Judging" and was meant to supplement her earlier accounts of "Thinking" and "Willing" in the same study—a structure that invokes the tripartite structure of Kant's critical philosophy and its three critiques of reason, practical reason, and judgment. My focus will be Arendt's account of the impartiality or "enlarged mentality" cultivated by the judge, and its possible implications for moral autonomy. I am helped in this regard by recent feminist interpreters of her work, especially Seyla Benhabib, who identifies Arendt's writings on judgment as an invaluable resource for feminists debating the value to women of the Enlightenment norms of autonomy and critical distance.[9] In *Situating the Self*, which locates these feminist debates in the larger context of postwar pessimism about the Enlightenment—as evinced by communitarians, postmodernists, and members of the Frankfurt school such as Max Horkheimer and Theodor Adorno—Benhabib looks to Arendt's oftentimes idiosyncratic reading of Kant to reclaim autonomy as a feminist value.[10] Arendt, she argues, helps us think about autonomy as a relative or contingent kind of independence: "Arendt intimated that intrinsic to Kant's model of 'reflective judgment' may be a conception of rationality and intersubjective validity which would allow us to retain a principled universalist moral standpoint while acknowledging the role of contextual moral judgment in human affairs."[11]

More broadly, Arendt's work, which is difficult to pin down in disciplinary terms, has been summoned as a critical resource in recent debates about modernity and its status as "an unfinished project," to borrow Jürgen Habermas's description of it. Indeed, Craig Calhoun and John McGowan, the editors of *Hannah Arendt and The Meaning of Politics*, suggest that Arendt's complication, in her writings on judgment, of such long-standing binary oppositions as reason/feeling and freedom/necessity, enables a substantial reframing of "debates that were becoming arid and pedantic or that were stuck in political name-calling."[12] Likewise, Ronald Beiner and Jennifer Nedelsky, the editors of *Judgment, Imagination, and Politics: Themes from Kant and Arendt*, suggest that Arendt's insightful contribution to a modern theory of judgment "provides a path to understanding the role of judgment in politics, in law, in science, and in daily life, at the same time that it invites a rethinking of the terms objectivity, subjectivity, truth, persuasion, and validity."[13]

Recent debates about the Enlightenment have tended to align Enlightenment modernity very closely with Kantianism. My aim is to give sentimentalism its due as a shaper of the eighteenth century's liberal legacies, and to do so, to begin with, by bringing it into dialogue with Kantianism. The German and the British Enlightenments, as noted earlier in this study, are often described as rationalist and empiricist, respectively. But when we summon the topic of judgment, the opposition of rationalism and empiricism, as well as of the two Enlightenments, becomes less stable.

REDEEMING THE PUBLIC REALM OF APPEARANCES: FROM AESTHETICS TO POLITICS

A few words are in order first about Kant's *Critique of Judgment* (1790). In completing his critical philosophy, Kant distinguished between two kinds of judgment, "determinant" and "reflective." Judgment, as he put it, is "the faculty for thinking of the particular as contained under the universal."[14] When the "universal" or "rule" or "law" is given, the judgment is called *determinant*; when only the particular is given and the universal must be found, the judgment is called *reflective*. The distinction between reflective and determinant judgments becomes important to Kant principally in the third critique, his work on aesthetics, because reflective judgments, according to him, have relevance only within the aesthetic domain. The kind of judgment that matters in the first two critiques, the *Critique of Pure Reason* (1781) and the *Critique of Practical Reason* (1788), is determinant. Kant interprets moral judgments, for example, as the work of reason alone; they determine whether particular actions conform to an a priori law given by reason. As stated in the *Groundwork of the Metaphysics of Morals* (1785), the law or categorical imperative of morality enjoins: "act only in accordance with that maxim through which you can at the same time will that it become a universal law."[15] Importantly, moral independence, as depicted here, is an assumption rather than an achievement. As Jerome Schneewind explains, "Autonomy, as Kant saw it, requires contracausal freedom; and he believed that in the unique experience of the moral ought we are 'given' a 'fact of reason' that unquestionably shows us that we possess such freedom as members of a noumenal realm."[16]

Kant understood aesthetic experience, however, to mobilize a different process of judging. We do not judge a rose to be beautiful, for example, by reasoning syllogistically, as in: "All roses are beautiful. This is a rose. Hence this rose is beautiful." Instead, we *feel* the rose to be beautiful. But this feeling, Kant contends, is something more than a subjective preference. Judgments of taste, on his interpretation, "have a subjective principle, which determines what pleases or displeases only through feeling and not through concepts, but yet with universal validity."[17] Hence, when we say "This rose is beautiful" we are saying something more than "I find this rose beautiful." According to Kant, we are claiming that others too should find this rose beautiful. In the *Critique of Judgment*, he suggests that taste is a kind of *sensus communis*: "By *'sensus communis'* . . . must be understood the idea of a communal sense, i.e., a faculty for judging that in its reflection takes account (a priori) of everyone else's way of representing in thought, in order as it were to hold its judgment up to human reason as a whole and thereby avoid the illusion which, from subjective private conditions that could easily be held to be objective, would have a detrimental influence on judgment" (173–74). Unlike the moral law, which is given a priori as a fact of reason, the lawfulness of aesthetic judgment is enabled by the free play of imagination and understanding. Kant explains, "only under the presupposition that there is a common sense (by which, however, we do not mean any external sense but rather the effect of the free play of our cognitive powers), only under the presupposition of such a common sense, I say, can the judgment of taste be made" (122).

The *Critique of Judgment*, as many Kant scholars have noted, has a curious singularity in the context of the larger critical philosophy because of the starring role it gives to feelings in theorizing judgment.[18] Hannah Arendt suggests that it is "the only [one of Kant's] great writings where his point of departure is the World and the senses and capabilities which made men (in the plural) fit to be inhabitants of it."[19] Crediting Kant with being the philosopher who had *discovered* the faculty of judgment in his aesthetics—determinant judgments, Arendt contends, do not really merit the name of judgment since they are determined by reason to the point of being indistinguishable from it—Arendt lamented that Kant "did not recognize the political and moral implications of his discovery."[20] This was a lacuna that she sought to fill herself by taking up the mantle, so to speak, of the most famous philosopher of her birthplace, Königsberg. And as Ronald Beiner, the editor of *Lectures on Kant's Political Philosophy* suggests, she took the task to be an urgent one. In "Understanding and Politics," for example, she described judgment as a particularly pressing question for a century that had witnessed the rise of totalitarianism and the explosion of "our categories of political thought and our standards of moral judgment."[21] Only those capable of independent judgment, she argued, had questioned the new "common sense" ushered in by Nazism's and Stalinism's rejection of the basic Enlightenment principle of universal moral respect—as theorized, above all, by Kant. Departing from her fellow German émigrés, anti-Enlightenment philosophers of the Frankfurt school such as Adorno and Horkheimer, Arendt urged a critical return to the thinker whose practical philosophy prohibits treating anyone as a means to an end rather than an end in himself or herself. More specifically, she prescribed a return to Kant's aesthetics and its account of reflective judgments—that is, judgments without clearly established rules or standards.[22]

In her writings on judgment, culminating in the *Lectures on Kant's Political Philosophy*, Arendt adapts Kant's aesthetics to develop, above all, a theory of political judgment. Kant, she suggests, never wrote a political philosophy or fourth critique because his understanding of political judgment is implicit in his interpretation of aesthetic judgment in the *Critique of Judgment*. Aesthetics and politics, she argues, are closely linked domains of human experience because in both, the claims of opinion trump the claims of truth. In an early essay, "The Crisis in Culture," she maintains that aesthetics and politics "belong together because it is not knowledge and truth which is at stake, but rather judgment and decision, the judicious exchange of opinion about the sphere of public life and the common world, and the decision what manner of action is to be taken in it, as well as how it is to look henceforth, what kind of things are to appear in it" (223).[23] On this understanding, art works and political "products" (words and deeds) are "phenomena of the public world" (218); both appear in a space shared with others, and offer themselves up to judgment, which Kant had described in the *Critique of Judgment* as the preeminent faculty for dealing with appearances.[24]

Arendt's contention that Kant was the first major philosopher of judgment—as she put it, "Not till Kant's *Critique of Judgment* did this faculty become a major topic of a major philosopher"—derives from her interpretation of him as the most important theorist of appearances within the Western philosophical tradition.[25] In *The Life of the Mind* she asserts that "In the work of no other philosopher has the concept of appearance, and hence of semblance (of *Erscheinung* and *Schein*), played so decisive and central a role as in Kant" (40). It is for this reason too that she sidelines Aristotle in her discussions of judgment, even though she draws upon his work extensively to develop an account of action in *The Human Condition*, and even though Aristotle is often described as the preeminent theorist of context-sensitive moral judgments in the Western philosophical tradition.[26] But for Arendt, as becomes clear in the Kant lectures and in a lecture entitled "Philosophy and Politics,"[27] Aristotle's philosophy is tarnished by a deep-rooted prejudice, shared by most philosophers, about "mere" appearances as opposed to supersensible truths.[28] She suggests that beginning with Plato's allegory of the cave in *The Republic*, philosophy depicted the public realm of appearances as an inferior realm of illusion that the philosopher must escape if his thought is to have integrity. In "Philosophy and Politics," she reinforces this argument by constructing a colorful narrative about the birth of political philosophy, an event that she equates with the death of politics. Political philosophy, Arendt suggests, came into being not because philosophers enjoyed writing about politics but because they feared it. It was the unseemly progeny of the battle between the philosopher and the city that erupted after the Athenian polis put Plato's beloved teacher Socrates to death. It originated in the trauma Plato suffered upon Socrates's trial and execution, an event that "in the history of political thought plays the same role of a turning point that the trial and condemnation of Jesus plays in the history of religion" (72). Despising the faulty *doxai* or opinions of the Athenians, Plato made the profoundly un-Socratic move, according to Arendt, of folding that which appears into that which is (through the creation of political philosophy). That is, he sought to transform *doxa*—from *dokei moi* or the "world as it opens itself to me" (80)—into truth:

> The spectacle of Socrates submitting his own doxa to the irresponsible opinions of the Athenians, and being outvoted by a majority, made Plato despise opinions and yearn for absolute standards. Such standards, by which human deeds could be judged and human thought could achieve some measure of reliability, from then on became the primary impulse of his political philosophy, and influenced decisively even the purely philosophical doctrine of ideas . . . [Plato] was the first to use the ideas for political purposes, that is, to introduce absolute standards into the realm of human affairs. (74)

Arendt contrasts Plato's absolutism with Socrates's own commitment to doxa—implicit not least in his enactment of the philosophical life as the life of a gadfly or midwife who moves among his fellow men in the marketplace, urging them to improve their opinions by airing them in the presence of others.

In the *Lectures on Kant's Political Philosophy*, Arendt identifies Kant, rather than Plato or Aristotle, as Socrates's best philosophical heir, owing to his greater fidelity to Socratic principles in two crucial respects: first, because aesthetic judgment, as theorized by him, respects appearances qua appearances, and second, owing to his transformation of philosophy into critique, with "critique" signifying a continuous checking of one's own thoughts and judgments through "the public use of one's reason." The judge, like the critical thinker Kant describes in his essay "What is Enlightenment?," must learn to apply critical standards to her own thoughts, and this, Arendt argues, "one cannot learn without publicity, without the testing that arises from contact with other people's thinking."[29]

Arendt's claims on behalf of reflective judgment—what she simply calls judgment—in the Kant lectures are framed by this larger discussion of critical thinking. Judgment, she argues, is distinguishable from taste because it is critical. While taste connotes a self-evident "it-pleases-or-displeases-me" (64), judgment requires bringing one's feelings of pleasure and displeasure under scrutiny. Kantian judgment, as Arendt interprets it, proceeds in two stages, through an "operation of the imagination" and an "operation of reflection." The first requires distancing the object by mentally re-presenting it. The second entails reflecting on one's pleasure or displeasure with the representation. The key question for Kant, Arendt observes, is how we come to approve or disapprove of our own pleasure or displeasure:

> One can approve or disapprove of the very fact of *pleasing*: this too is subject to "approbation or disapprobation." . . . [At] the time you are doing scientific research you may be vaguely aware that you are happy doing it, but only later, in reflecting on it, when you are no longer busy doing whatever you were doing, will you be able to have this additional "pleasure": of *approving* it. In this additional pleasure it is no longer the object that pleases but *that* we judge it to be pleasing . . . Hence the question: How does one choose between approbation and disapprobation? One criterion is easily guessed if one considers the examples given above: it is the criterion of communicability or publicness. One is not overeager to express joy at the death of a father or feelings of hatred or envy; one will, on the other hand, have no compunctions about announcing that one enjoys doing scientific work. (69)

Critical independence, as imagined here, does not imply social isolation. The enlarged mentality that enables judgment solicits the judgments of others. It is in interpreting the role of other people's judgments that Arendt departs from Kant most radically. As already noted, Kant had argued that judgments of taste are never simply personal but enjoy a certain (subjective) universality; by this he means that they automatically take into account the judgments of others. Arendt challenges this account by highlighting the interest of an actual community of judgment and opinion sharing. The validity or objectivity of judgment, she argues, comes from using one's reason publicly, from sharing one's opinions. "No opinion is self-evident," she asserts in "Truth and Politics." Hence, in "matters of opinion, but not in matters of truth, our thinking is truly discursive, running, as it were, from one part of the world to another, through all kinds of conflicting views" (242). As conceived here, the itinerant imagination of the judge requires something more than Kant's free play of the faculties; it is strengthened by engaging diverse perspectives in the actual public sphere.

In the *Lectures on Kant's Political Philosophy*, Arendt reinforces this argument by identifying impartiality as a contingent achievement, as "that relative impartiality that is the specific virtue of judgment" (73). Reflective judgment, she suggests, mobilizes a general standpoint that is only as general or objective as the standpoints it engages:

> The greater the reach—the larger the realm in which the enlightened individual is able to move from standpoint to standpoint—the more "general" will be his thinking. This generality, however, is not the generality of the concept—for example, the concept "house", under which one can then subsume various kinds of individual buildings. It is, on the contrary, closely connected with particulars, with the particular conditions of the standpoints one has to go through in order to arrive at one's own "general standpoint". This general standpoint we earlier spoke of as impartiality; it is a viewpoint from which to look upon, to watch, to form judgments, or, as Kant himself says, to reflect upon human affairs. (43–44)

On this understanding, the judge does not seek to transcend bias—an impossible task—but to complicate it by submitting her judgments to peer review. Impartiality, Arendt clarifies, "is not the result of some higher standpoint that would then actually settle the dispute by being altogether above the melée" (42). While the Platonic philosopher looks for standards of judgment that transcend the human world, the judge of matters aesthetic and political looks for a standard that is at once immanent and transcendent. It is immanent because it presupposes participation in the public domain. It is transcendent because it is not the same as public opinion. This latter point is crucial for Arendt and makes her discussion of judgment especially pertinent to debates about autonomy. In "Truth and Politics," for example, she emphasizes that the enlarged mentality is not a species of empathy; it does not require entering the heads of others or collapsing the difference between one's own standpoint and the standpoints of others.[30] The judge, she explains, "does not blindly adopt the actual views of those who stand somewhere else, and hence look upon the world from a different perspective; this is a question neither of empathy, as though I tried to be or to feel like somebody else, nor of counting noses and joining a majority but of being and thinking in my own identity where actually I am not" (241–42).

Arendt's account of reflective judgment and the enlarged perspective bears comparison with more recent constructivist or proceduralist interpretations of Kant—for example, as developed by John Rawls in *Political Liberalism* and other writings.[31] Kantian constructivism, Rawls suggests, "holds that moral objectivity is to be understood in terms of a suitably constructed social point of view that all can accept."[32] On this account, the principles of justice cannot be justified by any "moral truth interpreted as fixed by a prior and independent order of objects and relations, whether natural or divine, an order apart from and distinct from how we conceive ourselves" (519). They are legitimated instead by an exchange of people's "considered convictions" (518).

While Rawls does not cite Arendt as a precursor of his constructivism, Seyla Benhabib turns to Arendt's writings on judgment in *Situating the Self* as a resource in developing her comparably postmetaphysical ethical understanding. Implicit in Arendt's account of the enlarged mentality, Benhabib argues, is a fundamentally "interactionist" (6) conception of reason and normativity. Benhabib grounds her own discourse ethics in a procedure of normative justification whereby "Instead of asking what an individual moral agent could or would will, without self-contradiction, to be a universal maxim for all, one asks: what norms or institutions would the members of an ideal or real communication community agree to as representing their common interests?" (24). Arendt, Benhabib adds, renews the liberal ideal of autonomy and renders it a useful concept for feminism by dissociating it from metaphysical paradigms of sovereign subjectivity and legislative reason. She helps us see that the moral point of view is not a view from nowhere. "The moral point of view," Benhabib enjoins, "is not an Archimedean center from which the moral philosopher pretends to be able to move the world." Instead, it articulates "a certain stage in the development of linguistically socialized human beings when they start to reason about general rules from the standpoint of a hypothetical questioning: under what conditions can we say that these general rules of action are valid not simply because my parents, the synagogue, my neighbors, my tribe say so, but because they are fair, just, impartial, in the mutual interest of all" (6). On this interpretation, critical independence from the force of tradition is postconventional but not postsocial, so to speak. This is because critical reasoning, as Arendt indicated, requires the public use of one's reason.

While Benhabib looks to Arendt, and Arendt looks to Kant, for an understanding of normative underpinnings that are respectful of "appearances" and the judgments of others, we can find such an understanding also in the writings of the British sentimentalists. It is implicit in their extensive concern with aesthetics and their representation of moral judgments as paralleling aesthetic judgments. Like Arendt, the sentimentalists deploy an aesthetic analogy for experiences extending beyond the aesthetic domain but their use of the analogy, more explicitly than Arendt's, highlights the ineluctably reflective nature of *moral* judgments.

A COMMON POINT OF VIEW: ETHICS AND AESTHETICS

Well before Hannah Arendt, though seemingly unbeknownst to her, the British sentimentalists also identified aesthetic judgment as a paradigmatic kind of judgment. From Shaftesbury to Adam Smith, sentimental moral philosophers looked to aesthetic experience to understand moral experience. They did so in part to underscore that moral judgments are not the work of reason alone. Instead, like aesthetic judgments, they involve feelings. Morality, David Hume famously argued in the opening pages of Book III of the *Treatise of Human Nature*, is a "matter of feeling" (470). Hume adds, however, that it is a matter of feeling because it is not a "matter of fact." The operative tension here is not between reason and feeling but between positive and normative domains, or fact and value. Hume takes aesthetic and moral judgments to be similar because, as *evaluative* judgments, they refer to matters that cannot be settled by reference to something "out there" in the real world. Comparable to Arendt's differentiation of that which can be known and that which appears, the sentimentalists' fact–value distinction, or Hume's law, receives its most trenchant formulation in the *Treatise*:

> Take any action allow'd to be vicious: Wilful murder, for instance. Examine it in all lights, and see if you can find a matter of fact, or real existence, which you call vice. In which-ever way you take it, you

find only certain passions, motives, volitions, and thoughts. There is no other matter of fact in the case. The vice entirely escapes you, as long as you consider the object. You never find it, till you turn your reflexion into your own breast, and find a sentiment of disapprobation, which arises in you towards this action. (488–69)

Values, on this interpretation, have no objective correlative, so to speak. Instead, they entail turning one's eyes inward in "reflexion." Elsewhere, Hume suggests that actions, sentiments, and characters are deemed vicious or virtuous because they produce in a spectator "a pleasure or uneasiness of a particular kind" (471). And he goes on to add, "The case is the same as in our judgments concerning all kinds of beauty, and tastes, and sensations." Focusing only on its implications for morality, Korsgaard paraphrases Hume's law as follows: "Strictly speaking, we do not disapprove the action because it is vicious; instead, it is vicious because we disapprove it."[33] According to Korsgaard, Hume and the other British sentimentalists give morality the decisive "inward turn" that culminates in Kant's concept of autonomy. Values, from this perspective, are subjective and intersubjective rather than things in the world. As Korsgaard puts it, "To talk about values and meanings is not to talk about entities, either mental or Platonic, but to talk in a shorthand way about relations we have with ourselves and one another."[34]

The connection between Kantianism and sentimentalism extends still further. Like Kant, as interpreted by Arendt, the sentimentalists also believed that judgment, despite its necessary subjectivity, claims a kind of objectivity. Taste, to invoke the title of Hume's famous essay of 1757, has a standard. In this context, however, crucial differences emerge within sentimentalism, between the moral sense theory of Francis Hutcheson—which draws, in turn, on Shaftesbury's ethics and aesthetics—and what might be described as Hume and Smith's moral constructivism. In his seminal work of sentimental ethics, *An Inquiry into the Original of Our Ideas of Beauty and Virtue* (1725), Hutcheson had argued that the objectivity of aesthetic and moral judgments is guaranteed by the internal senses of beauty and morality.[35] These are perceived to be a priori disinterested, as is underscored by Hutcheson's comparison of them to the external senses; like the external senses they work instantaneously and independently of the will.

Hutcheson observes of the sense of beauty, for example, that "this superior Power of Perception is justly called a Sense, because of its Affinity to the other Senses in this, that the Pleasure does not arise from any Knowledge of Principles, Proportions, Causes, or of the Usefulness of the Objects; but strikes us at first with the Idea of Beauty."[36] Moral judgments, too, are the work of an internal sense which approves benevolent actions and motives without the mediation of reflection. "The Author of Nature," Hutcheson argues, "has much better furnish'd us for a virtuous Conduct, than our Moralists seem to imagine, by almost as quick and powerful Instructions, as we have for the preservation of our Bodys. He has made Virtue a lovely Form, to excite our pursuit of it; and has given us strong Affections to be the Springs of each virtuous Action" (9).

Hutcheson's moral sense parallels Kant's *sensus communis* in the *Critique of Judgment* in that it too assures an a priori disinterestedness and universality. By contrast, Hume and Smith anticipate Arendt by treating judgment as a reflective and deliberative process rather than an ineffable intuition.[37] Whereas for Hutcheson the moral sense approves or disapproves independently of the will, for the later sentimentalists the sentiments of approval and disapproval must themselves be approved or disapproved by reflecting upon them.[38] The emphasis on reflection links Hume's and Smith's writings to the work of such rationalists of the day as Richard Price and Kant.[39] Nonetheless, they can be distinguished from the rationalists by their more capacious understanding of reflection. Michael Frazer characterizes this difference as the sentimentalists' greater holism: "While sentimentalism describes reflection as a matter of feeling and imagination as well as cognition, rationalism describes reflection as a matter of rational cognition alone."[40] Hence, when sentimentalists describe the process by which individuals approve or disapprove of their own sentiments of approval and disapproval, they refer to "a process of reflection in which the mind as a whole repeatedly turns on itself as a whole, and winnows out those sentiments which cannot past the test of reflection . . . Only those moral sentiments which endure when we reach reflective equilibrium can be treated as authoritative, for only minds in reflective equilibrium are capable, as Hume puts it, of 'bearing their own survey.'"[41]

The sentimentalists' test of reflection has, however, another dimension, in addition to the holism of which Frazer speaks, which is implicit in their treatment of ethics and aesthetics as parallel domains of experience. This is, to return to an Arendtian locution, the "basic other-directedness of taste and judgment." For the sentimentalists, too, taste and judgment are other-directed, and just as Arendt speaks of an enlarged mentality so too Hume writes in the *Enquiry* of "enlarged reflections" (274) and Smith waxes lyrical in the *Theory* about the Stoic ideal of world citizenship. All three thinkers take the objectivity of judgment to be intersubjectively enabled. The only standard belonging to taste, Hume suggests in "Of the Standard of Taste," rests in "a considerable uniformity of sentiment among men" (234). In the *Enquiry* he indicates:

When a man denominates another his *enemy*, his *rival*, his *antagonist*, his *adversary*, he is understood to speak the language of self-love, and to express sentiments, peculiar to himself, and arising from his particular circumstances and situation. But when he bestows on any man the epithets of *vicious* or *odious* or *depraved*, he then speaks another language, and expresses sentiments, in which he expects all his audience to concur with him. He must here, therefore, depart from his private and particular situation, and must choose a point of view, common to him with others; he must move some universal principle of the human frame, and touch a string to which all mankind have an accord and symphony. If he mean, therefore, to express that this man possesses qualities, whose tendency is pernicious to society, he has chosen this common point of view, and has touched the principle of humanity, to which every man, in some degree, concurs. (272)

Moral claims, unlike statements of preference, solicit the agreement of others. Like Rawls's "social point of view," Hume's common point of view invokes as a regulative ideal a widely shareable standpoint from which to judge. Elsewhere, Hume makes a similar argument about aesthetic judgments: "When any work is addressed to the public, though I should have a friendship or enmity with the author, I must depart from this situation; and considering myself as a man in general, forget, if possible, my individual being and my peculiar circumstances" (239).

A principal question for the sentimentalists, as for the Kantian theorists of aesthetic judgment, is how we cultivate such a standpoint. We will recall that for Arendt the general standpoint enjoins inserting oneself into a community of real and imagined judges. The sentimentalists uphold a similar dialogism, as in Hume's contention in the *Enquiry* that "a false relish" in both taste and moral judgment can "frequently be corrected by argument and reflection" (173). The standards of taste, he suggests in both his aesthetic and moral writings, are determined by consensus among experts.

The other-directedness of judgment, as delineated by the sentimentalists, is a consequence also of their social theory of selfhood. Posed as a challenge to philosophical egoism, this theory suggests that human beings are fundamentally sociable and rely upon one another not only to meet their physical needs but also because the inner life, so to speak, demands it. Smith argues, for example, that moral and aesthetic concepts have no meaning outside of society:

> Were it possible that a human creature could grow up to manhood in some solitary place, without any communication with his own species, he could no more think of his own character, of the propriety or demerit of his own sentiments and conduct, of the beauty or deformity of his own mind, than of the beauty or deformity of his own face. All these are objects which he cannot easily see, which naturally he does not look at, and with regard to which he is provided with no mirror which can present them to his view. Bring him into society, and he is immediately provided with the mirror which he wanted before. It is placed in the countenance and behaviour of those he lives with, which always mark when they enter into, and when they disapprove of his sentiments; and it is here that he first views the propriety and impropriety of his own passions, the beauty and deformity of his own mind. To a man who from his birth was a stranger to society, the objects of his passions, the external bodies which either pleased or hurt him, would occupy his whole attention. The passions themselves, the desires or aversions, the joys or sorrows, which those objects excited, though of all things the most immediately present to him, could scarce ever be the objects of his thoughts.[42]

On this account, there would be no reflection on inner "objects"—that is, on sentiments and motives—in a state of nature. We only start to reflect on first-order desires, and to develop, as a consequence, moral and aesthetic concepts, once our desires become somehow visible to us; and they become visible to us, at least initially, through the reactions of other people to them, reactions that are inscribed in the demeanor and behavior of others.

On Smith's interpretation, other people hold the key also to the impartial standpoint that individuals must cultivate in order to make judgments. Frequently personifying this standpoint as the "impartial spectator," the "man within the breast," the "inhabitant of the breast," "the great judge and arbiter of our conduct," Smith develops an intriguing Bildungsroman about this character in Part III of *The Theory of Moral Sentiments*, which is entitled "Of the Foundations of our Judgments concerning our own Sentiments and Conduct, and of the Sense of Duty."[43] Drawing on the accounts of sympathy and the spectator–agent distinction he develops in his study's first two parts, Smith traces morality to sociability, to the social experience of viewing and being viewed. On this understanding, we begin subjective life as spectators of other people, and our first judgments of right and wrong concern the conduct and sentiments of other people. Soon, however, we become aware that not only are we judging other people but that they too are judging us.[44] We face one another as at once spectators and actors or agents (each of us is a spectator of the other as actor or agent).[45] Because, according to Smith, it is natural to desire the approbation of others, agents rapidly become spectators of themselves in addition to being spectators of others. They come to exercise the same kind of critical scrutiny in relation to their own motives, passions, and actions that they habitually exercise in relation to those of other people. This self-scrutiny requires imagining how one's actions would appear to others who have no direct stakes in the consequences of one's actions. Impartiality entails bringing the eyes of others, so to speak, to bear upon one's own private reflections. This argument is compactly presented in Part III of the *Theory*:

> We can never survey our own sentiments and motives, we can never form any judgment concerning them; unless we remove ourselves, as it were, from our own natural station, and endeavour to view them as at a certain distance from us. But we can do this in no other way than by endeavouring to view them with the eyes of other people, or

as other people are likely to view them. Whatever judgment we can form concerning them, accordingly, must always bear some secret reference, either to what are, or to what, upon a certain condition, would be, or to what, we imagine, ought to be the judgment of others. We endeavour to examine our own conduct as we imagine any other fair and impartial spectator would examine it. If, upon placing ourselves in his situation, we thoroughly enter into all the passions and motives which influenced it, we approve of it, by sympathy with the approbation of this supposed equitable judge. If otherwise, we enter into his disapprobation and condemn it. (110)

The impartial standpoint, as depicted here, does not require precisely the critical debate of which Arendt speaks in her descriptions of the enlarged mentality. Smith's explanation is more psychological than Arendt's; he is primarily interested in the "secret" or implicit reference to the judgments of others that the judge makes in trying to view her own motives and actions with impartial eyes.[46] Like Arendt, however, Smith suggests that impartiality requires complicating bias and enlarging personal perspective; further, the enlargement of perspective is nurtured on his understanding, as it is on Arendt's, by engaging actual others.

Some critics have argued that the sentimentalists' thoroughly socialized individual appears fundamentally incapable of autonomy. One such critic was Smith's friend, Sir Gilbert Elliot, who wrote to the philosopher that his theory of moral sentiments left underspecified how individuals might become critics of their communities. If the impartial standpoint is achieved in an interactive context, how can it register substantial critical disagreement with one's community? In response, Smith highlighted the priority of the inner over the outer tribunal of judges.[47] "Man," he argues in his revisions to the first edition of the *Theory*, "naturally desires, not only to be loved, but to be lovely; or that thing which is the proper object of love" (113). For the best judge, "The most sincere praise can give little pleasure when it cannot be considered as some sort of proof of praise-worthiness" (114). On this account, while self-evaluation inevitably and productively engages the evaluations of others, it acquires a relative autonomy not least through the principles that individuals give to themselves—principles that can and should be engaged in gauging the prescriptions of an outer tribunal comprised by specific others and the community.

Smith's account of the "general rules of morality" and of the sense of duty that enjoins respect for rules is one of the most intriguing aspects of his moral theory. It links his sentimentalism very explicitly with the Kantian ideal of self-legislation.[48] But whereas Kant takes the general rules of morality to be given a priori, Smith interprets them as, at least in the first instance, developments of experience: "Our continual observations upon the conduct of others, insensibly lead us to form to ourselves certain general rules concerning what is fit and proper to be done or to be avoided" (159). These serve as "the standards of judgment, in debating concerning the degree of praise or blame that is due to certain actions of a complicated and dubious nature" (160). Respect for rules, Smith suggests, is "a principle of the greatest consequence in human life and the only principle by which the bulk of mankind are capable of directing their actions" (162). It ensures that one's actions accord with one's own reflectively endorsed highest principles even when circumstances or dispositions plead otherwise. According to Smith, rules equalize action, if not intention, both across time for particular persons and across persons through education since there is "scarce any man . . . who by discipline, education, and example, may not be so impressed with a regard to general rules, as to act upon almost every occasion with tolerable decency, and through the whole of his life to avoid any considerable degree of blame" (163). Smith places the sense of duty at the center of his moral theory:

> When our passive feelings are almost always so sordid and so selfish, how comes it that our active principles should often be so generous and so noble? . . . It is not the soft power of humanity, it is not that feeble spark of benevolence which Nature has lighted up in the human heart, that is thus capable of counteracting the strongest impulses of self-love. It is a stronger power, a more forcible motive, which exerts itself upon such occasions. It is reason, principle, conscience, the inhabitant of the breast, the man within, the great judge and arbiter of our conduct. It is he who, whenever we are about to act so as to affect the happiness of others, calls to us, with a voice capable of astonishing the most presumptuous of our passions, that we are but one of the multitude, in no respect better than any other in it. (137)

This account of principle looks forward to the famous passage in the *Critique of Practical Reason* (1788) where Kant speaks of his reverence for the moral law: "Two things fill the mind with ever new and increasing admiration and awe, the more often and steadily we reflect upon them: the starry heavens above me and the moral law within me."[49] Smith, however, shuns the transcendentalism that accompanies the Kantian picture of self-respect and respect for rules. He contends that the reverence due to self-legislating morality should not confuse us into according morality a transcendental status, the mistake of "several very eminent authors" who "draw up their systems in such a manner, as if they had supposed that the original judgments of mankind with regard to right and wrong, were formed like the decisions of a court of judicatory, by considering first the general rule, and then, secondly, whether the particular action under consideration fell properly within its comprehension" (160). Moral judgments, on this understanding, are first and foremost reflective rather than determinant. Concomitantly, the freedom of individuals specifies an experiential and relational kind of autonomy.

Autonomy is a controversial norm in contemporary literary studies and critical theory but its critique, as mobilized by various poststructuralist writers, often presupposes that to endorse autonomy is to endorse a subject of Reason that controls its fate by standing above all worldly determinants. Hence, poststructuralist arguments against autonomy often highlight the pressures exerted upon the mind and subjectivity by the body, the other, by social norms or hegemonic networks of power. Interestingly, this contextualism links poststructuralism to sentimentalism. But by contrast with poststructuralist theorists who take considerations of context to disable the norm of autonomy, sentimentalists take the subject's social embedment to be its only grounds. We are linguistic and embodied beings, they suggest, who are socialized into specific communities, and even the goals that frame our actions and the judgments that we bring to bear upon them are, in important ways, established in relation to others. As such, autonomy is not an absolute independence but the contingent freedom that we all exercise, in one way or another, when we reflect upon our goals, choices, desires, needs, capabilities, and actions. Autonomy, the philosopher Marilyn Friedman argues, presupposes heteronomy: "Implicit in the idea of acting according to wants, desires, cares, concerns, values, or commitments that are one's own is the idea that one might have acted according to the wants, desires, cares, concerns, values, or commitments of *others* but did not do so . . . Socially deracinated, autonomy would be a pointless and meaningless notion."[50]

One could argue, too, that to preserve the thesis of the subject's social constitution or social embedment one needs to have a *subject* that is socially constituted. Insofar as it makes the social impinge too heavily on the individual, poststructuralism does not complicate the binary opposition of subjectivity and sociality but collapses the one into the other. This produces a strain not least because the self-reflective subject is a pertinacious construct, even an assumption of language, and tends to resurface in the most autonomy-resistant arguments. Consider, for example, Judith's Butler's delineation, in *The Psychic Life of Power*, of the kind of agency that belongs to the socially constituted subject.

> Agency exceeds the power by which it is enabled. One might say that the purposes of power are not always the purposes of agency. To the extent that the latter diverge from the former, agency is the assumption of a purpose unintended by power, one that could not have been derived logically or historically, that operates in a relation of contingency and reversal to the power that makes it possible, to which it nevertheless belongs. This is, as it were, the ambivalent scene of agency, constrained by no teleological necessity.[51]

Butler's aim here is to redefine agency in accordance with the imperatives of power. The agency of the socially constituted subject, she contends, can be formulated only by challenging the paradigm of self-reflective individuality that we have inherited from the Enlightenment. It should be seen to reside not in the individual's capacity for critical deliberation but in the unexpected and unwilled misalignment of "the purposes of power" and "the purposes of agency." It is striking, however, that Butler uses the language of purpose and intention in order to critique the self-same language. On her account, the referent of agency has changed—agency belongs to a personification (power) rather than a person—but the paradigm of agency remains untouched.

We do not challenge metaphysical understandings of purpose and intention by trying to make them go away. The sentimental and

Kantian theories of judgment I have described in this chapter offer an alternative path: They reformulate agency by attending to questions of perspective and standpoint, questions that preserve an interest in the individual but that, at the same time, militate against the atomistic and self-grounding individual of earlier modes of thought. Sentimentalism and Kantianism merit our continued attention owing to their forceful delineation, at once, of the claims of the subject and of context.

3. Judging Clarissa's Heart

IN *LETTRE À d'Alembert sur les spectacles* (1758), Jean-Jacques Rousseau declared that "In no language whatsoever has a novel the equal of *Clarissa*, or even approaching it, ever been written."[1] Denis Diderot was hardly less effusive, assigning *Clarissa's* author a place in the history of letters alongside Homer, Euripides, and Sophocles.[2] That Samuel Richardson's second novel struck such a chord with the Enlightenment vanguard would appear to have had something to do with its riveting invocation of a question dear to the hearts of liberals and *philosophes*: the question of what, if any, legitimacy could be ascribed to a traditional morality of obedience in a modern or enlightened world. Questions of obedience and self-governance had figured prominently also in Richardson's bestselling first novel, *Pamela; or, Virtue Rewarded* (1740), but the treatment accorded them there had been milder: The virtuous servant-girl, Pamela Andrews, challenges class hierarchies by disobeying her lascivious master but she does so guided by widely accepted social and moral laws, like the code of chastity. The eponymous heroine of *Clarissa; or, The History of a Young Lady* (1747–48), by contrast, finds herself at odds with *the* most fundamental moral code of her culture, the law of filial obedience, which symbolized all other laws enjoining obedience—as was highlighted, for example, by Robert Filmer's *Patriarcha; or, The Natural Power of Kings* (1680).[3] The story of a virtuous young woman whose parents tyrannically enjoin her to enter a mercenary marriage, *Clarissa* renders strikingly unpalatable the putatively "natural authority" that parents exercised over their children and that society exercised over young unmarried women—that is, the so-called respectable society which urges Clarissa to marry her rapist to preserve her reputation. Obedience, Richardson's heroine finds, is no guarantee of virtue in the world in which she finds herself, a world in which "the good," as she observes, has become "strangely mixed" (224). Unable to look to her elders or to society for moral guidance, Clarissa must look to herself for such guidance. She must look, as she writes to her friend Anna Howe, to "what offers to my own heart, respecting, as I may say, its own rectitude, its own judgement of the *fit* and the *unfit*" (596).

Clarissa's striking figure of the judging heart situates her narrative in established biblical and Anglican traditions of inwardness, in which the heart was routinely figured as the seat of conscience and also as the most essential part of the self—symbolic of a *deiform* or godlike human nature.[4] As Clarissa explains to Anna, she can trust her heart because it reveals principles that are "in my mind; that I *found* there, implanted, no doubt, by the first gracious Planter" (596).[5] Interpreting Richardson's figure of the heart against the backdrop of Latitudinarian devotional writings, John Dussinger suggests that "Whether he calls it 'conscience' or 'feeling heart', Richardson implies throughout [*Clarissa*] that man has within him an intuitive judge to which he must answer for all his actions and that furthermore this inner voice is directly related to the Holy Spirit."[6]

Notwithstanding its roots in the more progressive trajectories of Christian thought, the trope of the judging heart ushers in a literary sentimentalism that engages the larger liberal culture of the Enlightenment in ambiguous ways. On the one hand, Clarissa's heart's judgment affords her a remarkable autonomy, an ability to take a stand against her elders and social convention. On the other hand, this judgment is not precisely her own, as is registered by her frequent representations of her heart as an autonomous entity, which judges quite independently of her.[7] Hence, when Clarissa invokes her heart's authority, as she frequently does, the role of the moral agent that she assumes is more passive than active. Consider, for example, her frequent lament that her family doesn't trust her heart. Writing to Anna, she exclaims: "Oh that they did but know my heart! It shall sooner burst, than voluntarily, uncompelled, undriven, dictate a measure that shall cast a slur either upon them, my sex, or myself" (141). While the "uncompelled" and "undriven" heart is a powerful symbol of moral self-direction, Clarissa, the owner of this virtuous heart, appears to have little to do in the drama of conscience. Her direct line to God, so to speak, diminishes the interest of her own will and judgment. Like Job, whose trials are invoked throughout *Clarissa* as prototypical of Richardson's heroine's tribulations, Clarissa, as the possessor of an especially virtuous heart, is meant to be seen as subservient, in the last analysis, to a judgment not her own.[8] She is subservient to what Lovelace, in a telling expression, describes as "the God within her."[9]

This is the principal message, too, of Richardson's intriguing postscript to *Clarissa*, in which he justifies his heroine's early death to the many readers who had pleaded for a happier resolution of her trials.[10] Shedding the editorial persona he adopts in his preface to the novel, Richardson issues a stern challenge to his readers in the name of Christianity: "And who that are in earnest in their profession of Christianity but will rather envy than regret the triumphant death of CLARISSA, whose piety (from her early childhood); whose diffusive charity; whose steady virtue; whose Christian humility; whose forgiving spirit; whose meekness; whose resignation, HEAVEN *only* could reward?" (1498).[11] Transforming a disobedient daughter into a "meek" saint, and his "history of a young lady" into a saint's life, Richardson's retrospective gloss also identifies Clarissa's filial disobedience as the highest instantiation of morality as obedience, one in which the earthly and fallible father is replaced by the heavenly Father as the figure to whom obedience is most properly owed.[12]

In this chapter I argue that the heart's judgment—which is associated with the meek saint of the above description—is not the only kind of judgment of interest in *Clarissa*.[13] Yet another understanding of judgment—and hence of the "freedom and independency" that Clarissa associates with the use of "my own judgement" (290)—is mobilized by Richardson's heroine through her varying judgments *of* her heart.[14] Clarissa, it is important to note, insistently questions her heart's authority. "Ought I not to suspect my own heart?" (104), she repeatedly asks Anna. The heart, she observes, is "very deceitful: do you, my dear friend, lay mine open (but surely it is always open before you!) and spare me not, if you find or think it culpable" (596). While Clarissa's doubts about her heart, as I explain momentarily, also have Christian antecedents, her frequent calls to Anna to help her view her heart—or rather, the motives and inclinations the heart symbolizes— more objectively do not. Not only does judgment, on this alternative

understanding, require a cultivated objectivity that can be distinguished from the "objectivity" of God's laws—the innate or a priori
principles that she finds within her, "implanted," as she suggests, by
"the first gracious Planter"—but, in a radical departure from Christian
paradigms of inwardness, Clarissa takes this objectivity to be reinforced through her epistolary exchange with her friend. The socialized
paradigm of judgment summoned by both friends through much of
the narrative—at least until the rape, after which Clarissa steadfastly
turns her eyes heavenward—pushes morality in an emphatically this-
worldly direction, consonant with the constructivism of sentimentalists like Hume and Smith, and theorists of reflective judgment like
Kant and Arendt.

Significantly, feelings do not cease to be important when the
heart becomes the object of judgment since the objectivity enabled
by epistolarity is also an objectivity enabled by friendship. In his
Theory of Moral Sentiments, Smith groups Richardson with the "poets
and romance writers, who best paint the refinements and delicacies
of love and friendship, and of all other private and domestic affections"
(143). But Richardson's *Clarissa*, I argue, is more important still
as a precursor text of the sentimental impartiality at the heart of
Smith's moral theory. Indeed, Richardson's epistolary technique can
be seen to render more explicitly interactive the impartiality that
Smith invokes through a genetic explanation of the "man within the
breast." There is no man (or, for that matter, God) within the
breast, Richardson's *Clarissa* suggests through its representation of its
heroine as a judge of her heart. Morality resides instead in the cultivation of a standpoint that has no gender and that can be adopted
by anyone—including, significantly, the letter-writing women who
challenge the paternalism of their culture by claiming the right of
private judgment.[15]

LOOKING WITHIN

A good place to begin a fuller consideration of the languages of judgment in *Clarissa* is letter 185, the letter in which Clarissa figures her
heart as a judge. It is written to Anna from London, not long after

Clarissa has left Harlowe Place with her libertine admirer, Lovelace. Its context is Anna's growing anxiety that her friend is unmarried even as she remains under Lovelace's equivocal protection. Anna urges Clarissa to lose no time in tying the knot, regardless of any scruples she might still have about Lovelace's character. Clarissa, she contends, can no longer afford such scruples since, in the eyes of the world, she has willingly eloped with a lover. "Punctilio," Anna had warned Clarissa even before she had left home, "is out of doors the moment you are out of your father's house" (355).

Clarissa, for her part, has hesitated to accept Lovelace's offer of marriage, in part because of the flippancy with which it was made but also because she remains troubled by his role in staging her departure from Harlowe Place (she senses that she has been tricked into throwing herself under his protection). "Let me," she writes to Anna, "once for all, endeavour to account for the motives of my behaviour to this man, and for the principles I have proceeded upon, as they appear to me upon a close self-examination" (596). The explanation is worth quoting in full:

> Be pleased then to allow me to think that my motives on this occasion arise not *altogether* from maidenly niceness; nor yet from the apprehension of what my present tormentor, and future husband, may think of a precipitate compliance, on such a disagreeable behaviour as his. But they arise principally from what offers to my own heart, respecting, as I may say, its own rectitude, its own judgement of the *fit* and the *unfit*; as I would without study answer *for* myself *to* myself, in the first place; to *him* and to the *world*, in the *second* only. Principles that *are* in my mind; that I *found* there, implanted, no doubt, by the first gracious Planter: which therefore *impel* me, as I may say, to act up to them, that thereby I may to the best of my judgement be enabled to comport myself worthily in both states (the single and the married), let others act as they will by *me*.
>
> I hope, my dear, I do not deceive myself, and instead of setting about rectifying what is amiss in my heart, endeavour to find excuses for habits and peculiarities which I am unwilling to cast off or overcome. The heart is very deceitful: do you my dear friend, lay mine open (but surely it is always open before you!) and spare me not, if you find or think me culpable. (596)

This excerpt offers one of the most striking endorsements of autonomy anywhere in eighteenth-century letters. While Anna's recommendation of marriage is premised on the understanding that the laws of respectable society are binding on Clarissa, Clarissa understands herself to be bound, first and foremost, by the dictates of her own conscience, or, as she puts it, the judgments of "my own heart."[16] The heart's judgment of right and wrong, or the "fit" and the "unfit," is morally binding, she explains, because it is underwritten by none other than God himself—the "first gracious Planter," whose laws are "implanted, no doubt" within the virtuous individual's innermost self.

The "no doubt" of this assertion of faith becomes complicated, however, in the very next paragraph of letter 185, in which Clarissa summons another crucial figurative meaning that her culture gives the heart, as the seat of self-interested desire. This alternative signification can be traced back to both religious and secular origins—to, on the one hand, Calvinist and Puritan doctrines of universal sinfulness, and, on the other hand, the doctrine of universal selfishness of philosophers of egoism such as Hobbes and Mandeville. Indeed, Clarissa's suggestion that the heart is "very deceitful" directly echoes the Mandevillian Lovelace's earlier representation of the heart as a "curs'd deceiver" (148). On this understanding, the promptings of the organ are revelatory not of God's laws but of the imperatives of self-love. Lovelace, Clarissa's sister Arabella suggests early in the narrative, "has got into your fond heart" (140). And Lovelace, a handsome and cultured man, does indeed prove to be a persistent serpent in the garden of Clarissa's heart; her attraction to him, as Anna also observes, has the potential to cloud her judgment about him and about how she should act in relation to him. From this other perspective then, the heart may indeed be a judge of sorts but its judgments are themselves susceptible to judgment by some authority other than itself—that is, by none other than Clarissa.

The difference between the heart's judgment and Clarissa's judgment is registered in letter 185 by the trope of the spectator, which identifies Clarissa as her heart's observer rather than its blind disciple. "[Do] you, my dear friend," she enjoins Anna, "lay my heart open," as though it were a book that could be placed on a lectern, or some other object for joint viewing by Anna and herself. Ocular imagery, as is signaled in *Clarissa* by the two young women's extensive vocabulary of "bystanders" and "standers-by," serves as a crucial second pole of the metaphorical grid of Richardson's sentimentalism, which must be considered alongside its language of the heart.

As it emerges in letter 185 of *Clarissa*, sentimental ethics mobilizes two kinds of inward turns or "looking within." On the one hand, what Clarissa looks at when she looks within is a heart or mind—heart and mind are often used interchangeably, by both Richardson's heroine and the Christian tradition of inwardness on which she draws—in which God's principles flourish like plants. On the other hand, she observes a heart that may not be what it appears. Judgment, on this second interpretation, does not require peering *into* the heart but objectifying and scrutinizing it—ideally with the help of a friend. The emphasis shifts here from *what* one sees when one looks within to *how* one looks—that is, to the looking itself. To make this point somewhat differently, the two paragraphs cited above uphold distinct understandings of why Clarissa's heart is noteworthy or spectacular: The first suggests that it is "spectacular" in the sense of spectacularly good, as in a heart blessed by God's grace. In the second, it becomes "spectacular" in the very different sense of a spectacle worthy of judgment and scrutiny.

Crucially, the whole question of point of view becomes important only in the second paragraph, when the emphasis shifts to how one looks at, rather than what one sees in, the heart. It is only there that the quality of Clarissa's spectatorship of her motives and intuitions becomes important. Clarissa's injunction to Anna to lay her (Clarissa's) heart open is predicated on her belief that there are better and worse ways of looking at her heart. More than one point of view can be brought to bear upon her spectacular heart—which becomes, in this sense, a public spectacle.

The figure of the spectator mobilized by Clarissa in letter 185 of her narrative is obscured by John Mullan in his reading of Richardsonian sentimentalism in *Sentiment and Sociability*. I argued earlier in this study that Mullan's interpretation of sentimental culture, like those of scholars such as Markman Ellis and Janet Todd, privileges its ethos of absorption in ways that elide its rhetoric of detachment. His reading of *Clarissa*, more particularly, anticipates Scott Paul Gordon's recent account, which ascribes to Richardson's novel a vision of affectivity that altogether circumvents the mediation of critical reflection.[17] For Mullan, this circumvention is forcefully registered by Richardson's symbolism of the heart. The heart, he argues, appears in Richardson's novels as a "guarantee of [his heroines'] truthfulness" (63) and even as a "general principle" that prohibits any "introspective ambivalence" (68); in its promptings "are combined will, judgement, and feeling" (64).[18] On this interpretation, Clarissa's letters to Anna are transcriptions of the heart that "purport to reproduce . . . a decorous yet guilelessly tremulous language of feeling" (63). They produce a community of feminine sentiments in which tears and blushes are perceived to be superior to words as the media of communication. In "Richardson's extraordinary version of femininity," Mullan asserts, women "are bound together . . . in sighs, in tears, in postures and movements instantly understood" (113).

This reading elides the considerable suspicion surrounding the heart's promptings in Clarissa and Anna's correspondence. It is curious also as an account of a friendship that is conducted principally through letters, letters that presume the distance of a narrator, even when the narrative in question details sighs and tears and postures instantly understood. Women do *not* seem bound in *Clarissa* by tears alone or even predominantly by tears. In the crepuscular moral world in which they find themselves, they become affiliated more urgently by the need for joint deliberation about "the fit" and "the unfit," Clarissa's formulation for moral distinctions. As Richardson's heroine indicates somewhat primly at one point, her friendship with Anna permits each "freely to *give* reproof and thankfully to *receive* it, as occasions arise; that so either may have opportunity to clear up mistakes, to acknowledge and amend errors, as well in behaviour as in words and deed; and to rectify and confirm each other in the judgement each shall form upon persons, things, and circumstances" (484).

Richardson's novel's interest in spectatorship and self-spectatorship is noted by Cynthia Griffin Wolff in *Samuel Richardson and the Eighteenth-Century Puritan Character*, which situates *Clarissa* in the context of the Puritan culture of self-examination.[19] Wolff observes that since the Puritan had no established church to guide and solace him, "he had to discover a pattern of salvation in his own life, and the proof of such a pattern could be denied by the most trivial offense."[20] In the absence of pastoral care, the individual would subject each of her actions to extensive critical scrutiny in order to determine the degree to which it was the product of selfish desire. Hence the relentless Puritan regimen of meditation, prayer, and self-examination: "The cardinal duty of each Christian," Wolff indicates, "was to discover through extensive self-examination his own secret sins and then to keep watch over them . . . Discovery of the secret sin—or, as we would call it, self-knowledge—was called 'Heart Knowledge' and the difficulty of obtaining this Heart Knowledge, even with prolonged and unremitting self-examination, was a major theme of the Puritan manual" (19). The diary, Wolff notes, was another means, and a more methodical one, of scrutinizing one's often-opaque heart. It permitted a sustained objectification of motives and actions, and provided solace by distinguishing between the self as sinful actor and as God-fearing spectator.

While Wolff's and others' studies of Puritanism shed a useful light on the forms of critical self-reflection permeating eighteenth-century culture, Clarissa's quest for self-awareness and impartiality differs from the Puritan's in crucial ways. To begin with, the Puritan seeks familiarity with personal sin—the self is prejudged to be essentially sinful under the credo of essential depravity—but Clarissa has no such preconceptions about herself. She is suspicious of her motives and inclinations rather than certain that they are sinful. Further, Clarissa's injunctions to Anna to help her gain the distance that she needs to become a better judge of her own passions and motives transforms what Wolff describes as the "lonely duty"(17) of the Puritan self-examiner into a "sociable" duty to see oneself as objectively as possible. As Mark Kinkead-Weekes also notes, "For Clarissa self-examination is not individual and private; it is a deliberate attempt to lay bare her heart and her behaviour for the judgement of her friend."[21] Like the Puritan diarists, Clarissa puts the self, the self as an actor or agent, into print, but unlike her predecessors she receives readers' reports on her self-representation. This ideological difference between Clarissa and her Puritan forefathers corresponds to the formal difference between the epistolary novel and the diary. The letter, unlike the diary, is perforce a sociable kind of writing; while it "presupposes isolation," as Kinkead-Weekes suggests, it also "equally implies communication and aspires to community."[22]

Epistolarity in *Clarissa* ascribes to virtue a sociable and immanent dynamic. Clarissa's correspondence with Anna is a principal source of intellectual and emotional nourishment for her, both inside and outside her father's house. The coolly deliberative tone that the two friends often take produces a striking contrast not only to the self-serving passions—lust, greed, and ambition—of the various men in Clarissa's life but also to the timidity of older women like her mother, representative of an earlier kind of womanhood, which leaves the judging to men. Anna's counsel helps Clarissa as she navigates uncharted moral waters—first, as she weighs whether parental injunction still carries the moral authority it did; second, as she considers how to treat Lovelace the suitor; and finally, as she deliberates about how to treat Lovelace the penitent rapist. Anna's love for Clarissa renders her a sympathetic spectator of her plight but Clarissa's friend contends that her sympathy does not disable her impartiality. Here Richardson directly anticipates Smith, who identifies the sympathetic imagination as crucial to judgment because it enables the enlargement of perspective that impartiality connotes. As Smith explains in the opening sections of the *Theory*, judgments of propriety—that is, judgments that establish the appropriateness or inappropriateness (a more flexible and context-sensitive measure than "right" or "wrong") of actions and motives—are made by cultivating an impartial standpoint, by combating the particularism that characterizes any one standpoint and imaginatively engaging other standpoints.

Impartiality is the principal norm underwriting Clarissa and Anna's shared understanding of judgment, and the standpoint that their correspondence seeks to enable. "Judge me," Clarissa implores Anna, "as any indifferent person . . . would do" (73). Anna's "kind correction," Clarissa indicates, will help her see her actions from another standpoint: "I may at first be a little pained; may *glow* a little, perhaps, to be found less worthy of your friendship than I wish to be; but assure yourself that your kind correction will give me reflection that shall *amend* me" (73). In response, Anna urges Clarissa, time and again, to trust her impartiality: "It would be an affront to your own judgement if you did not; for do you not ask my advice? And have you not taught me that friendship should never give a bias against justice?" (67–68). The greatest proof of friendship, it appears, is to vivify the imperatives of justice.

It is important that the young women are peers or participants in a reciprocal dialogue. There is an ease and candor in their exchange that is lacking in Clarissa's letters to her family and to mentors such as her nurse, Norton. Anna and Clarissa are equal but different, with Anna's writing voice readily distinguishable from Clarissa's: It is more worldly, often satirical and humorous, and far less pious than the title character's. Clarissa's desire, she observes at one points, to "at least give a patient hearing to what may be said on the other side," produces the injunction to Anna to "write your whole mind" (66). The intimate but independent friend who writes long letters—here is where the minuteness of Richardson's "formal realism," as Ian Watt designates its representational detail, becomes important—helps the self cultivate a flexibility of perspective that can then be extended toward more radical imaginings, such as imagining how an adversary might view one's actions.[23] Clarissa enjoins Anna: "I charge you as I have often done, that if you observe anything in me so very faulty, as would require from you to others in my behalf the palliation of friendly and partial love, you acquaint me with it; for, methinks, I would so conduct myself as not to give reason even for an *adversary* to censure me; and how shall so weak and so young a creature avoid the censure of such, if my friend will not hold a looking-glass before me to let me see my imperfection?" (73).

We will recall the prominence of mirror imagery in Smith's *Theory of Moral Sentiments*. Society, Smith suggests, is a necessary mirror for the self since the self only learns to see itself as a differentiated individual as a consequence of its social embedment. Further, moral and aesthetic judgments are made by complicating personal bias, by engaging the points of view of others. The "eyes of other people," Smith observes, are the "only looking-glass by which we can, in some measure . . . scrutinize the propriety of our own conduct" (112). Judgments of the appropriateness or inappropriateness of one's own actions are not made by noumenal selves but by participating in a worldly community of other judges, by seeing one's actions "with the eyes of other people, or as other people are likely to view them" (110).

Perhaps the reason that so many of Richardson's readers, from the earliest to the most recent, have found the tragic ending of *Clarissa* distasteful is not because they crave the romantic resolution of the marriage plot but because the otherworldliness of the ending—summoning, as it does, a Christian system of otherworldly rewards—jars with Clarissa's worldliness, implicit in her friendship with Anna and her commitment to worldly procedures of judgment.[24] The *contemptus mundi* motif of the postscript, Richardson's suggestion there that "HEAVEN only could reward" (1498) his heroine's virtue, militates against Clarissa's own identification of Anna's eyes as a "looking-glass" in which she *can* find a measure of her worth. Indeed, even in death, Clarissa appears to want to maintain contact with the eyes of other people. The "eye-attracting coffin" (1409) she designs in anticipation of her demise, with its elaborate iconography of what Lois E. Bueler identifies as interrupted and resurgent virtue, might be interpreted as an attempt to render her virtue "spectacular," not in the sense of the beatifying or canonizing work of the postscript (Clarissa-as-saint, at the apex of a moral hierarchy) but in the aesthetic sense of opening it up to the interpretations of others.[25]

Richardson underscores, moreover, that the worldliness that becomes attached to virtue when the heart becomes an object of judgment does not detract from his heroine's independence. Clarissa's desire to engage Anna in joint deliberation in no way diminishes the independence of her judgment. While Clarissa would like Anna to approve her actions and motives, she cherishes, above all, her own approval of them. This last point is vivified by her decision, after she is raped, not to marry Lovelace to save her reputation, even though this is what she is advised to do by many others, including Anna and Lovelace's aunt, Lady Betty Lawrence—people whose opinions she respects. To Anna she writes in justification of her decision: "Do you think your Clarissa Harlowe so lost, so *sunk* at least, as that she could for the sake of patching up in the world's eye a broken reputation, meanly appear indebted to the generosity, or *compassion* perhaps, of a man who has, by means so inhuman, robbed her of it?" (1116). Ultimately it is one's own eyes rather than the world's eye or even the friend's eye that matter in distinguishing "the fit" and "the unfit."

In "Philosophy and Politics," Hannah Arendt describes the Socratic understanding of conscience—one that she broadly endorses—in similarly visual terms, as a matter of seeing and being seen. Conscience, she suggests, means that "I do not only appear to others but also to myself" (87). Put somewhat differently, "It is better to be in disagreement with the whole world than, being one, to be in disagreement with myself." One can be in disagreement with oneself, according to Arendt's Socrates, because one is at once a thinking and an acting being.[26] Morality becomes susceptible to education because of this difference, because one can learn to think differently about what one has done or should do. The "underlying assumption of [Socratic] teaching," Arendt clarifies, is "thought and not action, because only in thought do I realize the two-in-one who I am" (89). Arendt underscores too the secularizing consequence of Socrates's language of self-appearance and self-agreement, which, she argues, obviates the need for an "all-knowing and all-caring God who will pass a final judgment on life on earth" (87). This God is necessary in the absence of the two-in-one of consciousness, since it is his eyes that guarantee the goodness of a good deed in the absence of earthly witnesses to it. By contrast, a good deed, on Socrates's understanding, is good even if it has no witnesses because of the witness of the moral agent's own consciousness. To religion's Golden Rule—do unto others as you would have them do unto you—Arendt's Socrates offers the secular counterpart: "appear to yourself as you would want to appear if seen by others" (87). On this account, it is because one doesn't want to live with a murderer that one doesn't commit murder, even if this murder were to remain hidden from the eyes of gods and men.

The example of Socrates, interestingly, is summoned on two occasions in *Clarissa*, in which Lovelace's friend and correspondent, Belford, establishes a direct parallel between the trials of the "divine Clarissa" and the "divine Socrates." The two invocations represent, in microcosm, the novel's vacillation between a worldly and an otherworldly ethics. In the first of these, Belford oddly summons the pagan philosopher by way of justifying the Christian principle of otherworldly rewards and punishments. Responding to Lovelace's report of the rape, he exclaims, "Oh LOVELACE! LOVELACE! had I doubted it before, I should now be convinced that there must be a WORLD AFTER THIS, to do justice to injured merit, and to punish such a barbarous perfidy! Could the divine SOCRATES, and the divine CLARISSA, otherwise have suffered?" (884). In the second instance, however, the example of Socrates appears in the service of a more secular ethics. Clarissa is able to face her death calmly, Belford reports to Lovelace, because "she has no willful errors to look back upon with self-reproach." This, Belford adds, "was the support of the divine Socrates, as thou hast read. When led to execution, his wife lamenting that he should suffer being innocent, Thou fool, said he, wouldst thou wish me to be guilty?" (1307).

The Socrates of the first invocation is a Job-like figure who needs a God or divine judge to justify his meaningless suffering. The Socrates of the second invocation is able to reject the judgment of his worldly judges on the authority of his own conscience. It is the autonomous moral agent of the second reference that Anna summons in the novel's opening letter when she describes Clarissa as someone above praise, "not wishing to be observed even for your silent benevolence, sufficiently happy in the noble consciousness which rewards it" (40).

That Clarissa's virtue lends itself to both beatifying and secularizing interpretations is implicit too in Anna and Belford's concluding commentaries on this virtue, offered after Clarissa's death. On Belford's interpretation, the "divine Clarissa" was guided throughout her trials by an unmatched "religious rectitude." Belford's highlighting of "that religious rectitude which has been the guide of *all her actions*" (1307; my emphasis) is syntactically parallel to Anna's earlier celebration, in a letter to Clarissa, of "that prudence which governs *all your actions*" (71; my emphasis). The woman that Clarissa calls "*the sister of [my] heart*" (1404) sticks by the secularizing interpretation of her friend's virtue even after her death, when the desire to "divinize" it would presumably be the strongest. In the final letter that she contributes to the narrative, which offers a summa of her friend's virtuous life, Anna observes that "*Propriety*, another word for *nature*, was her law, as it is the foundation of all true judgement" (1468).

Anna's vocabulary of "propriety," "judgement," and "prudence" locates Clarissa's virtue in the trajectory of a broadly secular sentimentalism hospitable to the new morality of autonomy. It also locates her narrative at the beginning of a fictional tradition that finds one

terminus in Jane Austen. It is, in other words, Anna's secularizing interpretation of Clarissa's virtue rather than Belford's abject worship that
locates her friend at the beginning rather than the end of a tradition.

JUDGMENT AND EDUCATION

The dual paradigms of judgment that emerge in *Clarissa* have different
implications not only for Richardson's heroine's commitment to her
"freedom and independency" but also for her author's commitment to
educating his readers in the ways of virtue. Like Arendt's Socrates,
Richardson too believed that virtue can be taught and learned, and
perhaps more than any other eighteenth-century novelist he was able
to fulfill the Socratic role of pedagogic gadfly in a marketplace of
ideas—a role that was enabled not only by his enormously successful
fiction but also by his profession as printer and publisher.[27] His belief
in moral development is undercut, however, by his novel's Christianizing
rhetoric of the judging heart that is bestowed by "the first gracious
Planter." This essentially good heart, a free gift of God, would not
appear to need much educating.

Lovelace forcefully recognizes the antipedigogical implications of
Clarissa's language of the heart when he traces her shifting responses
to his overtures to her vacillation about his heart. As he puts it to
Belford while reporting one of their quarrels, "She must plainly tell me
that I appeared to her incapable of distinguishing what were the req-
uisites of a pure mind. Perhaps had the *libertine* presumption to imagine that there was no difference in *heart*, nor any but what proceeded
from *education* and *custom*, between the pure and the impure—And
yet custom *alone*, as she observed, would make a second nature, as well
in good as in bad habits" (702). On the one hand, as Lovelace suggests,
Clarissa understands human nature as, in significant ways, a social
construction or second nature produced by education. On the other
hand, she appears to believe in an essential difference of persons that is
in excess of any difference in education (figured by her as the difference between a "pure" and an "impure" heart).[28] Her attitude toward
Lovelace varies depending upon the understanding of human nature
that is uppermost in her mind. On the one hand, building upon the

reports she receives of his noble behavior toward Rose, the country girl whose marriage he enables, she grants him the full potential of moral reform. On the other hand, she views Lovelace as irredeemably immoral because of what she sometimes describes as his "black heart" and at other times as his heartlessness. Early on, for example, she observes to Anna that "I am still of opinion, that he wants a *heart*; and if he does, he wants everything. A wrong *head* may be convinced, may have a right turn given it: but who is able to give a *heart*, if a heart be wanting?" (184). Against the grain of her own belief that "All human excellence . . . is comparative only" (853), Clarissa frequently asserts an absolute superiority over Lovelace, as in her claim that "my soul is immeasurably thy soul's superior." From this angle, Lovelace is "vice itself" (892), just as Clarissa, in Belford's reverent eyes, is "virtue itself" (959). The beatification of the "divine Clarissa," which Belford begins even before she dies, and which has its roots in what he describes as his "holy love for this angel of a woman" (1080), merely reproduces the logic of Clarissa's assertion to Lovelace that "there is not, I will be bold to say, a sincerer heart in the world than hers before you" (833).

In some respects, indeed, Lovelace serves as a better spokesperson for his author's program of moral education than Clarissa. In a striking rewriting of the plant metaphor deployed by Clarissa in letter 185— that is, her representation of God's laws as plants blooming in the garden of her heart—he observes to Belford, "Then her LOVE OF VIRTUE seems to be *principle*, native, or if *not* native, so deeply rooted that its fibres have struck into her heart, and, as she grew up, so blended and twisted themselves with the strings of life that I doubt there is no separating of the one, without cutting the others asunder" (657). Here it is not the moral law but character that is represented as a plant. Clarissa, Lovelace suggests, has loved and cultivated virtue from so early an age that her virtue *seems* to be innate or "native." While Lovelace's rake's creed denies to women a love of virtue for its own sake, his confident knowledge of the other sex is shaken by his encounters with Clarissa. "Can education," he asks Belford, "have stronger force in a woman's heart than nature?—Sure it cannot. But if it can, how entirely right are parents to cultivate their daughters' minds, and to inspire them with notions of reserve and distance to our sex; and indeed to make them think highly of their own?" (695). While Belford's interactions with Clarissa encourage him to deify women, Lovelace's encounters encourage belief in a program of education that is grounded in the principle of women's self-respecting individuality.

Lovelace's apparent openness to the claims of education jars, however, with his rake's creed, which is as absolutist as Clarissa's saintly discourse of the heart. When Richardson, in the preface, cautions young women not to subscribe to "that dangerous but too commonly received notion, *that a reformed rake makes the best husband*" (36), he might have added this reason: that the rake is a fanatic of sorts, whose life has been structured so fully by fixed rules that loosening their hold is a Herculean task. Confronted with the novel particular that is Clarissa, Lovelace is unable to bend existing rules or create new rules to accommodate the particular character he confronts. Unable to make judgment reflective, his actions, often at odds with his feelings about Clarissa, embody the rake's maxim that a woman's nature triumphs over nurture—that women are, in effect, fundamentally uneducable. The rape, for example, is plotted by Lovelace to prove the "triumph of nature over principle" (1147). He aims to give the lie—through the awakening of sexual desire, or failing that, through an enforced pregnancy—to Clarissa's program of constructing a moral character for herself over and above her reproductive character as a woman.

In his energetically polemical deconstructive study *Reading Clarissa*, William Warner elides Lovelace's absolutism when he figures the clash of worldviews of Lovelace and Clarissa as a battle between a rigidly moralistic Christian woman and a proto-Nietzschean proto-postmodernist, who is as playfully unconcerned with rules as the deconstructive critic himself.[29] As I do, Warner highlights the importance of the languages of judgment in *Clarissa* but he situates them in the recherché humanism that he, like other poststructuralist critics of the novel genre, associates with Enlightenment modernity. While many of the particulars of Warner's study have been vigorously debated by subsequent readers, its interpretation of humanism, or what he calls "the humanist sublime," still enjoys considerable critical currency. By way of conclusion, I consider the implications for Warner's argument about humanism of the two paradigms of judgment I have ascribed to Richardson's *Clarissa*—the heart's judgment and the judgment of an impartial observer.

Echoing Mandeville, Warner interprets humanism as a program of unending self-flattery. The humanist sublime, as he describes it, attributes moral seriousness and psychological depth to individuals in order to glorify a fundamentally inglorious creature, man. *Clarissa*, he argues, has a privileged place in the development of this ideology because it is the novel that initiates fiction's inward turn to the psychological individual. Anticipating critics of the British novel such as Nancy Armstrong and Deidre Shauna Lynch, Warner suggests that a principal problem with the inward turn instantiated by *Clarissa* is that it takes the individual out of history and sociality; it is premised on a disavowal of the self's contingency and social embedment.[30] On this reading, Richardson's heroine's principal labor is to preserve humanism's myth of an essential and essentially good self. Clarissa, Warner argues, repeatedly stages a "scene of judgment" in which she turns the tables on those who would judge her by representing her virtue as a "self-present virtue" (18). Interestingly, Warner identifies the novel's discourse of the heart as the principal culprit behind this humanist ideology:

> At the center of [Clarissa's] self is the heart, the purest and most precious part of the self, which will not admit of the entrance of any foreign matter. The heart becomes the locus of virtue by being planted with principles that are the laws of God and man. If these principles are strictly adhered to, the self may become a paragon of virtue which shines in the eyes of men. But to do this the self must encourage the natural inclinations of the heart, those feelings of "pity" and compassion that link it with all men. All these activities require an immense and patient investment of time and energy, and a willingness to make headway slowly. Sometimes, quite unexpectedly, external adversity reveals something is wrong with the self. An examination of the heart leads to the discovery of a flaw or stain, which can only be removed through an arduous act of meditation. This act reintegrates the self and puts it back on course. (17)

By contrast with John Mullan's and Scott Paul Gordon's interpretations of Richardsonian sentimentalism as lachrymose sensibility, Warner highlights its concern with reflection. Humanism, as Warner understands it, takes men and women to be deliberative agents, but deliberative by way of serving an uncritical essentialism, as in Clarissa's faith in her essentially good heart. Clarissa works hard, Warner argues, to make us believe that her virtue is a metaphysical substance, and she and her author deploy cardiac imagery as a resource in this context. Her heart emerges in the narrative as an inherently good thing and personal flaws are represented as foreign matter in its native soil (to be removed with surgical precision). Self-satisfied in her goodness, Richardson's heroine, Warner contends, seeks a "radical autonomy, an existence quite apart from all human ties." Indeed, it is humanism's archenemy, Lovelace, who emerges on Warner's reading as committed to the world of sociability and relationship: "Lovelace's life is a function of Clarissa as antagonist in struggle, and of Belford as recipient of his narratives. Each gives him the possibility of playing, performing, feeling alive. That he is a function of the manifold of struggle and the interplay between self and other means that he is an uncertain and changing quantity, but also that he acknowledges, with every story and gesture, that he needs the other person and will feel the most acute sense of loss on their departure" (39).

Warner's point about selfhood being a social construction is well taken, as is his argument about the essentializing work of Richardson's language of the heart. But Warner neglects the extensive questioning of the heart's authority by Clarissa in her capacity as her heart's judge, as well as Anna's role in the novel's rhetoric of impartiality. On his reading, Anna and Clarissa's friendship is "chill and uninteresting"— a reading again very different from Mullan's interpretation of the friendship as instituting a lachrymose community of women—because it is structured by a "mediating concept of virtue" (39). This obscures, however, the ways in which friendship in *Clarissa* enables the most difficult construction of all, the construction of general standards that are really standpoints, or that are only as legitimate as the individual standpoints that enable them. While Warner reads the "scene of judgment" in *Clarissa* as enabling its heroine's judgmentalism—her judgment of Lovelace as evil and of herself as innately good—I have suggested that the novel's discourse of judgment only equivocally implies such judgmentalism.[31] It is worth noting too that insofar as the critique of humanism is meant to be a critique of essentialism, it appears fractured by its own continued investment in "*the* humanist self," which it exposes, again and again, to be a social construction.[32]

In recent times, several critics have opened up contexts other than "humanism" or "anti-humanism" as important to understanding the form and moral theme of Richardson's fiction. In *Samuel Richardson's* Clarissa *and the Eighteenth-Century Reader*, Tom Keymer attributes to *Clarissa* a dialogic ethos reminiscent of earlier traditions of casuistry, an ethos implicit in the novel's epistolary format and the letters' multiplication of interpretations around single events.[33] Casuistry, Keymer points out, "starts from a recognition that system-building is a precarious enterprise, and takes as its special field particular instances in which the automatic application of rules appears most questionable." It is "at such points, where daily life appears to deny the validity of laws and the efficacy of systems, that [Richardson's] novels are typically located."[34] Formally, this juridical paradigm produces, among other things, the disappearing author of *Clarissa's* first edition, in which Richardson performed a *deus absconditus* and left to his reader the difficult role of casuist-judge: "Meanings remain vexed, controversial, indeterminate; and in the absence of synthesis, or of any objective guidance in matters of evaluation and judgment, the reader is pushed into the most exacting and creative of roles."[35]

Situating *Clarissa* in an ongoing tradition of Kantian constructivism, exemplified by John Rawls's theory of justice, Amit Yahav-Brown also highlights the challenge it poses to absolutist and metaphysical ideologies. Yahav-Brown takes as her point of departure the rhetoric of "reasonableness" in Richardson's novel, which, she suggests, finds an intriguing parallel in Rawls's *Political Liberalism*.[36] For Rawls, Yahav-Brown explains, "reasonable" can be distinguished from "rational" as a criterion for choice because it summons collective deliberation. Hence, "while rationality is derived from the deliberation of a single agent, reasonableness is derived from deliberations among multiple agents. To establish the rationality of a claim, we can reason alone; but to establish the reasonableness of an act or claim we must reason with others" (806). In a telling comparison of Richardson and Defoe, Yahav-Brown suggests that point of view becomes important in the history of the novel only once norms acquire this collaborative character. Defoe "presents the narrative only from the hero or heroine's point of view, thus suggesting that there is no crucial distinction to be made between his characters' reasoning and the reasoning of others." By contrast, "In developing reasonableness and distinguishing it from rationality, Richardson introduces point of view as a crucial variable. One's reason, he suggests, may differ from another's not only in quantity but also in substance; reasoned motivation may entail different things when viewed from Clarissa's perspective, or when viewed from Lovelace's" (809).[37]

My complementary argument here has been that before many of the philosophers of judgment who also establish the claims of sentiment in the eighteenth century, Richardson opens up an ethical understanding that pivots around standpoints rather than standards, and that identifies the social world to be an ineluctably perspectival public space. Yahav-Brown's delineation of "reasonable" as distinct from "rational" offers one important lens for thinking through this novel concern with perspective. Another, highlighted by the present study, is the Kantian distinction between reflective and determinant judgments. Reflective judgments, as I noted in the previous chapter, are judgments that have no pre-established rules or standards and that are legitimated instead by an interactive procedure of deliberation and dialogue. When Hannah Arendt, for example, controversially deemed evil "banal" in *Eichmann in Jerusalem*, she was arguing against the elision of such procedures of legitimation, against the foreclosure of reflective judgment by moral absolutes like "evil." Identifying "the nature and function of human judgment" as "one of the central moral questions of all time," Arendt gave it a central role in the fight against totalitarianism:

Since the whole of respectable society had in one way or another succumbed to Hitler, the moral maxims which determine social behavior and the religious commandments—"Thou shalt not kill!"—which guide conscience had virtually vanished. Those few who were still able to tell right from wrong went really only by their own judgments, and they did so freely; there were no rules to be abided by, under which the particular cases with which they were confronted with could be subsumed. They had to decide each instance as it arose, because no rules existed for the unprecedented.[38]

Totalitarianism, as described here, destroyed all preexisting conventions of morality. It produced a new moral order in which so-called respectable society felt free to disrespect human life. Only those who could judge reflectively were able to oppose these new codes of "respect." Only those who were able to "think without a banister"—a formulation that Arendt repeatedly deploys in her writings on judgment—could refrain from the new injunction to kill.

"What a world is this!" Clarissa exclaims at the height of the conflict at Harlowe Place. "What is there in it desirable? The good we hope for, so strangely mixed, that one knows not what to wish for" (224). The aspirations of the virtuous individual, in the new moral order Richardson depicts in *Clarissa*, are no longer guided by a clearly given good since fathers have become tyrants and dictators. Clarissa's recourse to her heart's judgment represents an attempt to deny the novel indeterminacy with which she is confronted. Her complication of the figure of the judging heart denotes an acceptance of the new disorder, and evinces a commitment to rules for judging that are more made than found. For Kant, we will recall, "The power of judgment in general is the faculty for thinking of the particular as contained under the universal. If the universal (the rule, the principle, the law) is given, then the power of judgment, which subsumes the particular under it . . . is determining. If, however, only the particular is given, for which the universal is to be found, then the power of judgment is merely reflecting" (66–67). Kant restricts "merely reflecting" or "reflective" judgments to the aesthetic domain. Richardson's *Clarissa* moves them to the moral domain.

4. A Sentimental Education:
Rousseau to Godwin

RICHARDSON'S *CLARISSA* SIGNIFICANTLY shaped one of the Enlightenment's key intellectual and literary projects, that of Jean-Jacques Rousseau. Rousseau's novel, *Julie; or, The New Heloise* (1761), is explicitly modeled on Richardson's masterpiece. Like *Clarissa*, *Julie* is an epistolary novel and like its precursor it takes as its theme the conflict between old and new moralities, the ethos of obedience and that of self-direction, as embodied in a battle of wills between a father and a daughter.[1] Published in the near proximity of the two most influential works of Rousseau's oeuvre—*Emile* (1762), a novel-cum-philosophical treatise on education, and *The Social Contract* (1762)—*Julie* is widely considered to have exercised considerable influence on both. But it has only recently begun to receive sustained attention, both as a novel and as a work of importance in considering Rousseau's idea of freedom.[2] The latter, as is well known, woke Kant from his moral slumbers—just as Hume's epistemological doubt woke him from his dogmatic slumbers—and it was identified by the French revolutionaries as the underwriting norm of their revolution.[3] Since *Julie* takes its inspiration from *Clarissa*, one might say that *Clarissa*'s, if not Clarissa's, afterlife ended up being far more revolutionary than Richardson had anticipated in the postscript to his novel—which, as was noted in the previous chapter, transformed the disobedient daughter of the narrative into a "meek" Christian saint.

Julie is, however, no mere imitation of *Clarissa*.[4] A major point of departure is Rousseau's treatment of his heroine's sexuality. While virtue and virginity become closely aligned in Clarissa's story, they are less so in Julie's. Unlike Richardson's heroine, Julie willingly enters a sexual union before marriage and, although this is represented by her author as a misstep, it is also identified as a bounded and reversible declension. In *Julie*, Rousseau seeks to revise *Clarissa* into a Bildungsroman of the passions, to show how the love of two people of refined sensibilities—Julie d'Étange and her tutor, known by no other name than "St. Preux" (the playful appellation Julie and her cousin Claire bestow upon him)—lends itself to affiliation with virtue and can be brought back into virtue's fold when it takes a wrong turn. In a letter to Julie, St. Preux suggests, "Love inspired in us sentiments too noble to derive from them the misdeeds of denatured souls" (261). Elsewhere, he describes their love as "a raging fire that carries its heat into the other sentiments, and breathes into them a new vigor" (49). But the "other sentiments" that love invigorates turn out to be very different for the two lovers. St. Preux's love for Julie prompts the development of reason and judgment, and finds its ends in the freedom of the moral man and the practical duties of the educator: St. Preux, we are told, will become the tutor of Julie's children, and also, through his writings, of society as a whole.[5] By contrast, Julie's experience of a supposedly ennobling love enables a very limited kind of judgment. She learns a gendered variant, a woman's judgment, which is mostly indistinguishable from instinct except in the aesthetic domain, where it is manifest as a reasoned taste. In her narrative, the "raging fire" of sexual passion becomes transmuted into the refined appetites of a chatelaine. While St. Preux learns to be free, Julie learns to garden and to adore good food and elegant—though not ostentatious—clothing.

Rousseau's sentimental alternative to Richardson encompasses then two divergent understandings of virtue, which are split along gender lines. These compare interestingly with the two virtues mobilized by Richardson's *Clarissa* and discussed earlier in this study: one grounded in its heroine's figure of the judging heart and the other in her judgments of her heart. Both, I suggested, are "sentimental" in their attempts to align the claims of judgment and feeling, but they are sentimental in different ways and situate Richardson's novel differently in the context of Enlightenment conversations about autonomy. Female virtue in *Julie*, as upheld by its mature heroine, resembles the virtue of obedience that comes into play in Richardson's novel through its heroine's representations of her heart as an authoritative inner judge—an entity that spontaneously reveals God's judgments to its bearer. Tellingly, both the heart and religion play a crucial role in Julie's

Bildung. Julie's "too-tender heart" (41), which becomes inflamed by her sexual passion for St. Preux, is soothed (and domesticated) by being filled with the counteracting lights of God's wisdom and the wisdom of the Enlightenment, as represented by her husband Monsieur de Wolmar. Indeed, by the end of the narrative, Julie is said to have achieved "the meekness of the Christian" (598–99), a phrase strikingly reminiscent of Richardson's description of his heroine in the postscript to *Clarissa*.

In some respects, St. Preux's virtue parallels the second conception of virtue operative in *Clarissa*, one grounded in its heroine's commitment to impartial judgment. But whereas Clarissa's impartiality and autonomy, I argued in the last chapter, situate her in the social world— they are epistolary developments and strengthened by peer review— St. Preux's autonomy has a strikingly antisocial cast. It finds its ends in the philosopher's life, which is described by Rousseau as a life that shuns involvement with other people beyond the asymmetrical exchange of pupil and tutor—strikingly unlike the life of the gadfly that Arendt ascribes to the Socratic philosopher and the Kantian critical thinker or judge.

Like *Clarissa*, *Julie* was a sensational success all over Europe and not least in Richardson's native country.[6] Together with *Emile*, it substantially shaped British literature and culture in the closing decades of the eighteenth century. But it did so not least through the criticism it evoked, which was directed especially at Rousseau's depiction of women's virtue. A particularly powerful challenge came from one of Rousseau's most ardent admirers, Mary Wollstonecraft. In *A Vindication of the Rights of Woman* (1792), Wollstonecraft developed a program of education for women that was inspired by Rousseau's belief that moral freedom is the proper goal of education; departing from Rousseau, however, Wollstonecraft identified it to be the goal of male and female education alike. Both men and women, she argued, have been sent into the world to cultivate their faculties and "acquire virtue."[7] Virtue, therefore, cannot be different for such similarly educable creatures.

In the one case anticipating, and in the other case building upon, Wollstonecraft's argument, are two novels that take *Julie* as their immediate points of departure: Henry Mackenzie's *Julia de Roubigné* (1777) and William Godwin's *Fleetwood; or, The New Man of Feeling*

(1805).[8] Just as *Julie* finds its inspiration in *Clarissa*, Mackenzie's sentimental novel invokes and revises Rousseau's bestselling work. *Fleetwood* is still more encompassing in its intertextual reference because it summons at once *Julia*, *Julie*, and *Emile*. Rousseau even appears offstage as a character in Godwin's novel, cast in the role of a close personal friend of the Scottish Macneil—reminiscent perhaps of David Hume, just as the Swiss Ruffigny brings to mind the Savoyard vicar of *Emile*.[9] Mackenzie's other work, and especially his immensely popular first novel, *The Man of Feeling* (1771), is clearly also important to Godwin's *Fleetwood*, as its subtitle, "The New Man of Feeling," suggests.

Godwin and Mackenzie question Rousseau's division of virtue along gender lines, as well as his association of female virtue with feelings only. A cautionary tale about a young woman who becomes a victim of her sympathetic responsiveness, and especially of the self-sacrificing pity that makes her subservient to husbands and fathers, Mackenzie's *Julia de Roubigné* complicates Rousseauvian sentimentalism's valorization of women's capacity to feel. By developing an extensive network of theatrical and other aesthetic metaphors, Mackenzie positions his heroine as a spectator of her own and others' feelings, as someone who could, but doesn't, sufficiently cultivate the critical distance that autonomy demands.

Godwin's challenge to Rousseau is still more far reaching. He questions not only the latter's gendering of virtue but also the essentialist cast of his sentimentalism, which upholds an ineffable "nature" as the basis of social arrangements.[10] If Rousseau's argument against Richardson is that the latter is too suspicious of human nature, as constituted by the natural passions, Godwin's rebuttal of Rousseau is that nature is a far more equivocal norm than the author of *Julie* and *Emile* imagines. In making this argument, Godwin draws upon sentimentalists like Hume, who memorably described nature in *A Treatise of Human Nature* as the trickiest of terms—"none more equivocal and ambiguous" (474)—because many human traits taken to be natural are in fact social constructions.[11] He builds also on his wife Mary Wollstonecraft's novel *Mary* (1788), which dramatizes the limits of a Rousseauvian education by representing its eponymous heroine, educated principally by nature, as a permanent exile from society.[12]

Fleetwood departs from the other sentimental novels considered in this study by abandoning the epistolary form in favor of first-person retrospective narration. While epistolarity, in a novel like *Clarissa*, registers a dialogic ethos by multiplying the points of view from which any given event can be interpreted, Godwin's formal choice reinforces one of his fundamental critiques of Rousseauvian sentimentalism: that it produces a training in solipsism. At the same time, he upholds the potential of education by highlighting the gap between the standpoints of the mature narrator, who offers his history as a "record of my errors" (59), and the protagonist of the history, his younger erring self. The narrative itself traces the emergence of the gap by depicting Fleetwood's education through experience and social engagement into more flexible habits of mind. This contrasts with the entrapment of the letter writers in *Julia de Roubigné*, whose letters seem to have been sent into a void because we never see the responses to them. Susan Manning tellingly describes Mackenzie's last novel as "a series of dramatic monologues which, fatally, fail to converge in an agreed or shareable version of reality. All the letter writers (and this is especially true of Julia and Montauban) live within inturned imaginations which fail to register modifying contact with another viewpoint."[13] While I would adapt this argument to account for what I described earlier as Julia and Maria's peer-reviewing activity, it is certainly the case that Mackenzie's novel registers a crisis in epistolary address that can be traced to the growing isolation of individuals in modern commercial society. As such, the shift to *Fleetwood*'s autobiographical mode seems nearly inevitable though Godwin reprises Mackenzie to register his fin de siècle moment with cautious optimism about the continued potential of modifying contact with others. Concomitantly, he revises Mackenzie's tragic conclusion by replacing death, caused by a failed marriage, with rebirth through a second marriage (with the same person). Godwin's hero is a "new man of feeling" because, unlike *Julia's* Montauban, he learns to be less rigid in his views and also because, unlike the paradigmatic man of feeling, Mackenzie's Harley, he doesn't die but lives to marry his Miss Walton—not once but twice. Like *Julie*, *Fleetwood* is principally a male Bildungsroman but the education it enjoins is the training of men not into philosophers but into thinkers capable of friendship with women.

NATURAL EDUCATION

Rousseau's fundamental thesis in *Julie* and *Emile* is that virtue has a story because virtue is a development. It is a development of the natural or primary passions that Emile's tutor pools together under the rubric of self-love or *amour de soi*. In a direct challenge to Hobbes, Rousseau contends that the natural passions enable self-preservation and hence must be distinguished from selfishness; they are morally neutral but are corrupted by society into *amour-propre*, a self-love that requires making comparisons with others and feeling superior to them (in brief, vanity). In an ideal Rousseauvian universe, like the counterfactual world of *Emile*, which imagines what it would be like to bring up a child in near-total isolation from society, other people are kept at bay by the tutor until the pupil develops the reason that controls *amour-propre*. Emile's education is a "natural education" because it develops the passions in conformity with nature rather than with society and its laws. Rousseau figures this as, to begin with, a "dependence on things," as opposed to a dependence on persons or wills:

> There are two sorts of dependence: dependence on things which is from nature: dependence on men, which is from society. Dependence on things, since it has no morality, is in no way detrimental to freedom and engenders no vice. Dependence on men, since it is without order, engenders all the vices, and by it, master and slave are mutually corrupted.

Emile is introduced into society, including the world of books, only after he is old enough to exercise rational self-control, and the first book he reads is, appropriately, *Robinson Crusoe*—a book that reinforces the Rousseauvian dictum of natural man as an island unto himself. In *Julie*, where the protagonists are older, society and the individual are never separate. But the society the lovers inhabit is described by the "editor" of their letters as a relatively simple mountain community far from the corruptions of Paris: *Julie* is subtitled "letters of two lovers who live in a small town at the foot of the Alps." In this rustic setting of great natural beauty, the lovers' passions are perceived to retain a purity that makes them ripe for a Rousseauvian education.

Rousseau's negative attitude toward society is accompanied by some self-irony since he also suggests that only society of some sort can prevent *amour de soi* from becoming *amour-propre* before the birth of reason. In *Emile*, "society" becomes Jean-Jacques himself in the guise of a tutor who shapes Emile's environment to conform to what he calls nature. In *Julie*, the lovers regain the path of nature and virtue after they have deviated from it with the help of the "tutor" that is Julie's husband. A man of very high birth and great intellectual powers, Wolmar is represented by Rousseau as the very best of his society, as someone who brings the spirit of rational philosophy to bear upon the traditional obligations of the landed gentleman.

A Rousseauvian natural education signifies, then, not a simple return to nature and away from society, as accounts aligning Rousseau's sentimentalism with cultural primitivism suggest, but rather a return to nature as prescribed by the best of society—by tutors who are perceived to be near-infallible guardians of the young.[14] The importance attached to the perspectives of peers in such key works of British sentimentalism as Richardson's *Clarissa* and Hume's "Of the Standard of Taste" finds no analogue in Rousseau's moral vision, which privileges a point of view—that of the tutor—that claims to be no point of view at all since it is described by the tutor himself as the point of view of nature, frequently personified as "Nature." But Nature turns out to constitute a double standard in *Emile* and *Julie*, by splitting into two natures—male and female—mobilizing different virtues and different educations.[15] Male virtue resides in autonomous judgment; female virtue, as Rousseau understands it, in attentiveness to men's judgments. In *Emile*, more conservative than *Julie* in its gender politics, female virtue entails a near-total reliance upon men and their perceptions of right and wrong. As Jean-Jacques, Emile's tutor, puts it:

By the very law of nature women are at the mercy of men's judgments, as much for their own sake as for that of their children. It is not enough that they be estimable; they must be esteemed. It is not enough for them to be pretty; they must please. It is not enough for them to be temperate; they must be recognized as such. Their honor is not only in their conduct but in their reputation; and it is not possible that a woman who consents to be regarded as disreputable can ever be decent. When a man acts well, he depends only on himself and can brave public judgment; but when a woman acts well, she has accomplished only half her task, and what is thought of her is no less important to her than what she actually is. From this it follows that the system of woman's education ought to be contrary in this respect to the system of man's education. Opinion is the grave of virtue among men and its throne among women. (364–65)

As represented here, female virtue thrives on the *amour-propre* that Rousseau deems fatal to male virtue. Woman's physical dependence, Rousseau believes, translates into moral dependence. Clarissa's insistence that her own judgments of "the fit" and "the unfit" take precedence over the judgments of others—including the other that is respectable society—is replaced in Rousseau's gendered moral universe by a highly conventional concern with reputation. "The Supreme Being," he suggests in *Emile*, "wanted to do honor to the human species in everything. While giving man inclinations without limit, He gives him at the same time the law which regulated them, in order that he may be free and in command of himself. While abandoning man to the immoderate passions, He joins reason to these passions to govern them. While abandoning woman to unlimited desires, He joins modesty to these desires in order to constrain them" (359). Elsewhere, he identifies good taste as one of the most important goals of a woman's education, as a quality that helps her render her home and person more desirable to her husband.

Julie is less blatantly sexist than *Emile* because it is a narrative about an exceptional woman rather than the everywoman who is Emile's partner Sophie. Concomitantly, Julia d'Etange's virtue appears to be of a higher order. It is embodied less in her reputation or her considerable arts of pleasing but, more prominently, in her exceptional heart, which is renowned for being a "too tender heart" (41). Julie's mature virtue is grounded in the spontaneous judgments of that precious organ. St. Preux writes of Madame de Wolmar's rule of judging: "As for Julie, who never had any rule but her heart and could not have a surer one, she gives in to it without scruple, and in order to do good, she does whatever it requires of her" (435).

However, with no other rule for judging than her heart, Julie is easily ruled by the judgments of others—those of her feudalistic father,

to begin with, and later, her enlightened husband's judgments. There
is a precise equivalent and precursor in *Julie* to Julia de Roubigné's
description, in letter XIX of Mackenzie's novel, of the pity that leads
her to marry the man of her father's, rather than her own, choice. We
will recall that Julia responds to her father's highly emotional staging
of his and Montauban's disappointments with "enthusiastic madness."
The spectacle of older men symbolically falling from the pedestal upon
which they have been placed by her culture brings Julia literally down
to her father's feet, avowing submission and reinstating the distance
between them. In *Julie*, Rousseau has the Baron d'Étange actually bend
before his daughter and petition for his friend. Weakened by grief at
her mother's death and stupefied by her father's genuflection, Julie
gives in to the latter's wishes. She describes the incident to St. Preux in
the very long letter XVIII of Part III, in which she also invites him to
exchange the role of Julie's lover for Madame de Wolmar's friend:

> He saw that my mind was made up, and that he would obtain noth-
> ing from me by authority. For a moment I thought I was delivered
> from his persecutions. But what became of me when I suddenly
> beheld at my feet the sternest of fathers moved and melting into
> tears? Without letting me rise he grasped my knees, and fixing his
> damp eyes on mine, he told me in a touching voice I can still hear
> within me: My daughter! Respect your father's white hair; do not
> send him in grief to the grave, like her who bore you in the womb!
> Ah! Do you want to inflict death on the entire family?
>
> Imagine my shock. That posture, that tone of voice, that gesture,
> those words, that terrible thought so unsettled me that I slid half-
> dead into his arms, and it was only after many sobs that were choking
> me, that I was able to answer him in a broken and faint voice: O my
> father! I had defenses against your threats, I have none against your
> tears. It is you who will be the death of your daughter. (286)

The scene is even more violent than its equivalent in *Julia de Roubigné*.
Julie's too-tender heart responds to the spectacle of her father's grief
with a "half-death" that foreshadows the almost automaton-like quality of her life as Madame de Wolmar. Just as she had earlier responded
with too much pity to the "dangerous spectacle" (78) of St. Preux controlling his sexual passion for her—she writes to Claire that "it was

pity that undid me" (79)—so too Julie is undone here by the potent spectacle of her aloof father becoming an uncontrolled and uncontrollable man of feeling.

Interestingly, this scene of the father's genuflection not only anticipates *Julia de Roubigné* but also looks back to *Clarissa*. The equivalent in the latter text is the least violent of the three because it entails a description of what James Harlowe senior *might* have done to force his daughter's hand but does not get the opportunity to do since Clarissa flees the paternal mansion. In letter 145, Clarissa writes to Anna Howe about a missive she has received from her aunt Hervey, who reports that the imperious Mr. Harlowe had intended to beg his daughter on bended knee to marry the man he had chosen as her husband. Here is Clarissa:

> And now to know that my father, an hour before he received the tidings of my supposed flight, owned that he loved me as his life: that he would have been all condescension: that he would—Oh! my dear, how tender, how mortifyingly tender, now in him! My aunt need not have been afraid that it should be known that she has sent me such a letter as this!—A father kneel to a daughter!—There would not indeed have been any bearing of that!—What I should have done in such a case, I know not. Death would have been much more welcome to me than such a sight, on such an occasion, in behalf of a man so very, very disgustful to me! But I had deserved annihilation had I suffered my father to kneel in vain. (506–7)

Clarissa's pious assertion that she could not have borne the sight of her father on his knees is qualified by her characteristic self-doubt: "What I should have done in such a case, I know not." Pity, Clarissa suggests, might have undone her. But then it might have not. And the possibility that it might have not is reinforced by her particularizing the imagined scene: If, in general, a kneeling father is a sight that a dutiful daughter cannot and should not endure, "*such* a sight, on *such* an occasion, in behalf of *a man so very, very disgustful to me*" is perhaps one *this* daughter would have been able to withstand (my emphasis).

The difference in these representations of kneeling fathers says a great deal about Richardson and Rousseau's ideological investments. While *Julie* is sometimes described as a more liberal novel than *Clarissa* because it is interpreted as endorsing its heroine's sexuality—Rousseau doesn't exactly do that since he represents Julie's sexual relationship with St. Preux as a problem to be overcome—Clarissa's narrative is by no means simply a narrative of replacing obedience with obedience (as Julie's becomes). As I argued in the previous chapter, the story of obedience to various fathers, heavenly and earthly, which is charted by the novel's discourse of the judging heart, appears alongside the narrative of self-governance implicit in Clarissa's judgments of her heart. Julie, by contrast, never lays claim to any judgment but that of her heart: Judgment, instinct, and affection become one and the same on Rousseau's understanding of female virtue in *Julie*.

Moving from obedience to obedience, Julie's education into virtue is so seamless as to be virtually unnoticeable. Indeed, the letter to St. Preux in which Julie describes it is made respectably voluminous only by the detailed recollections it offers of their past relationship. As represented by Julie, her transition from fallen woman to virtuous wife happens at exactly the moment that she becomes Wolmar's wife. Julie depicts the marriage ceremony as a highly somber rite of passage:

> The dim light in the building, the profound silence of the Spectators, their modest and meditative demeanor, the procession of all my relatives, the imposing sight of my revered father, all these things lent to what was about to take place an atmosphere of solemnity that summoned me to attention and respect, and would have made me shudder at the very thought of perjury. I thought I saw the instrument of providence and heard the voice of God in the minister's grave recitation of the holy liturgy. The purity, the dignity, the holiness of marriage, so vividly set forth in the words of Scripture, those chaste and sublime duties so important to happiness, to order, to peace, to the survival of mankind, so sweet to fulfill for their own sake; all this made such an impression on me that I seemed to experience within me a sudden revolution. It was as if an unknown power repaired all at once the disorder of my affections and re-established them in accordance with the law of duty and nature. (291–92)

At the altar, Julie experiences a "sudden revolution" of sentiments rather than the "progress of sentiments" (500) of which David Hume speaks in *A Treatise of Human Nature* when he describes how

the "artificial" sense of justice is cultivated by individuals as a development of their more primary perceptions of right and wrong. She
understands that she is entering the fold of a better community than
the community of which her bigoted father was the authoritative
spokesperson. Or rather, the community is the same but has a better
guardian—not the traditionalist father but a forward-looking hus-
band-philosopher, an Enlightenment version of Plato's philosopher-
king in *The Republic*. In God's house-turned-meeting place for family
and friends, Julie places her too-tender heart under the tutelage of
"fathers" superior to her biological father—God and her husband.

As if unsure of the role she will play after the spectacle of her con-
version plays itself out, Julie looks around the ranks of the spectators
for suggestions and is especially struck by the message she finds in the
compassionate eyes of Claire and her husband: "A fortuitous glance in
the direction of Monsieur and Madame d'Orbe, whom I saw side by
side with compassion in their eyes, moved me even more powerfully
than had all the other objects. Amiable and virtuous couple, are you
the less united for knowing less of love?" Their marriage represents,
and Julie enters, a union that "wisdom sanctions and reason directs"
(292). Yet their compassion also appears to signal the limits of this kind
of marriage; they seem almost regretful that she is entering a union
like theirs. Indeed, Julie's somber marriage ceremony, represented by
her as an initiation into a higher community, might also be read as a
scene of sacrifice—as a staging, for instance, of Mackenzie's Julia's
favorite play, Racine's *Iphigénie*.

Rousseau makes it appear as though a passionless marriage is the
only union compatible with Julie's virtue. Julie's heart, as various
onlookers indicate, was unable to bear the "devouring flame" of her
passion for St. Preux. Her love is repeatedly described as a "corroding
poison" (32) that renders her a victim, "floating amidst contrary passions" (164). Against this representation stands the image of love's
effects on St. Preux. While love consumes Julie's heart, it only animates
St. Preux's. Claire writes to Julie's lover that "your love although of
equal strength on both sides is not similar in its effects. Yours is ebul-
lient and animated, hers is gentle and tender: your sentiments are
vehemently vented outwardly, hers return toward her, and by pene-
trating the substance of her soul gradually denature and change it.

Love quickens and sustains your heart, it wilts and oppresses hers" (265). St. Preux's friend, the enlightened Englishman, Edward Bomston, reinforces this argument when he suggests to Claire, "A love such as [St. Preux's] is not so much a weakness as a strength put to the wrong use. An ardent and unhappy flame can occupy for a time, forever perhaps, part of his faculties; but it is itself a proof of their excellence, and of the advantage he could draw from them to cultivate wisdom: for sublime reason is maintained only by the same vigor of soul that makes for great passions, and philosophy is properly served only if it is practiced with the same ardor one feels for a mistress" (158). While love occupies only a fraction of St. Preux's superior faculties, it dominates Julie's, by implication, inferior ones. Looking forward to Julie's own deathbed account of love's effects upon her, Bomston describes her subjectivity as identical with her love for St. Preux. Offering to Julie the option of eloping to England with her lover, he writes, "Love has too deeply infiltrated the fabric of your soul for you to have the power of driving it out" (162).

St. Preux's moral education is, in many respects, reminiscent of the unidirectional ascent up the ladder of love described by Diotima in Plato's *Symposium*: first one learns to love beautiful things, then beautiful people, and finally beauty or goodness itself.[16] Invoking this parallel, St. Preux indicates to Julie that she is the person "whom I worshipped when I was *beginning* to perceive genuine beauty" (301; my emphasis). Julie is similarly instrumentalized by Bomston, who describes her as a vehicle for St. Preux's growth out of interested, and implicitly, infantile love, and into the disinterestedness of the philosopher and the moral man. In a letter to his friend, he asks, "Do you know what it is that caused you always to love virtue? It took on in your eyes the appearance of that adorable woman who so well represents it, and it would be very unlikely indeed for so dear an image to allow you to lose the taste for it" (430). In other words, Julie has taught St. Preux to learn virtue so well that he learns to un-love her.

Elsewhere Bomston argues that St. Preux has confused ends and means with respect to his true vocation, that of the philosopher:

My dear man, your heart has long deceived you with respect to your understanding. You have meant to philosophize before you knew how; you have mistaken sentiment for reason, and content with judging things by the impression they have made on you, you have been ignorant of their true value. A righteous heart is, I admit, the *first organ* of truth; he who has felt nothing is incapable of learning anything; he merely floats from errors to errors, he acquires nothing but vain knowledge and sterile learning, because the true relation of things to man, which is his *principal science*, remains ever hidden to him ... It is little to know human passions, if one knows not how to appreciate their objects; and this *second study* can only be accomplished in the calm of meditation. (429)

As represented here, the philosopher's education begins with knowledge of human things and human passions but proceeds to a more abstractive study of objects and relations. Wolmar is the principal agent of St. Preux's second education. His strategy is to replace the image of the ravishing Julie that St. Preux carries in his heart with new objects of attention. To begin with, he lessens the hold of Julie's image by directing attention to the less exciting real-life matron: "In the place of his mistress I force him to see always the spouse of an honorable man and the mother of my children: I overlay one tableau with another, and cover the past with the present" (419).

Eventually the spouse and mother also fade into the background, and the background that is Clarens, Julie and Wolmar's home, becomes the foreground. St. Preux is prompted to philosophical reflection by the "lovely and moving spectacle" of "a simple and well-regulated house" (363); significantly, this spectacle is moving rather than ravishing, as was the idolatrous image of the unmarried Julie. The latter had prohibited the transition to knowledge of impersonal things: As St. Preux himself writes to Julie upon their first separation, early in the narrative, love prohibits attention to objects other than the beloved. In the first flush of love, he is self-avowedly capable only of the simplest observation, of the landscape and the agrarian peasant society of the Valais. Only later does he move on to the more complex spectacle of Parisian society.

Wolmar's Clarens requires considerably greater powers of observation than Paris or the Valais because it represents, in one household, the laws that should regulate society as a whole. As understood by

Rousseau, this ideal society, like the ideal person and the ideal education, follows a path dictated by nature—in this case, nature as interpreted by Wolmar. It is a society so natural that one might mistake it
for a state of nature even though the master's hand, we are told, can be
seen in everything by the discerning eye. St. Preux is educated into the
requisite discrimination by spending time in the Elysium, Julie's carefully cultivated garden which nonetheless looks like the "wildest, most
solitary place in nature" (387). Julie holds up her garden to St. Preux
as an example of the principles structuring Clarens as a whole: "nature
did it all, but under my direction, and there is nothing here that I have
not designed" (388). Julie's direction is placed by her author under her
husband's superior rule, which is characterized by St. Preux as representative of the highest principles of man and nature. To Bomston, he
suggests that the "order [Wolmar] has brought into his house is the
image of the one that prevails in his heart, and seems to imitate in a
small household the order established in the governance of the earth"
(305–6). As in *Emile*, the tutor's and nature's points of view become one
and the same. While St. Preux the lover finds the image of his beloved
engraved in his heart, Wolmar the philosopher-king carries within
him a picture of the ideal society, which his actual household merely
reproduces. This difference in vision, Rousseau suggests, derives from
the two men's varying attachments to the world of other people.
Wolmar is a man of reason rather than feeling. Like Addison's taciturn
Mr. Spectator, he prefers to observe rather than to participate in the
whirlpool of the passions that comprises social life. As he explains to
St. Preux, "I enjoy observing society, not taking part in it"; "I like to
read what is in men's hearts; as my own little deludes me" (404).
Wolmar indeed wishes that he could free himself altogether from
social embedment by becoming a disembodied eye: "If I could change
the nature of my being and become a living eye, I would gladly make
that exchange" (402). According to Julie, her husband "likes to make
judgments on men's characters and on the actions he observes. He
makes them with profound wisdom and the most perfect impartiality.
If an enemy did him harm, he would discuss his motives and means as
calmly as if it were a matter of complete indifference" (305).

Wolmar upholds the interest, then, of a very different impartiality
than that ascribed by Richardson to Clarissa in her capacity as a judge

of her heart. He represents a God's-eye viewpoint rather than the enlarged perspective of a judge who engages other judges. If St. Preux is the Socrates of the *Symposium*, Wolmar is the philosopher in Plato's *Republic*, who has ascended out of the cave of opinion and into the realm of the intelligible or Ideas.

The ends toward which both men gravitate are, however, the same. At Clarens, through Wolmar's example and teaching, St. Preux learns to become a disembodied eye of sorts, a monkish Wolmar or castrated Abelard, the historical figure whose unhappy love story is invoked by *Julie*'s title. But while his medieval prototype experienced the loss of love as tragic, St. Preux equates his symbolic castration with the freedom of self-governance, or a mastery of the passions so complete that they no longer create distracting participation. Bomston suggests that St. Preux has lived so intensely in so short a time that he has all the experience he needs to enjoy the freedom of the vita contemplativa, figured by him as a fundamentally solitary life. The final object awaiting him on the ladder of love is himself, his own mind and its rich reflections. Observing St. Preux's progress with delight, Bomston confirms, "There is nothing remaining for you to feel or see that merits your attention. The only object left for you to behold is yourself" (429). At this point, St. Preux still claims to love Julie, but as the means to the end of his self-return. As he suggests to her, "I love you as much as ever, it is true; but what attaches me to you most is the return of my reason. It presents you to me such as you are; it serves you better even than love" (554). Bringing Julie down to earth, her former lover rises above it: "the flames with which I have burned have purified me; there is nothing of the ordinary man left in me" (557).

The case is very different for Julie. As her posthumous letter to St. Preux indicates, she never stopped loving him passionately. Indeed, her final communication to her lover represents her life as Wolmar's wife as a "deception" and a "delusion," albeit a "salutary" one (608). As she describes events, Wolmar prolonged her life by provisionally taming her destructive passion but the passion itself was never eradicated. She confides to its object, "You have believed I was cured, and I thought I was . . . Aye, however much I wanted to stifle the first sentiment that brought me alive, it crystallized into my heart. There it awakens at the moment when it is no longer to be feared; it sustains me when my strength fails me; it revives me as I lie dying" (608). While Julie represents her rekindled love for St. Preux as her sustenance in the final moments of life, her image of love as a crystal in her heart renders it, more tellingly, the cause of her untimely death.

Ultimately, Julie's too-tender heart becomes a disembodied house-hold deity, a better spouse for Wolmar's disembodied eye than was the living Julie. Julie urges St. Preux to hasten back to Clarens after her death so that he can be part of the community revolving around a heart that exists best in memory: "You lose of Julie only what you have long since lost. Come rejoin her family. May her heart remain in your midst. May all those she loved gather together to confer on her a new being" (609). Claire reinforces Julie's wish: "May her spirit inspire us: may her heart unite all of ours" (612).

The fallen woman does end up dying in *Julie*. Her rehabilitation into useful citizenship of the little republic that is the family, to borrow Oliver Goldsmith's phrase, doesn't work. The revision of *Clarissa* into the Bildungsroman that is *Julie* represents the *Bildung* not of woman but of man, and of a man whose love for women is merely a step on a ladder of love that leads beyond other-regarding sentiments altogether. Instead of being a progress of the sentiments, a Rousseauvian (male) education is a progress out of the sentiments. The story of virtue, as mobilized by St. Preux's cultivation of freedom, is a sentimental unlearning.

ALL THE WORLD'S A STAGE: MACKENZIE

In *Julia de Roubigné*, Henry Mackenzie reprises *Julie* to dramatize the tragic consequences of treating women as second-class citizens in the republic of virtue.[17] The plots of the two novels are very similar: Each is a story of star-crossed lovers in which a young woman is in love with a companion-tutor whom she cannot marry because of the prejudices of her traditionalist father. In each, the father manipulates his daugh-ter into marrying a friend, a more principled man than the father himself. However, in Mackenzie's novel, the tragic consequences of the loveless union are far more violent than in *Julie*. Julia's inability to forget her long-time companion, Savillon, prompts her jealous husband to kill her—and this even though Julia and Savillon, unlike Julie and St. Preux, never bed, and only declare their love for one another at their final meeting. Mackenzie questions the sanitizing resolution of the Wolmars' marriage by importing into his sentimental novel the plot of imagined infidelity and jealous rage at the center of Shakespeare's *Othello*.

Women, Mackenzie suggests, are all too often treated as commodities in a barter between men, a point that is underscored by the parallels he draws between Julia and the slaves working on the West Indian estate of Savillon's uncle.[18] Julia too is highly self-conscious of her objectification at the hands of men. She describes her oft-sorrowful heart—a too-tender heart like Julie's—as her husband's property: "this bosom," she writes to her friend Maria, "is the property of Montauban" (132). Reinforcing the economic metaphor, Monsieur de Roubigné describes his daughter's hand, which he gives in marriage to the Count Louis de Montauban, as his wealth: "That hand . . . is the last treasure of Roubigné" (69).

Mackenzie is critical, too, of Rousseau's uncritical celebration of Julie's too-tender heart, the heart that causes her so much grief. This aspect of his critique of Rousseau's sentimentalism moves in two directions. On the one hand, he worries that the tender hearts of susceptible young people will lead them into imprudence and even immorality. This point is reinforced later in his career in his well-known critique of sentimental novels of the French type—clearly a jibe at *Julie*—in the *Lounger*, the weekly periodical that he edited from 1785 to 1787. In such novels, Mackenzie writes, "The duty to parents is contrasted with the ties of friendship and of love; the virtues of justice, of prudence, of economy, are put in competition with the exertions of generosity, of benevolence, and of compassion: and even of these virtues of sentiment there are still more refined divisions, in which the overstrained delicacy of the persons represented always leads them to act from the motive least obvious, and therefore generally the least reasonable."[19] Echoing Samuel Johnson's fears about the effects of novel reading on impressionable young minds, Mackenzie contends that sentimental fiction misleads by conflating virtue and unreasonable delicacy.[20] Also invoking Shaftesbury's cautionary essay against religious enthusiasm in *Characteristics* (1711), he indicates that "In the enthusiasm of sentiment there is much the same danger as in the enthusiasm of religion, of substituting certain impulses and feelings of what may be called a visionary kind, in the place of real practical duties."

But the argument against a virtue grounded in the feeling heart extends beyond such prudential and moralistic considerations. In *Julia de Roubigné*, Mackenzie anticipates Wollstonecraft's suggestion in *A Vindication of the Rights of Woman* that the traditional association of women and sensibility victimizes women by depriving them of agency and autonomy. Taught to cultivate their sensibility at the expense of reason and judgment, women, Wollstonecraft argues, "become the prey of their senses, delicately termed sensibility, and are blown about by every momentary gust of feeling" (136). A critic of excessive sensibility rather than of the passions per se, Wollstonecraft adds that "A distinction should be made between inflaming and strengthening [the passions]." It is only when the passions are "pampered, whilst judgment is left unformed" that "madness and folly" ensue (136–37).[21]

While Mackenzie's Julia, unlike the sensitive plant of Wollstonecraft's description, is an intellectual woman—as her opening letter to Maria indicates, she is very pleased by the latter's appellation for her of the "little philosopher"—her intellect has little room to expand in the socially isolated environment in which she is placed after her family's loss of wealth and status. Julia claims to love the joys of a sequestered country life but her confinement to a community comprised only by her immediate family is represented by Mackenzie as a debilitating imprisonment. Emotions run high in this narrow community because its guardian, Monsieur de Roubigné, is unable to accept his family's fallen fortunes with any composure. Julia frequently yearns for an enlargement of the family circle, for "the intervention of a third person, in a society, the members of which are afraid to think of one another's thoughts" (8). The balance of sense and sensibility that her earlier relationship with her childhood companion Savillon had encouraged is destabilized by her participation in the negative community of affect produced by her father's self-indulgent sufferings and her own self-punishing pity. Recalling her happy time with Savillon, Julia writes to Maria: "He used to teach me ideas; sometimes he flattered me, by saying, that, in his turn, he learned from me. Our feelings were often equally disgusted with the common notions of mankind, and we early began to form a league against them. We began with an alliance of argument; but the heart was always appealed to in the last resort" (39). Notwithstanding the differences of gender and accomplishment, the young people emerge here as fundamentally equal interlocutors in an evolving conversation to which each has something to contribute. Their intellectual friendship, which turns into love, is reminiscent of Julie and St. Preux's relationship at the beginning of *Julie*, which is represented by Rousseau as ennobling precisely because it addresses both head and heart. Like the lovers in Rousseau's novel, moreover, Julia and Savillon assert a certain independence of the world and its conventions (though they do not disturb its code of chastity, as do Rousseau's lovers). Their "league" against the world specifies an independence fostered by the exchange of opinion, and one in which the heart has a key role to play: "We began with an alliance of argument; but the heart was always appealed to in the last resort." This interpretation of judgment resonates with that proffered by Mackenzie's friend and compatriot Hume, who, as I noted earlier, described judgment as a sentiment that has been reflectively endorsed, in communication with others. As Hume writes in the *Enquiry Concerning the Principles of Morals*, "the final sentence" in the process of judgment "depends on some internal sense or feeling." But "in order to pave the way for such a sentiment, and give a proper discernment of its object, it is often necessary, we find, that much reasoning should precede, that nice distinctions be made, just conclusions drawn, distant comparisons formed, complicated relations examined, and general facts fixed and ascertained" (172–73).

Julia's epistolary friendship with Maria sustains the pattern of peer review characterizing her relationship with Savillon. Maria's importance to Julia's sense of herself and her judgments is registered by the very first letter of the novel which begins with Maria's, rather than Julia's, words, transcribed by Julia to reopen a conversation that the young women first began at the convent where they were schooled. The image of the convent as a hospitable space for women's friendship suggests, however, that such friendship is a precarious and fragile thing, which must be protected from the demands of the larger world that intrudes in the shape of fathers and husbands. Thirty years after *Clarissa*, moreover, the epistolary address has itself become attenuated by the growing internal differentiation of modern society, with the country and the city sustaining fewer connections than in the past. While letters are the traditional means of bridging distance, the distance between Julia and Maria, as well as between their families, is far greater than that between Clarissa and Anna—even after Clarissa goes to London. The Howes and the Harlowes are part of a tightly knit community of families and intervene in one another's lives quite freely. By contrast, Julia and Maria's families appear to inhabit radically different worlds—in part, of course, because of Julia's family's fallen fortunes—and the potential for what Susan Manning calls modifying contact with another becomes considerably diminished in their case. Unlike Anna Howe, whose spirited letters to Clarissa render her a force to be reckoned with, Maria de Roncilles is a ghostly presence in Mackenzie's novel, as is reinforced by the absence of her letters within it. Her voice is registered only indirectly, through Julia's comments on letters that the reader never sees, or directly only in fragments, through Julia's interpolation, in several of her own letters, of suggestions from Maria's letters.

Mackenzie suggests too that the parent–child relationship is no substitute for a relationship between peers as an enabler of independent judgment. This point is made in his portrayal not only of Julia's relationship with her aggrieved and aggressive father but also of her relationship with her mother, who resembles Clarissa's mother in Richardson's novel in that she is her husband's superior in talents and better equipped to head their household. While her dyspeptic husband rails against his misfortunes, Madame de Roubigné tries to make the best of their family's reduced circumstances. Montaubon comments upon her composure and self-possession in the face of adversity: "She talks of the world as of a scene where she is a spectator merely, in which there is something for virtue to praise, for charity to pardon; and smooths the spleen of her husband's observations by some palliative remark which experience has taught her" (24). Madame de Roubigné's mere spectatorship is shown to be a problem, however, in relation to her daughter's struggles. Like Mrs. Harlowe in *Clarissa*, she is clearly sympathetic to her daughter, who resembles her in abilities, but like her precursor in Richardson's novel, Madame de Roubigné finds her role as supportive mother complicated by her role as the wife of an unreasonable man. Like Mrs. Harlowe, too, she interprets wifely duty very strictly, as her posthumous letter to Julia indicates. Because she perceives herself as, in the last analysis, her husband's agent in all domestic matters, she is unable to serve as a confidante for her suffering daughter. Julia perceives that her mother's role as Roubigné's helpmeet produces a struggle within her and Madame de Roubigné's sufferings and hard-won composure grieve her loving daughter. Writing to Maria after one of her father's outbursts, Julia indicates: "I met my mother in the parlour, with a smile of meekness and serenity on her countenance; she did not say a single word of last night's incident; and I saw that she purposely avoided giving me any opportunity of mentioning it; such is the delicacy of her conduct in relation to my father. What an angel this woman is! But I fear, my friend, she is a very woman in her sufferings" (16). The angel turns out to be very much a woman, whose sufferings, a consequence of an unequal marriage, lead to an early death.

With only the remote Maria as the sharer of her thoughts and feelings, Julia finds it difficult to cultivate the distance she needs to critically assess the demands made upon her by her importunate father and by her own importunate feelings. Her sympathy for Monsieur de Roubigné and Montauban is shown to be dangerous because it places her still more securely under the control of those her culture deems her superiors. Letter XIX of the novel, which I discussed at some length in chapter 1, makes her danger clear. The episode it delineates, in which Julia's heart swells to madness at the sight of her father's suffering, is preceded by other "scenes," to deploy the novel's theatrical metaphor, of disabling absorption, as in an earlier episode in which Julia actually witnesses Montauban's tears, at which point her pity nearly leads her to agree to his proposals; and also a scene between her parents in which an uncharacteristically composed Roubigné reveals to his wife and daughter how fallen in fortune they really are. Anticipating its own swelling to "enthusiastic madness" later in the narrative, Julia's heart is "roused as with the sound of a trumpet" by the moving spectacle of her parents' self-command:

> I started up, I know not how; I said something, I know not what; but, at that moment, I felt my heart roused as with the sound of a trumpet.

My mother stood on one side, looked gently upwards, her hands, which were clasped together, leaning on my father's shoulder. He had one hand in his side, the other pressed on his bosom, his figure seeming to rise above itself, and his eye bent steadily forward.—Methought, as I looked on them, I was above the fears of humanity. (47)

Julia's careful reconstruction above of the poses of the "actors" and the orchestral music accompanying them speaks to the intensely theatrical quality of her thoughts, the accuracy of her memory, and the extent of her vulnerability. Insofar as she is a too-absorbed spectator of the tableaus and scenes that comprise her life, she becomes a victim of her filial feelings. As her later actions reveal, she is willing to sacrifice her own happiness at the altar of her parents' sufferings.

However, the trope of aesthetic spectatorship also specifies other possibilities: a more detached standpoint, a more flexible positioning of the viewer, and engagement with other viewers. Julia and Maria's letters enact and reinforce these alternatives. Their epistolary exchange or heart-to-heart—Julia indicates to Maria that "I will speak to you on paper when my heart is full, and you will answer me from the sympathy of yours" (9)—renders Julia's heart cooler or less full of self-punishing passions. Hence, Julia's invocation, at one point, of her feelings as her "rule of judging" is at least partially self-ironic. Writing to Maria about her reasons for refusing Montauban's first proposal of marriage, she indicates:

> while you argue from reason, I must decide from my feelings. In every one's own case, there is a rule of judging, which is not the less powerful that one cannot express it. I insist not on the memory of Savillon . . . But should I wed any man, be his worth what it may, if I feel not that lively preference for him which waits not for reasoning to persuade its consent? . . . "But I already esteem and admire him".— It is most true!—why is he not contented with my esteem and admiration? If those feelings are to be ripened into love, let him wait that period, when my hand may be his without a blush. This I have told him; he almost owned the injustice of his request, but pleaded the ardour of passion in excuse. Is this fair dealing, Maria? that his feelings are to be an apology for his suit, while mine are not allowed to be a reason for refusal? (58)

This is a highly reasoned defense of the rule of feeling and identifies that rule, as deployed by Julia, to be ineluctably open to the claims of reason. Julia's invocation of justice as the grounds of her complaint against Montauban reinforces the centrality of that norm to her story, a story about the injustice to women within paternalistic society. Feelings, her author appears to suggest, might indeed be a good enough rule for judging, but only after their justice or injustice has been determined through reflection.

"Justice" gets the last word in Mackenzie's novel—or, rather, justice tempered by pity is invoked as the most important of the virtues. Reporting on Montauban's violence against his wife and himself, his relative Monsieur de Rouillé concludes his letter to Maria with the suggestion that justice and pity must join hands to ensure a better world for all.

> While I mourn the fate of his most amiable wife, I recal the memory of my once dearly-valued friend, and would shelter it with some apology if I could. Let that honour which he worshipped plead in his defence.—That honour we have worshipped together, and I would not weaken its sacred voice; but I look on the body of Montauban—I weep over the pale corpse of Julia!—I shudder at the sacrifices of mistaken honour, and lift up my hands to pity and to justice. (163–64)

In life, Julia and Montauban become representatives, respectively, of excessive sympathy and rigidity of principle. The tragedy that Rouillé's closing image captures derives from Montauban's, and to a lesser extent, Julia's, failure to marry principle and feeling. This interpretation of Mackenzie's moral intention is reinforced by his friend Walter Scott's account of how *Julia de Roubigné* originated in a conversation between Mackenzie and Henry Homes, Lord Kames. In response to Kames's observation that most stories gain narrative momentum from the interventions of a villainous character, Mackenzie, Scott reports, sought to construct a narrative in which villainy had no role to play. Instead, the tragedy would derive from "the excess and over-indulgence of passions and feelings, in themselves blameless, nay, praiseworthy, but which, encouraged to a morbid excess, and coming into fatal though fortuitous concourse with each other, lead to the most disastrous consequences."[22]

When, in letter XIX of the novel in which she appears, Julia de Roubigné is prompted by her swollen heart to step onto the figurative proscenium where her father is staging a tearful rendition of Addison's *Cato*, she claims a role for herself that foreshadows the end depicted by Rouillé's letter: her role as the obedient daughter and sacrificial victim of Racine's *Iphigénie*. By treating her death as a senseless sacrifice, Mackenzie distinguishes his sentimentalism from that of Rousseau, whose *Julie* presents its heroine's death as a beautiful gesture of undying love for her philosopher-lover. Concluding with the tragic theater of violence against women, Mackenzie's novel asks its readers to take their pity for the dead and to marry it with justice in order to honor the claims of the living.

UNNATURAL EDUCATION

In the first edition of *An Enquiry Concerning Political Justice and Its Influence on Modern Manners and Morals* (1793), William Godwin famously declared that if confronted with the choice, he would save the Archbishop Fénelon from a fire over the latter's chambermaid who might be "my wife or mother."[23] In subsequent editions of *Political Justice* the example was modified to replace the chambermaid with a valet, and "my wife or mother" with "my brother, my father." The second and third editions (1796 and 1798, respectively) of Godwin's major philosophical treatise made other more substantial changes, to reflect Godwin's growing unhappiness with the rationalism and ethical consequentialism (judging an action by its consequences) of the first edition. Even so, he was never fully satisfied with *Political Justice*, as he indicates in 1800:

> The *Enquiry concerning Political Justice* I apprehend to be blemished principally by three errors. 1. Stoicism, or an inattention to the principle, that pleasure and pain are the only bases upon which morality can exist. 2. Sandemanianism, or an inattention to the principle that feeling, and not judgment, is the source of human actions.

3. The unqualified condemnation of the private affections. It will easily be seen how strongly these errors are connected with the Calvinist system, which had been so deeply wrought into my mind in early life, as to enable these errors long to survive the general system of religious opinions of which they formed a part . . . The first of these errors . . . has been corrected with some care in the subsequent edition of *Political Justice*. The second and third owe their destruction to a perusal of Hume's *Treatise of Human Nature* in the following edition.[24]

The mention of Hume's *Treatise* is significant, and scholars including Mark Philp, Gary Handwerk, Louise Joy, and Rowland Weston have recently shown that Godwin's mature thought is far more indebted to the eighteenth century's culture of sentiment than the first edition of *Political Justice* suggests.[25] *Fleetwood* offers Godwin's most extensive statement on his relationship with this culture by taking as its starting point the precedent sentimentalisms of Rousseau and Mackenzie. Like *Julia de Roubigné*, it challenges the ideal of marriage at the center of *Julie* and dramatizes the dangers to women of Rousseau's association of women and feeling. More explicitly than Mackenzie, however, Godwin highlights the inadequacies of the norm of nature that underwrites both Rousseau's understanding of education and the gendered moral universe of works like *Emile* and *Julie*. The eponymous hero of *Fleetwood* is the monstrous progeny of a Rousseauvian education. A latter-day Emile, brought up as Rousseau would have liked, Fleetwood is a misogynist and despot who nearly kills his young wife, Mary, after he suspects her of adultery (as in *Julia de Roubigné*, the Othello plot is prominent in *Fleetwood*). Unlike Montauban, however, Fleetwood learns the error of his ways and is given a second chance at marriage and happiness. Unlike Emile and St. Preux, he concludes his narrative with a newfound respect for the opinions and tastes of others, and especially of the woman who serves as his principal companion in life.

Godwin's critique of Rousseau builds on the earlier critique developed by Mary Wollstonecraft in her novels and educational writings, writings that are greatly influenced by the rationalism and ethical cognitivism of contemporaries like the dissenting minister and philosopher, Richard Price, but that also extensively engage Rousseau's sentimentalism. Rousseau is the most important of the male theorists of female education that Wollstonecraft summons in *Vindication of the Rights of Woman*, a sign of her admiration for many aspects of his writings. Wollstonecraft agrees, in particular, with Rousseau's argument that existing social institutions and conventions tend to corrupt morals and that critical distance from tradition is a crucial register of the individual's maturity. Wollstonecraft is critical, however, of Rousseau's structuring norm of nature because she recognizes its fundamental arbitrariness and injustice to women. In *Vindication*, she argues that the citizen of Geneva confuses nature and nurture, especially with regard to women, when, for example, he attributes to them a "natural" love of finery and admiration, a love that is really the unnatural imposition of convention: "the effect of habit is insisted upon as an undoubted indication of nature" (160). Rousseau's *Julie* makes a cameo appearance in Wollstonecraft's novel *The Wrongs of Woman; or Maria*, published by Godwin after her death in 1798, in which it serves as an unfortunate example to the beleaguered heroine, who is inspired by Julie and St. Preux's relationship to enter a second relationship (following upon her disastrous marriage) that ends in a broken heart. But it is in her first novel, *Mary*, that Wollstonecraft takes to task most fully Rousseau's ideas on education. The eponymous heroine of *Mary* is a child of nature whose education has been neglected by her parents and whose isolation from the larger world is ensured by her growing up in the country, without the benefit of like-minded companions. This isolation is represented by the narrator as, on the one hand, a good thing: Mary is not subjected to the false training for women that fashionable society enjoins and that Wollstonecraft would go on to decry at length in *Vindication of the Rights of Woman*. Instead, she learns to develop judgment and reason through her encounters with her beautiful natural surroundings. But this judgment, the narrator suggests, does not have the advantage of modifying contact with others until later in Mary's life, when she meets a man of talents comparable to hers. At this point, however, Mary is already married, a consequence of her excessive pity for a dying mother who wishes to see her daughter married before she dies, and who is represented by Wollstonecraft as a pattern-book fashionable lady, given to cultivating sensibility at the expense of sense. Mary's plight becomes symbolic, then, of the pathos of intelligent women of her class: She develops intelligence by being freed from society's strictures only to fall victim to a sensibility that remains unsharpened by social intercourse. She cannot be a natural woman because she needs other people; nor can she be a full member of a society that does not value her talents. Her place in society is determined instead by unjust marriage laws that render her her husband's property in perpetuity—a husband, notably, that she did not choose for herself. Not unlike *Clarissa*, *Mary* concludes on a note of despair, with the afterlife represented as the only hospitable environment for the virtuous female soul. Invoking the gospel of Matthew, the narrator indicates, "Her delicate state of health did not promise long life. In moments of solitary sadness, a gleam of joy would dart across her mind—She thought she was hastening to the world *where there is neither marrying*, nor giving in marriage."[26]

Fleetwood might be read as a companion piece to *Mary*, one that upholds the possibility of a better fate for the Marys of the world—a fate that derives from educating their husbands on principles other than the Rousseauvian ones. Godwin is especially critical of Rousseau's suggestion that the first education takes place outside society. For Emile's tutor, we will recall, "up to the time when the guide of *amour-propre*, which is reason, can be born, it is important for a child to do nothing because he is seen or heard—nothing, in a word, in relation to others; he must respond only to what nature asks of him, and then he will do nothing but good" (92–93). By contrast, Godwin, like Hume and Smith, suggests that society is the necessary venue for the development of moral self-consciousness. In the essays on education collected in *The Enquirer* (1797), he identifies society as "the true awakener of man."[27] Further, he depicts the best such society as the society of peers, a point reinforced by his advocacy of public over private education. As he puts it, "there can be little true society, where the disparity of disposition is so great as between a boy and his preceptor ... A boy, educated apart from boys, is a sort of unripened hermit, with all the gloom and lazy-pacing blood incident to that profession" (429–30).

Fleetwood's isolated upbringing in sublime natural surroundings cultivates his passions and sensibility but no consciousness of another who is an equal. His father is a reclusive widower, broken down by grief at his wife's death. Fleetwood's overly accommodating tutor is perceived by him as "part of the furniture of our eating-room" (67). His most active relationships as a child and adolescent are with the poor, with objects of charity toward whom he adopts the godlike role of "a patron and a preserver" (64). Charity produces a false sense of superiority in the young, as the adult narrator of *Fleetwood* acknowledges: "in the cottage to which my benevolence led me, I appeared like a superior nature" (60). Highlighting the asymmetrical exchange of the giver and the receiver of alms, Godwin exposes the sometimes-smug benevolence of earlier men of feeling like Mackenzie's Harley or Sterne's Yorick in *A Sentimental Journey Through France and Italy* (1766).

Nature—the sublime nature of the remote Welsh countryside—is the young Fleetwood's principal companion. He describes himself as "the spoiled child of the great parent, Nature" (223). Nature performs the role of indulgent caregiver by offering little resistance to the child's will. It is a spectacle that cannot in turn become a spectator of Fleetwood—the kind of spectator that, Adam Smith argued, reinforces the powers of judgment. By contrast with Rousseau's Emile, whose isolation from society is perceived to preserve the passions in their uncorrupted natural form, Fleetwood's dependence on things rather than wills produces unwarranted self-aggrandizement and a fantastic inner life: "I was engaged in imaginary scenes, constructed visionary plans, and found all nature subservient to my command. I had a wife or children, was the occupier of palaces, or the ruler of nations" (56). Bred as a hermit or "solitary savage" (70), Fleetwood becomes rigid and unflexible. As he succinctly observes, "I had been little used to contradiction" (54).

Lacking perspective-making contact with a broad spectrum of other standpoints, Fleetwood's sensibility is pitched at too high a note. Like Goëthe's Werther or Mackenzie's Harley, Fleetwood is too sensitive for the world. On his own account, "The strings of my mind . . . were tuned to too delicate and sensitive a pitch: it was an Eolian harp, upon which the winds of heaven might 'discourse excellent music'; but the touch of a human hand could draw from it nothing but discord and dissonance." Complicating the association of the harp and the poet that figured prominently in the poetry of his romantic contemporaries, Godwin suggests that there are limits to the analogy. Fleetwood's sensitivity to nature is no guarantee of his sensitivity to human others. The deleterious consequences of Fleetwood's natural education are apparent at every stage of his sojourn beyond the paternal home. He first becomes aware of the difference of other people's perspectives in his university days, but unfortunately the most significant others he encounters at Oxford are bullies who render miserable the lives of weaker classmates. A sorry substitute for his erstwhile companion, blind Nature, these unimpressive classmates become, as Fleetwood puts it, the peers "whose applauses I sought, whose ridicule awed me, and whose judgment I looked to for the standard of my actions" (90).

The adult Fleetwood's difficulty establishing reciprocal relationships is especially evident in his encounters with women, and nowhere more so than in his dealings with his wife. Like Fleetwood, and also like her namesake, Wollstonecraft's Mary, the talented and beautiful Mary Macneil is also something of a child of nature. She too has had a natural education owing to the relative social isolation of her family, the consequence of her mother's youthful imprudence, which prevents other families from visiting them. But the isolation of the Macneil clan is mitigated by their numbers and also by the high cultural accomplishments of each member of the family. Like Rousseau's Julie, Mary is also a gardener, but her gardens are unlike Julie's Elysium in that they are not dedicated to hiding the human influence that has gone into shaping them. Mary's ambitions are not directed at recovering a prelapsarian innocence or state of nature. She views gardening as an art, and her accomplishments as a landscaper, a botanist, and a painter of flowers are represented by the narrator as by no means lower in stature than those of a philosopher: The closest we get to the figure of the philosopher in the Macneil household is the genial Mr. Macneil, who is a man of the world in the Humean sense.

Fleetwood likes to think of Mary, as he does of himself, as a tender flower (259) or nature's pet. He treats her as he did the nature of his childhood, as an other whose identity is wholly bestowed by its observer. The transparency of Mary's complexion encourages him in this regard because he imagines that he can "read every state of mind of the angelic creature" (278). But Mary resists Fleetwood's projections. While she is placed by her considerably younger age and by the loss of family and fortune in a relation of near-total dependency on her father's friend, she reminds Fleetwood of her autonomous individuality before marrying him: "I am not idle and thoughtless enough," she contends, "to promise to sink my being and individuality in yours. I shall have my distinct propensities and preferences . . . I hope you will not require me to disclaim them. In me you will have a wife, and not a passive machine" (281).

By the time Mary enters Fleetwood's life, he craves the companionship of equals. Tired of the isolation of his paternal home, as well as of the asymmetrical social relationships he has established through much of his adult life, he desires a friend or "the brother of my heart" (215). Alluding to Smith's *Theory*, Fleetwood observes that even the most self-sufficient of persons needs the confirming gaze of others: "However worthy and valuable he may endeavour to consider himself, his persuasion will be attended with little confidence and solidity, if it does not find support in the judgments of other men. The martyr, or the champion of popular pretensions, cheerfully encounters the terrors of a public execution, provided the theatre on which he is to die is filled with his approvers."[28]

Instead of a brother, Fleetwood finds a wife who fully merits the appellation he gives her of "the companion of my heart" (288). She is his peer, with tastes and talents to match his. Their companionship is facilitated by their many shared interests, including a love of nature and literature. With Mary at his side, Fleetwood learns to appreciate nature's beauties with new eyes—with the distance that was lacking in his youthful personification of it as a caregiver who mirrored back to him all his deepest convictions. Of the early days of marriage, he writes:

> When we looked down upon the rich and fertile plains, when we hung over the jutting and tremendous precipice, I perceived, with inexpressible pleasure, that mine was no longer a morose and unparticipated sensation, but that another human creature, capable of feeling all my feelings, rejoiced and trembled along with me. When I retired to my inn after the fatigues and dangers of the day, I did not retire to a peevish and forward meal among drawers and venal attendants; I sat down with the companion of my heart, and shared the pleasures of idleness, as we had before shared the pleasures of activity. How many agreeable topics of conversation did the rivers and the mountains suggest! how many occasions of mutual endearment did

they afford! It seemed that the spirit of kindness still gained new strength, as the scene was perpetually shifted before our eyes, and we breathed an atmosphere for ever new. (287–88)

Unlike the nature of his youth, nature, as figured by Fleetwood here, is no longer a cipher into which he can pour his feelings but the occasion of many "agreeable topics of conversation." His conversations with Mary encourage a flexibility of perspective that was lacking in his earlier encounters with nature so that "the scene was perpetually shifted before our eyes, and we breathed an atmosphere for ever new." The companionship afforded by his marriage profoundly changes his whole emotional landscape: "When I retired to my inn after the fatigues and dangers of the day, I did not retire to a peevish and forward meal among drawers and venal attendants; I sat down with the companion of my heart." While Julie and St. Preux must separate for their respective educations to proceed, Fleetwood and Mary trade opinions and endearments in a reciprocal exchange. While Rousseau's hero's education becomes a sentimental unlearning, Godwin's hero's ascent up the ladder of moral and aesthetic discrimination is accompanied by a parallel progress of the passions: "My passion, beginning in the instinct of the sexes, had been consecrated by sentiments so generous, so elevated, so spiritual! We had lived together" (366).

But Fleetwood's married life soon turns ugly because it is his first experience of living "familiarly, every day, and all day long, with a person claiming to have a will of her own" (313). Unused to the difference of another's distinct individuality, Fleetwood readily confuses shared interest with perfect harmony, as in his deployment of Hume's musical analogy—an analogy that Hume himself complicated in the *Treatise* and elsewhere by representing sympathy as the feelings of a spectator—to describe his experience of reading John Fletcher's *Wife for a Month* with his wife: "we are like instruments tuned to a correspondent pitch, and the accord that is produced is of the most delightful nature!" (299). While Fleetwood and Mary's joint viewing of nature's splendors during their honeymoon sparks debate and strengthens companionship, their reading of a play that foreshadows the premature conclusion of their first marriage has a very different result.

The intense feelings inspired in both by the reading is overinterpreted by Fleetwood into a seamless unanimity of opinion:

> How exquisite a pleasure may thus be derived from reading with a woman of refined understanding so noble a composition as that which engaged us . . . [We] are like instruments tuned to a correspondent pitch, and the accord that is produced is of the most delightful nature! We communicate with instantaneous flashes, in one glance of the eye, and have no need of words. When we have recourse to their aid, I instruct at once and am instructed. I see how my companion feels the passages as they succeed; I learn new decrees of taste, and am confirmed in the old. Male and female taste are in some respects of different natures; and no decision upon a work of art can be consummate, till it has been pronounced on by both. (299)

Forgetting that their reading is only the first step in a critical appreciation of the text at hand, Fleetwood confuses judgment with first impressions. He imagines that Mary's considered opinions are simply the same as her initial enthusiasm and while he avows respect for female taste, he simplifies it as a species of instinct: "I see how my companion *feels* the passages as they succeed" (my emphasis).

The fragility of this circle of taste is underscored by Fleetwood's response to the interruption of their reading, caused by Mary's departure to keep a prior appointment to collect rare plants. He experiences his wife's assertion of different interests—she leaves their reading to further her studies in botany—as a personal insult. Recalling the vehemence of his former self's anger, the mature narrator enjoins: "Human beings, who enter into engagements of domestic life, should remember, that however man and wife may in interests and affections be one, yet no interests and affections can prevent them from being in many respects distinct . . . He who flies from all contradiction, must dwell alone, or dwell with those to whom he never opens his soul" (303–4).

Fleetwood's excessive disappointment in the face of Mary's continued espousal of tastes and opinions that are not identical to his produces a growing estrangement of husband and wife. Replacing Mary as companion with his servile and manipulative cousin, Gifford, Fleetwood makes of Mary a wife of only a few months by divorcing her on the grounds of an imagined adultery. His solipsism and need for total control culminates in a frenzied staging of Mary and her putative lover's union with wax figures that become emblems of Fleetwood's others (that is, of other people as he views them). He becomes like the paranoid Rousseau of Macneil's description, who lived "towards the close of his life in a world of his own, and saw nothing as it really was" (244).

It is only when Fleetwood becomes the auditor of his neighbor Mr. Scarborough's forceful retelling of the story of Mary's supposed adultery that he acknowledges the extent of his solipsism and the enormity of the gap between his version of events and those of others. Mr. Scarborough, significantly, is a reformed sentimental father, the dyspeptic patriarch of *Clarissa*, *Julie*, and *Julia* turned into a compassionate parent who concedes that his daughter has wishes and desires other than his own. His personal narrative of education, within which the story of the Fleetwoods' marriage becomes embedded, begins likes the other sentimental novels considered in this study, with a call to filial obedience. Like *Clarissa*'s Mr. Harlowe, Mr. Scarborough enjoins his daughter to marry a man she does not love for the (supposed) greater good of their family. He addresses his daughter with the same combination of command and entreaty that structures the scene of the genuflecting father in *Clarissa* and its heirs. As he recalls to Fleetwood, "I talked much of parental authority and the duty of a child. I even condescended to entreat her to yield to a plan upon which my heart was entirely bent" (406). Like Julia's other father, her husband Montauban, Mr. Scarborough is ready to murder his daughter when he hears of her intended elopement with Fleetwood's kinsman, Kenrick. Unlike the hapless Julia, however, Louisa Scarborough escapes from the paternal mansion before her intended murderer has a chance to make an Iphigénie of her. Louisa's departure from her father's house, however, does not lead to a fast-tracked entry into the heavenly Father's mansion, as in the case of Clarissa. Indeed, her elopement is short-lived since her lover is not Lovelace. Rather, Kenrick is a resuscitated Harley from *The Man of Feeling*, equally prone to tears and other physical proofs of sensibility, but also, in a departure from his prototype, most anxious to wed and bed his beloved (Harley's sensitivity to the world extends even to his lover, in whose arms he falls only to expire). Unlike the gloomy sacrifice that is Julie's wedding ceremony, Kenrick and Louisa's marriage, the former asserts to Mr. Scarborough, must take place in "the face of day" (411) or not at all—that is, it must be sanctioned not only by God, the community, and the father, but also by the bride herself, who must see as clearly as possible the path upon which she embarks.

Won over by his future son-in-law's sincerity and generosity, Mr. Scarborough joins the latter to swell the ranks of new men of feeling, men who view wives and daughters less as objects of control than as independent moral agents with desires and judgments all their own. Mr. Scarborough's example encourages Fleetwood, too, to change, to exchange the role of irascible hermit for that of a respectful husband who ceases to treat his wife's tastes and opinions merely as extensions of his own.

And what of a new woman of feeling? Does the end of the eighteenth century spell new possibilities too for the Clarissas and Julias and Julies of fiction? *Fleetwood*'s Mary Macneil is like her prototypes in the sentimental novel in that she combines intellect and sympathy. Unlike her precursors, however, she has a wider scope for her talents; at the end of her narrative, companionship and intellectual vocation (if not a public profession) are both granted to her. As such, *Fleetwood* stands at a critical juncture between sentimental tragedy and the comic resolutions of many nineteenth-century realist novels. Insofar as it culminates in marriage, rather than the combination of love and work that Mary Fleetwood enjoys, the nineteenth-century novel is more reticent than early examples like *Fleetwood* about the full spectrum of women's potential. Nonetheless, it reflects and enables the greater freedom of nineteenth-century middle- and upper-class women to choose their partnerships (if not professions outside the home). Its focus shifts from what to do in the context of unhappy alliances, a key concern of sentimental fiction, to how to find a companionate partnership. This constitutes the heroine's story in the writings of one of sentimentalism's most important literary heirs, the novelist Jane Austen.

5. Judgment, Propriety, and the Critique of Sensibility: The "Sentimental" Jane Austen

Richardson's power of creating, and preserving the consistency of his characters, as particularly exemplified in "Sir Charles Grandison," gratified the natural discrimination of her mind, whilst her taste secured her from the errors of his prolix and tedious narrative.[1]

Her knowledge of Richardson's work was such as no one is likely again to acquire.[2]

IT IS NO EASY TASK to determine where Jane Austen's fiction stands in relation to eighteenth-century sentimentalism. We have, of course, the biographical testimony of Austen's brother and nephew, which identifies Richardson as her favorite novelist and as the novelist from whom she learnt the art of rendering character. But then we also have Austen's career-long critique of late-century sensibility—a critique that took the form of pointed satire in her early fictional forays in the juvenilia, and in the unfinished *Sanditon*, and that assumed a more somber character in her first published novel, *Sense and Sensibility* (1811). Richardson's fiction itself does not escape Austen's criticism, as is evidenced by her characterization of the unsavory Sir Edward Denham of *Sanditon*.[3] A would-be Lovelace, his fancy, the narrator observes, had been "caught early by all the impassioned, and most exceptionable part of Richardsons."[4]

Beginning with Walter Scott, many of Austen's readers have interpreted her critique of sensibility as signaling a radical break in the history of the British novel, as a consequence of which a Gothic and sentimental literature of individualistic excess gave way to a prosaic nineteenth-century realism committed to depicting rounded characters

in highly wrought social milieus.⁵ One of the best-known instantia-
tions of this reading is Ian Watt's in *The Rise of the Novel*, which represents Austen as the first great English novelist to hit the literary
scene after Richardson and Fielding, and as a quintessentially realistic
novelist with little tolerance for a putatively fluffy sentimentalism.
Watt abides by this interpretation even though he acknowledges
that Richardson's character-centered fiction was crucial to Austen's
development as a novelist. But Richardson himself emerges on Watt's
account as a realist rather than a sentimentalist. In the concluding
chapter of his pioneering history of British fiction, Watt dismisses
sentimentalism as one of "various fugitive literary tendencies" of
the second half of the eighteenth century, predicated in a moral theory
of sappy emotionalism, and embodied in bad novels flooding the literary marketplace to satisfy an uncritical (and predominantly female)
reading public.⁶

It is these "fugitive" novels that are brought to the fore, however, in
Marilyn Butler's influential *Jane Austen and the War of Ideas*, perhaps
the most extended consideration to date of sentimentalism as a context
for Austen's fiction.⁷ Butler offers a salutary corrective to Watt's sum-
mary dismissal of sentimental culture by rehabilitating it as a crucial
development of the British Enlightenment, and as integral to understanding the intellectual and political climate within which Jane
Austen wrote. But she deploys her reconstruction to reach a conclusion
remarkably similar to his—that Austen was an "anti-sentimental"
novelist. A pioneering work of politically engaged historicist criticism,
Jane Austen and the War of Ideas urges us, moreover, to see Austen's
antisentimentalism as something more than a set of apolitical aesthetic
and stylistic choices. Butler contends, for example, that the novelist's
choice of satire in early works like *Love and Freindship* (1790) and
Lesley Castle (1792) links her directly to the poets and caricaturists of
sensibility behind "The New Morality," perhaps the 1790s' most striking symbol of the "anti-Jacobin" or conservative British reaction to the
French Revolution. Exploding the myth of the kindly "Aunt Jane" of
posterity, who modestly restricted herself to chronicling the fortunes
of "3 or 4 Families in a country village,"⁸ she presents us with a novelist who was a direct participant in the key ideological battle of her
lifetime: the battle between Jacobins and anti-Jacobins, or, as Butler

characterizes these positions, between "the advocates of a Christian conservatism . . . with their pessimistic view of man's nature, and their belief in external authority" and "progressives, sentimentalists, revolutionaries, with their optimism about man, and their preference for spontaneous personal impulse against rules imposed from without" (165). Against the backdrop of this "war of ideas," Jane Austen's novels, Butler argues, reveal "the lineaments of the committed conservative" (165).

While Butler's reading of the politics of Austen's fiction has been vigorously challenged in important studies by Margaret Kirkham, Claudia Johnson, and Susan Morgan, these challenges have operated at some remove from the question of sentimentalism.[9] A crucial exception in this regard is Peter Knox-Shaw's incisive recent book, *Jane Austen and the Enlightenment*, which offers a sustained rebuttal of Butler's conservative, antisentimental Austen by directly engaging sentimental moral and political theory.[10] However, Knox-Shaw's choice of "scepticism" rather than sentimentalism as the rubric under which to rehabilitate the Scottish Enlightenment concedes too much to critics of the antisentimental-Austen persuasion by letting them retain a monopoly on what sentimentalism means.[11] In the meantime, the charge of antisentimentalism has stuck, as is evidenced by Clara Tuite's recent *Romantic Austen: Sexual Politics and the Literary Canon*. Tuite begins her chapter on *Sense and Sensibility* by characterizing it as an antisentimental novel and sustains Butler's coupling of antisentimentalism and anti-Jacobinism, but without an extended discussion of either trend.[12] Indeed, if one marker of the dynamic and burgeoning critical industry that has developed around Austen's fiction in the last three decades is a book bearing the title *Jane Austen and . . .*, then it would appear that the second oldest book of this sort, Butler's *Jane Austen and the War of Ideas*, has decisively settled at least the question of Austen's assessment of sentimental culture. The "and" of the title has been followed by, among other things, "Food," "Leisure," and "Sigmund Freud," but no "Sentimentalism" and no "Samuel Richardson."

Since truths universally acknowledged must be taken with a grain of salt in Austen's fiction, it is well worth asking what sentimentalism means on Butler's authoritative account and why Jane Austen is productively described as an antisentimental novelist. While Butler aligns sentimentalism with a wide range of literary, philosophical, and political writings from the eighteenth and early nineteenth centuries, she looks, above all, to Henry Mackenzie's fiction to flesh out its ideological presuppositions. Mackenzian sentimentalism, she contends, moves Enlightenment liberalism's "faith in man" (47) in a radically affective direction. As a development of novels like *The Man of Feeling* and *Julia de Roubigné*, sentimentalism accords moral authority to "innately good" feelings (196), and even the "truth of instinct" (27), as against the "cerebral judgment" (19) and "formalized ethical code" (12) of an earlier eighteenth-century neoclassicism.[13] Further, it evinces enormous distrust of society and its conventions: The sentimental novelist, Butler argues, views society "with hostility, and presents it angled through a single consciousness: it is an environment which at best puts pressure on his hero, at worst imprisons."[14] By contrast, the conservative novelist takes society itself to be the real hero: "The most typical plot has the central character, gradually schooled to objective reality, renouncing the private delusions that once tempted him to see the world other than it is" (124).

Jane Austen is certainly an antisentimental writer if we take sentimentalism to signal the belief that the relationship between the individual and society is perforce a hostile one, or that the spontaneous responses of individuals are "innately good." But then Richardson, Hume, Smith, and Mackenzie would also count as antisentimentalists since all of these writers, I have argued in this study, endorse various forms of critical distancing from the claims of feelings, and a broad morality of judgment under which the sentiments of approval and disapproval must themselves be approved or disapproved by subjecting them to reflective scrutiny and peer review. While I agree with Marilyn Butler that the sentimental contexts of Austen's fiction are crucial to understanding its politics, I take sentimentalism itself to pivot around the capacious motif of judgment rather than the narrower one of sensibility. Judgment is a key concern in all of Austen's six major novels, in which young women learn to become increasingly judicious observers of their own and other people's actions and motives—as is evidenced, for example, by their excellent choices in husbands at the conclusion of their stories. It is an especially important motif of *Sense and Sensibility*, the novel that marked Austen's debut on the literary scene and that situates her oeuvre as a whole most explicitly in relation to a precedent sentimental culture. *Sense and Sensibility* takes as its primary heroine a young woman distinguished by her discriminating judgment and as a secondary heroine her younger sister by two years, who has yet to learn such discernment when the novel begins. The older Elinor Dashwood's judgments are remarkable for their "coolness" (6) while those of the younger Marianne are distinguished by their warmth and spontaneity. Alongside this difference, the narrator highlights another crucial point of divergence between the sisters, their respective attitudes to the norms of decorum—and especially the codes of politeness—that structure much of their sociability as middle-class women of the late eighteenth and early nineteenth centuries. Elinor is represented as an emphatically polite young woman, who ascribes considerable importance to the manners that oil drawing-room exchange, while Marianne is shown to be impatient of their artifice. The laws of the drawing room, she argues early in the narrative, are relics of a bygone era that disable rational exchange by prohibiting the free expression of what one really thinks or feels.

Many modern readers tend to agree with Austen's younger heroine, and *Sense and Sensibility* is often characterized as a novel with an uneasy relationship to modernity, even as a work propelled by a fundamental clash of cultures—between conventional and postconventional social orders, conformism and individualism, a conservative ethos of propriety and a liberal one of sensibility. In *Romantics, Rebels, and Reactionaries*, Butler argues, for example, that Austen's defense of Elinor's manners affiliates her with the archaic Edmund Burke of *Reflections on the Revolution in France* (1790), who upheld the spirit of medieval chivalry as a corrective to the modern spirit of revolution and its doctrine of universal rights. Likewise, Mary Poovey describes Elinor as a pattern-book "proper lady" who represses personal desire in order to conform to patriarchal expectations.[15] By contrast, Marianne emerges on Poovey's reading as a modern heroine of individualism, whose spirited assertion of desire is viewed by Austen, alongside the male moralists of her day, as something to be feared and contained.

Recent scholarship by David Kaufmann and Peter Knox-Shaw has complicated these readings by placing *Sense and Sensibility*, respectively, at "the cusp of modernity,"[16] and in the midst of a pragmatic, scientifically minded Enlightenment committed to debunking "that form of moral heroism known as enthusiasm."[17] In this chapter, I contribute to such sympathetic reassessments by bringing the sentimental discourses of judgment to bear upon an interpretation of Austen's first published work. I suggest that rather than reading the plot-propelling conflict between the Dashwood sisters as a battle between sentimentalism and antisentimentalism, or modernity and tradition, we can productively interpret it as a family quarrel *within* a modern sentimental culture that was riven from its very beginnings, in works like Richardson's *Clarissa*, by competing understandings of judgment. That Elinor and Marianne Dashwood are sisters is no coincidence because through them, Austen asks us to distinguish between two patterns of judgment that are intimately related. Like the sentimental heroines preceding them, both sisters take judgment and feeling to be inextricably intertwined. They differ, however, in the importance they attach to critical reflection upon primary responses, and hence in their understandings of impartiality. As I will explain, Marianne interprets her feelings as perforce disinterested while Elinor understands disinterestedness to be a cultivated posture. Their differing attitudes toward the rules of politeness are a consequence of this primary difference, which invokes a conflict familiar to us from the eighteenth century's sentimental and aesthetic discourses, and indicated in paradigmatic form in *Clarissa*: the clash between the heart's judgments and judgments of the heart, between the moral sense and moral constructivism, or between intuition and reflective judgment.

In foregrounding the interest of sentimentalism as a context for Austenian judgment, I offer a different lens from which to view judgment's dynamics than the tradition of epistemological skepticism that Claudia Johnson invokes in "The 'Twilight of Probability': Uncertainty and Hope in *Sense and Sensibility*." Johnson argues that to attend to the motif of judgment in *Sense and Sensibility* we need to shift attention away from Austen's chosen title because sentimentalism and sensibility have little to say about this capacity.[18] "The stock terms of sensibility," she maintains, "surface [in *Sense and Sensibility*] only occasionally and somewhat vestigially" (172). On this reading, Austen's claims on behalf of judgment, and, in particular, her emphasis on judgment's tentativeness, find an important precursor instead in John Locke's theory of knowledge. Locke, Johnson suggests, "argues that our understandings are so narrow and the world so complex that our certainty is limited to very few kinds of propositions and that we live in the 'twilight . . . of *probability*' with respect to just about everything" (172).

I agree with Johnson that Austen seeks to highlight judgment's tentativeness in *Sense and Sensibility* but I maintain that the kind of tentativeness at stake has less to do with epistemological questions, or questions of probability, than with the contingency that the sentimentalists ascribe to moral and aesthetic judgments.[19] Anne Elliot, the heroine of *Persuasion* (1818), becomes a spokesperson for her author when, toward the end of her narrative, she represents the interpersonal domain as provoking "difference[s] of opinion which do not admit of proof."[20] I argue that Austen's endorsement of the coolness of Elinor Dashwood's judgments is due not to her distance from sentimentalism but to her very "sentimental" recognition that judgments can be hot or cool, that feelings have a crucial role to play in the judgments of motives and actions that we, consciously or unconsciously, make every day. That judging and feeling are closely correlated is signaled too by the extensive parallels Austen establishes between ethics and aesthetics, or judgment and taste—not only in *Sense and Sensibility* but in all her novels. From the juvenilia to *Persuasion*, Austen represents characters responding to motives and actions in ways that parallel their responses to poems, paintings, landscapes, music, and other aesthetic objects. Through her deployment of an extensive aesthetic analogy for social and moral experience, she identifies her new kind of fiction, as Walter Scott described it, as a vital heir of a precedent culture of sentiment, a culture that prioritized aesthetics as a means of understanding ethics.

While the full extent of Austen's knowledge of writers like Hume or Smith is unknown, her intimate knowledge of Richardson's fiction—"such as no one is likely again to acquire," according to her nephew—makes it possible to speak with some confidence of this nineteenth-century novelist's sentimental inheritance: an inheritance that must be distinguished from the late-century culture of sensibility to which characters like Marianne Dashwood subscribe. It is unsurprising that Austen would prefer Richardson's *Grandison* to *Clarissa*, since *Grandison* looks forward to the comic resolutions of her own novels. It is unsurprising, moreover, that a satirist and ironist would find the sometimes-melodramatic display of emotion in *Clarissa* distasteful. But, in *Sense and Sensibility*, Elinor Dashwood's commitment to impartial or "candid" (60) judgment links her directly to the eponymous heroine of Richardson's most complex work, who spends much of her narrative struggling to become a more detached judge of her feelings and motives.[21] Like the various heirs of *Clarissa* discussed in this study—Rousseau's revision of *Clarissa* in *Julie* and Mackenzie's revision of *Julie* in *Julia de Roubigné*—*Sense and Sensibility* attends to a question of Enlightenment culture raised with particular intensity in Richardson's second novel: How are judgments to be made in a world in which established rules have lost authority, in which the good, to quote Clarissa Harlowe, has become "strangely mixed"?

As in the case of *Clarissa* and its heirs, the good becomes mixed in Austen's fiction owing to the absence or corruption of paternal authority. All of Austen's novels are novels about fatherless daughters—fatherless in the sense that the father is too detached (*Pride and Prejudice*), or too self-absorbed (*Emma, Persuasion*), or too severe (*Mansfield Park*) to play an active role in a daughter's life. Alternatively, he is simply absent from the scene of action by virtue of distance (*Northanger Abbey*) or death (*Sense and Sensibility*). And mothers in Austen's fiction, as in *Clarissa, Julie*, and *Julia*, are by no means practicable mentors, as the youthful example of Mrs. Dashwood in *Sense and Sensibility* and the soporific example of Lady Bertram in *Mansfield Park* suggest. As a consequence, Austen's heroines, like their sentimental precursors, are constantly placed in situations that call for independent judgment. And their independence, I suggest, lies in their ability to make judgment reflective.

JUDGMENT, PROPRIETY, TASTE

Any discussion of the politics of Austen's fiction, and of its relationship with sentimentalism, must take account of the place of manners in Austen's social vision. *Sense and Sensibility* is often deemed Austen's gloomiest and most conservative work precisely because manners

assume center-stage in the narrative. The most polemical interpretation of their function remains Marvin Mudrick's, whose *Jane Austen:
Irony as Defense and Discovery* appeared in the same year as Marilyn
Butler's *Jane Austen and the War of Ideas*. Mudrick characterizes
Marianne Dashwood's education into a greater appreciation of
the codes of civility as nothing short of a "betrayal" of "the heart
of passion" on her author's part—indeed as a "burial" in "the coffin of
convention" of Austen's heroine of sensibility and of Jane Austen
herself.[22] Likewise, in *Jane Austen and the War of Ideas* Butler describes
Sense and Sensibility as "the most obviously tendentious of Jane Austen's
novels and the least attractive" (195); its investment in propriety
speaks pointedly, she argues, to Austen's ideological kinship with
Burke. Indeed, Austen emerges on Butler's reading, as developed
not only in *Jane Austen and the War of Ideas* but also in *Romantics,
Rebels, and Reactionaries*, as occupying the same place in the history
of the novel that Burke occupies in the history of political thought.
Burke, Butler suggests, was "the most splendid apologist for the gentry
in the Enlightenment" and Jane Austen "the gentry's greatest artist."[23]
Both, she contends, enjoin a conventional morality of manners against
the new morality of sensibility. Both "proclaim that the old style of
social responsibility is accepted, *duty* (the idealized reading of upper-
class motivation) put before the new individualism" (105).

A long line of feminist and queer interpretations confirms Butler's
and Mudrick's insights. In *The Proper Lady and the Woman Writer* and
The Madwoman in the Attic, feminist scholars Mary Poovey, Sandra
Gilbert, and Susan Gubar argue that the key Austenian topos of the
heroine's education is handled particularly crudely in Austen's first
novel, with Marianne Dashwood being subjected to a punitive "school-
ing and scolding" that brings her to the brink of death, and from which
she is saved only by becoming the antithesis of her former self—that is,
by becoming more like her proper older sister, Elinor.[24] And in "Jane
Austen and the Masturbating Girl," a classic of queer criticism, Eve
Sedgwick maintains that the disciplinary subject is constituted in *Sense
and Sensibility* by taming Marianne Dashwood's "autoerotic" sensibility
into conformity with the requirements of heteronormative society.[25]

Sense and Sensibility, however, is a remarkably self-conscious novel
in which Austen anticipates later interpretations of her work as

conservatively opposed to the individualisms of sensibility and romanticism. She anticipates them through her younger heroine, who explicitly associates her older sister's manners with an abject renunciation of self-directing agency. As noted earlier, Marianne argues that the laws of the drawing room condone insincerity and dullness, and oil the social machine at the expense of intelligent individuals. By subscribing to such unreasonable injunctions, Elinor, she suggests, sacrifices her own judgment to the collective judgment of society: Her decorum implies that "our judgments were given us merely to be subservient to those of our neighbours" (71).

In response, the narrator of *Sense and Sensibility* associates the novel's highly developed vocabulary of judgment more extensively with Elinor than with Marianne. Elinor is distinguished in the novel's opening pages by the coolness of her judgment and the "strength of [her] understanding," which "qualify her, though only nineteen, to be the counsellor of her mother" (6). She spends much of the narrative as though she were in a court of law: doubting, acquitting, and condoning. But she also spends a great deal of time beholding other people as though they were works of art, and an explicit parallel is established in *Sense and Sensibility* between judgments of character and aesthetic judgments.

Austen's association, in her characterization of Elinor Dashwood, of the languages of judgment and propriety, substantially complicates Butler's argument about the novelist's affinity with Burke because the latter upholds a morality of manners as an *alternative* to one based on private judgment. In the *Reflections* he suggests, "When antient opinions and rules of life are taken away, the loss cannot possibly be estimated. From that moment we have no compass to govern us; nor can we know distinctly to what port we steer."[26] The best kind of moral compass, according to Burke, is the collective judgment of the society, as embodied in inherited traditions or the "general bank and capital of nations, and of ages" (251). This championing of tradition is underwritten by a social psychology whereby individuals are perceived to be creatures of little sense but ample sensibility. Burke enjoins the French, for example, to recognize something that the English (supposedly) already know, that "We are generally men of untaught feelings" (251), by no means ripe to assume the rights that the revolutionaries mistake for a birthright. "We are afraid," he indicates, "to put men to live and trade each on his own stock of private reason; because we suspect that this stock in each man is small" (251). Against the Enlightenment norm of autonomy, Burke suggests that private morality and civil society flourish when the customs of the country control the passions of individuals: "Society requires not only that the passions of individuals should be subjected, but that even in the mass and body as well as in the individuals, the inclinations of men should frequently be thwarted, their will controlled, and their passions brought into subjection. This can only be *done by a power out of themselves*" (219). This view echoes Mandeville's representation of morality as something externally imposed on self-interested individuals. Also reminiscent of Mandeville's argument is Burke's contention that the most effective subjection is that which has been rendered most desirable. The beauty of the laws and the persons who subjugate render those to be subjugated pliant and ready for discipline. Hence, "There ought to be a system of manners in every nation which a well-formed mind would be disposed to relish. To make us love our country, our country ought to be lovely" (241).

Burke's system enjoins the cultivation, then, not of judgment but of the feelings that bind individuals to their communities and its traditions. The English, he proudly proclaims, are an ethnocentric type, unlikely to be swayed by abstract arguments about universal rights: "We know that we have made no discoveries; and we think that no discoveries are to be made, in morality; nor many in the great principles of government, nor in the ideas of liberty, which were understood long before we were born . . . In England we have not yet been completely emboweled of our natural entrails; we still feel within us, and we cherish and cultivate, those inbred sentiments which are the faithful guardians, the active monitors of our duty, the true supporters of all liberal and manly morals" (250).

In her spirited rejoinder to Burke in *Vindication of the Rights of Men* (1790), Mary Wollstonecraft nicely exposes the limitations of this nebulous appeal to feelings. "What do you mean by inbred sentiments?" (32), she asks. "From whence do they come? How were they bred? Are they the brood of folly? . . . Why [then] is passion or heroism the child of reflection, the consequence of dwelling with intent contemplation on one object?" (32). An enormous gap exists between Burke's untaught feelings and Wollstonecraft's passion, represented here as "the child of reflection," as also between Burke's understanding of aesthetic experience and that of sentimentalists like Mackenzie. We will recall that Mackenzie invokes the *theatrum mundi* metaphor in *Julia de Roubigné*, for example, to show that feelings are susceptible to the distancing work of the spectator. Burke, by contrast, figures the theater as a "school of moral sentiments" (244) because it appeals to feelings alone, because it reveals right and wrong at first glance. At one point in the *Reflections* he wagers that if the French revolution were staged as a theatrical performance it would be short-lived because an enraged audience would put an end to the show: "In the theatre, the first intuitive glance, without any elaborate process of reasoning, would shew, that this method of political computation, would justify every extent of crime" (244). While Julia de Roubigné's inability to cultivate the proper aesthetic distance from her father's theatrics is represented by Mackenzie as a problem, Burke eschews aesthetic distance to enjoin audience participation.

Burke's conservative reprisal of the man of feeling in the *Reflections*, as Claudia Johnson argues in her deft account of his "chivalric sentimentality,"[27] complicates Marilyn Butler's sketch of the ideological landscape of the 1790s, since, as it turns out, it is conservatives like Burke who extol excessive sensibility, and radicals like Wollstonecraft and Godwin who view it with suspicion.[28] For Johnson and other feminist critics more sympathetic than Butler to the politics of Austen's fiction, Wollstonecraft's two *Vindications* delineate a better measure of Austen's ideological investments than does Burke's *Reflections*. The point is well taken, and Austen sounds remarkably like Wollstonecraft in her depiction, through Marianne Dashwood's story, of the damage women inflict upon themselves by cultivating sensibility alone.[29] Nonetheless, Austen's interest in propriety marks something of a departure from Wollstonecraft, whose often-suspicious stance toward manners is greatly influenced by Rousseau's critique of the artifice of modern civilization. Austen's alignment, in *Sense and Sensibility*, of the languages of judgment and propriety finds a more fitting context instead in the broadly liberal sentimentalisms of Hume and Smith.

David Kaufmann's reading of *Sense and Sensibility* in "Law and Propriety, *Sense and Sensibility*" is illuminating in this regard. Kaufmann contends that Austen invokes propriety in her first novel not as "the atavistic outcropping of tradition but [as] the expression of an experience of radical change."[30] She builds in this regard on a rich eighteenth-century tradition of theorizing manners as a mechanism for protecting a newly emergent civil society from state interference.[31] For Hume, for example, manners ensure justice in everyday interactions and as such replace (and render irrelevant) the laws that enable state surveillance. In the *Enquiry* Hume suggests, "As the mutual shocks, in *society*, and the oppositions of interest and self-love have constrained mankind to establish the laws of *justice*, in order to preserve the advantages of mutual assistance and protection: in like manner, the eternal contrarieties, in *company*, of men's pride and self-conceit, have introduced the rules of Good Manners or Politeness, in order to facilitate the intercourse of minds, and an undisturbed commerce and conversation" (261).[32] Interpreting Hume, Kaufmann observes: "the law stands over and above civil society: it protects property and rights and thus ensures peace in voluntary commercial associations. Manners, which resemble laws, are the rules that govern social interactions not covered by the law. They allow society to exist, free from the intervention of government" (390).

I would suggest that the sentimentalists' distinctively modern investment in manners emerges still more forcefully in Smith's *Theory of Moral Sentiments* where it is framed by a larger discussion of the general rules of morality. As noted in chapter 2 of this study, general rules and the sense of duty that ensures respect for rules take centerstage in Smith's *Theory* and align his sentimentalism very explicitly with Kantian discussions of morality as self-governance. Unlike Kant, however, Smith gives self-legislation a markedly experiential character. Autonomy, as he understands it, derives from the independence of one's judgments, and such independence is ensured by a cultivated impartiality (rather than by a supersensible reason, as in Kant). On this account, rules have a second-order importance since they rely on individual acts of judgment, which alone reveal moral and aesthetic distinctions. They are "ultimately founded upon experience of what, in particular instances, our moral faculties, our natural sense of merit and propriety, approve, or disapprove of. We do not originally approve or condemn particular actions; because, upon examination, they appear to be agreeable or inconsistent with a certain general rule. The general rule, on the contrary, is formed, by finding from experience, that all actions of a certain kind, or circumstanced in a certain manner, are approved or disapproved of" (159). Rule-bound behavior, as conceived here, by no means represents the highest form of morality. Nonetheless, rules, Smith contends, shape (or should shape) a great deal of everyday action since it is difficult to be impartial in the heat of the moment, or in the context of choices where there is little or no time for reflection. Smith gives the example of an unwelcome visitor:

> Your friend makes you a visit when you happen to be in a humour which makes it disagreeable to receive him: in your present mood his civility is apt to appear an impertinent intrusion; and if you were to give way to the views of things which at this time occur, though civil in your temper, you would behave to him with coldness and contempt. What renders you incapable of such a rudeness, is nothing but a regard to the general rules of civility and hospitality, which prohibit it. That habitual reverence which your former experience has taught you for these, enables you to act, upon all such occasions, with nearly equal propriety, and hinders those inequalities of temper, to which all men are subject, from influencing your conduct in any very sensible degree. (163)

Mitigating the "inequalities of temper" to which all are liable, general rules ensure justice for all. The "all" here includes, notably, the self, insofar as the civil person abides by principles that have been reflectively endorsed by her in cooler moments and that seem to her to accord with the moral imperatives of justice. In the example above, irritation at the unwelcome guest gives way to civility not because one respects the judgments of others (enshrined in the codes of civility) over one's own but because one respects rules sanctioned by one's *own* considered judgment.

Smith's account of general rules as a supplement to private judgment informs Austen's defense of manners in *Sense and Sensibility*. What Edward Ferrars characterizes as Elinor Dashwood's "*plan* of general civility" (71; my emphasis) is represented by Austen as a self-conscious use of rules that in no way preempts the desirability of independent judgment. When Marianne accuses her sister of renouncing her own judgment by subscribing to the judgments of her neighbors, Elinor responds: "My doctrine has never aimed at the subjection of the understanding. All I have ever attempted to influence has been the behaviour" (71). Civility, Elinor underscores, is a behavioral code rather than a strictly moral one. It entails *acting* as though the feelings and opinions of others matter even if they do not or should not. As such, it preserves a justice-friendly distinction between the thinking and the acting self (as in Smith's example, where subscription to rules permits justice of action in the absence of just intention). At least as importantly, however, Austen's heroine's distinguishing of thought and action connotes a commitment to thinking *before* acting. Her quest for impartiality, or her wish, as she puts it to her mother, to "be candid in my judgement of every body" (60), requires "giving oneself time to deliberate and judge" (71). Decorum, as Susan Morgan notes in her fine reading of *Sense and Sensibility*, is interpreted by Austen as a "social principle for keeping our judgments from becoming irretrievable in our acts."[33] The reserve that Elinor's politeness often entails enables her to keep her initial impressions of actions and characters to herself until she had time to think them through. Her candor comports well with the polite reserve with which she greets the many new acquaintances she encounters in the early chapters of *Sense and Sensibility*, which depict the Dashwood women catapulted from the only home they have known (when the older Mr. Dashwood dies and his son from a prior marriage takes over their entailed estate) and into a world dominated by strangers.

Austen suggests that Elinor's goal of impartiality is no luxury but rather a necessity for a disinherited family of women who must make their way in the world by relying on the patronage and goodwill of strangers. The intimacy that shapes the epistolary form of sentimental novels like *Clarissa* and *Julie* is no longer a given in the atomistic social world Austen depicts in *Sense and Sensibility* (a world in which a half-brother acts like no brother at all) but must be found by exercising discriminating judgment. Love, Elinor implies to Marianne in describing her relationship with Edward Ferrars, has much to do with distancing judgment:

He and I have been at times thrown a good deal together, while you have been wholly engrossed on the most affectionate principle by my mother. I have seen a great deal of him, have studied his sentiments and heard his opinion on subjects of literature and taste; and, upon the whole, I venture to pronounce that his mind is well-informed, his enjoyment of books exceedingly great, his imagination lively, his observation just and correct, and his taste delicate and pure. His abilities in every respect improve as much upon acquaintance as his manners and person. At first sight, his address is certainly not striking; and his person can hardly be called handsome, till the expression of his eyes, which are uncommonly good, and the general sweetness of his countenance, is perceived. At present, I know him so well, that I think him really handsome; or, at least, almost so. (16)

Love and justice emerge as conjoined values in Elinor's explanation, which, as Morgan also observes, expresses at once a judgment of Edward's character and strong feelings for him. Justice to others, Elinor suggests, demands withholding judgment of their motives and actions, just as justice to oneself requires choosing one's affiliations with care. Beginning with a dispassionate cataloguing of Edward's qualities, Elinor ends on a passionate note, re-presenting a plain man as a handsome man. While Marianne worries that Edward is not the best match for her sister because "his figure is not striking" and his "eyes want all that spirit, that fire, which at once announce virtue and intelligence" (14), Elinor finds the expression of Edward's eyes "uncommonly good" and his countenance uniformly sweet. She does so because her judgment of Edward, and hence her love for him, are shaped not by first impressions—first impressions being an enduring Austenian topos and the original title of *Pride and Prejudice* (1813)— but by a developing acquaintance. Distance precedes affection on this understanding, and it is enabled, albeit in varying ways, by Edward's habitual diffidence and Elinor's more controlled and sophisticated civility.

The passage above speaks nicely also to the novel's omnipresent metaphor of screens, as in the screens of politeness that Elinor deploys in her interactions with the various men who come to woo the Dashwood sisters. Appropriately, Elinor, who can hide her feelings, paints screens, while Marianne, who wants to express them unreservedly, plays the piano. Elinor's account of her feelings for Edward suggests, however, that screening is not merely the business of hiding and expressing. It also betokens a certain contentment with appearances over truths, to invoke a critical Arendtian distinction. Hence, if Elinor screens herself in the early phases of her acquaintance with Edward through her distancing politeness she also screens Edward in the more ethical sense of according him a standpoint of his own, one that is at least provisionally worthy of respect and further engagement. More peculiarly, she screens him even after she knows him well by "mistaking" his plainness for good looks. Screens are at once the masks politeness enforces (or enables) and the veils willingly bestowed upon others. Screening is both an act of dissimulation as well as an act of moral respect, fairness, and even love. Elinor's willingness to screen herself and others opens up an understanding of the social world as a perspectival public space in which other people are always at some level strangers and in which the hope of community rests in making a stranger a discussant in the "unreserved conversation" (16) that Elinor specifies as her ideal of sociability.

Austen suggests that Marianne is prohibited by the maxims of sensibility from enjoying this kind of community. The narrator contrasts Elinor's account of her developing relationship with Edward with Marianne's first full exchange with Willoughby:

> It was only necessary to mention any favourite amusement to engage her to talk. She could not be silent when such points were introduced, and she had neither shyness nor reserve in their discussion. They speedily discovered that their enjoyment of dancing and music were mutual, and that it arose from *a general conformity of judgment in all that related to either*. Encouraged by this to a further examination of his opinions, she proceeded to question him on the subject of books; her favourite authors were brought forward and dwelt upon with so a rapturous a delight, that any young man of five and twenty must have been insensible indeed, not to become an immediate convert to the excellence of such works, however disregarded before. *Their taste was strikingly alike*. The same books, the same passages were idolized by each—or if any difference appeared, any objection arose, it lasted no longer than till the force of her arguments and the brightness of her eyes could be displayed. He acquiesced in all her decisions, caught

all her enthusiasm; and long before his visit concluded, they con-
versed with the familiarity of a long-established acquaintance. (36;
my emphasis)

The narrator's ironic commentary about "the general conformity of
judgment" and strikingly similar tastes of the two young people frames
a dialogue that is really a monologue initiated and sustained by
Marianne's enthusiasm. She opens up in conversation only once a
favorite topic has been introduced, and then proceeds with a deeply
felt exposition of her judgments and tastes which leaves Willoughby
admiringly acquiescent—in deference, however, to "the brightness of
her eyes" more than to the "force of her arguments." Nor is the narrator herself without admiration for the talented Marianne, who, she
suggests, will easily win converts. The problem with this exchange,
from the narrator's standpoint, is not Marianne's spiritedness but her
instrumentalist stance toward Willoughby, who appears to her, from
the beginning to the end of their conversation, only what she wants
him to be.

While Elinor screens herself and others, Marianne dislikes a world
of screens. Even though Marianne's contempt for the masks of polite
society is guided by the noble goal of sincerity, it often translates as a
judgmental (as opposed to judicious) posture toward others. With the
best intentions, but not the best results, she lifts the screens off of people
too quickly. Hence, Willoughby's vivacity and striking good looks
identify him to her almost instantaneously as a true man of feeling.
Shortly after her first meeting with him, she observes to her sister: "It
is not time or opportunity that is to determine intimacy;—it is disposition alone . . . [Of] Willoughby my judgment has long been formed"
(44–45). Likewise, Colonel Brandon's reserve and age brand him
immediately as the very antitype of the sentimental hero. Marianne
declares to her mother and sister that "if he were ever animated enough
to be in love, [he] must have long outlived every sensation of the kind"
(29). Relenting a bit, she concedes to Brandon the possibility of union
with a twenty-seven-year-old woman, someone who is similarly past
the years of feeling, but remarks that such a marriage would be merely
"a compact of convenience."

At one point in the narrative, Marianne revealingly confides to
Mrs. Dashwood that she wants to affiliate herself with a man who is

both a lover and a connoisseur. This argument is made in the context of a discussion of Edward's suitability for Elinor, and in relation to Marianne's judgment that his disinterested contemplation of Elinor's drawings—like his tame reading of Marianne's (and Jane Austen's) favorite poet, Cowper—is indicative that he lacks real taste. As she puts it, "He admires as a lover, not as a connoisseur. To satisfy me, those characters must be united" (14).

The parallelism of love and connoisseurship that Marianne establishes is an important one, one that Austen broadly endorses. How one responds to others is not unlike how one responds to aesthetic works, as Edward's attentiveness to Elinor's character and her paintings suggests. Marianne, Austen suggests, is not wrong to demand that a lover also be a connoisseur. She is only mistaken in thinking that either love or connoisseurship is best manifest as the rapturous delight with which she espouses her tastes to Willoughby and which she upholds as her own considered formula for taste. Hence, when Elinor praises the simplicity of Edward's taste, Marianne, we are told, "said no more on the subject; but the kind of approbation which Elinor described as excited in him by the drawings of other people, was very far from the rapturous delight, which, in her opinion, could alone be called taste" (15).

The limits of this understanding of taste are amply shown up by effusive but undiscriminating characters like Mrs. Palmer, whose admiration of the Dashwoods' home, for example, is as meaningless as it is unstinting: Hence, on her first visit to Barton cottage, Mrs. Palmer "was hardly seated before her admiration of the parlour and every thing in it burst forth" (81). Her "examination" of Elinor's drawings take the following form: "'Oh! dear, how beautiful these are! Well! how delightful! Do but look, mama, how sweet! I declare they are quite charming; I could look at them for ever'. And then sitting down again, she very soon forgot there were any such things in the room" (82). Rapture is Mrs. Palmer's forte, as is confirmed by a London shopping expedition in which Mrs. Palmer, like Harriet Smith in *Emma*, is distracted by everything and unable to choose anything: Marianne "could with difficulty govern her vexation at the tediousness of Mrs. Palmer, whose eye was caught by every thing pretty, expensive, or new; who was wild to buy all, could determine on none, and dawdled away her time in rapture and indecision" (123).

Austen distinguishes between rapture and taste also in an early representation of various characters responding to Marianne's musical performance:

> Marianne's performance was highly applauded. Sir John was loud in his admiration at the end of every song; and as loud in his conversation with others while every song lasted. Lady Middleton frequently called him to order, wondered how any one's attention could be diverted from music for a moment, and asked Marianne to sing a particular song which Marianne had just finished. Colonel Brandon alone, of all the party, heard her without being in raptures. He paid her only the compliment of attention; and she felt a respect for him on the occasion, which the others had reasonably forfeited by their shameless want of taste. His pleasure in music, though it amounted not to that extatic delight which alone could sympathize with her own, was estimable when contrasted against the horrible insensibility of the others. (27)

Here Austen reverts to the satire of the juvenilia, chaffing her characters for their blatant self-contradictions—especially the talented Marianne, whose formula for taste as rapturous delight is complicated by her own experience here of the rapturous delight of others as "horrible insensibility." Significantly, Colonel Brandon's attentiveness to her performance, as to her character, identifies him as a man close to her ideal of a husband—a man who combines the talents of love and connoisseurship.

Tony Tanner has argued that Coleridge's distinction of fancy and imagination is pertinent to Austen's characterization of the Dashwood sisters, with Elinor being associated by her author with the lesser principle of fancy.[34] But it is Elinor who is more imaginative about others than Marianne, and it with Elinor that the narrator associates the most complex aesthetic imagery in *Sense and Sensibility*. While Marianne is unable to build on her poetic "passion for dead leaves" (67) in responding to the autumnal Colonel Brandon, Elinor approaches him as though he were a painting or a sculpture: "She liked him—in spite of his gravity and reserve, she beheld in him an object of interest" (38). This talent for beholding a person is one that Marianne still has to learn when the novel begins.

I would argue that a better context for thinking about the aesthetic paradigms summoned by the two sisters is Hannah Arendt's distinction between reflective judgment and spontaneous taste in the *Lectures on Kant's Political Philosophy*. Arendt suggests that in the *Critique of Judgment* Kant renamed the faculty of taste the faculty of judgment to underscore that judgment has a reflective and critical dimension:

> It is not important whether or not [the beautiful object] pleases in perception; what pleases in perception is gratifying but not beautiful. It pleases in representation, for now the imagination has prepared it so that I can reflect on it. This is "the operation of reflection" . . . [One] then speaks of judgment and no longer of taste because, though it still affects one like a matter of taste, one has now the remoteness or uninvolvedness or disinterestedness, that is requisite for approbation and disapprobation, for evaluating something at its proper worth. By removing the object, one has established the conditions for impartiality.[35]

Judgment, Arendt contends, is closely tied to feeling (the beautiful "affects one like a matter of taste") but it is not reducible to feeling. The most important characteristic of the judge instead is the "enlarged mentality" (Kant and Arendt), or "impartiality" (Smith), or "general point of view" (Hume) that enables him or her to reflect upon spontaneous likes and dislikes.

Notwithstanding the importance it attaches to judgment, the cultish program of sensibility to which Marianne subscribes is represented in *Sense and Sensibility* as a sorry devolution of the culture of sentiment: It has lost sight of judgment's most important requirement, a cultivated impartiality, a requirement that, according to Austen, is highly compatible with the norms of politeness. As portrayed by her author, Marianne's contempt for the conventions of polite society denotes less an autonomous rejection of other people's judgments than a commitment to personal preferences. Her perceptions of right and wrong, like her aesthetic judgments, risk conflating judgment and instinct, as is highlighted by an early conversation between Marianne and Elinor, in which they are discussing the propriety of Marianne's unchaperoned trip to Allenham in Willoughby's company. When Elinor observes that "the pleasantness of an employment does not always evince its propriety," Marianne responds, "On the contrary, nothing can be a stronger proof of it, Elinor; for if there had been any real impropriety in what I did, I should have been sensible of it at the time, for we always know when we are acting wrong, and with such a conviction I could have had no pleasure" (52). Marianne's suggestion that pleasure and displeasure are appropriate guides to moral discrimination identifies judgment as a priori, determinant, and unmediated by personal reflection.

Austen's critique of Marianne's sensibility, then, is a critique of a pattern of judgment in which "untaught feelings," to deploy Burke's phrase, unwittingly triumph over considered reflections. The standard constituted by such feelings is impervious to alternatives, as Marianne herself affirms when she observes to Edward, "At my time of life opinions are tolerably fixed" (71). One of these fixed opinions is Marianne's belief, inherited from the cult of sensibility, that one can love only once in a lifetime. While Marianne is herself the child of a second marriage, she does not consider the possibility that feelings are fluid and can change with time and experience. As such, she espouses, early in her story, a commitment to the inevitability of feelings—a principle that all of Austen's novels are dedicated to upturning. Beginning with *Sense and Sensibility*, second love, second proposals, second chances, become the very stuff of a Jane Austen novel. Both Darcy in *Pride and Prejudice* and Wentworth in *Persuasion* must propose to their respective love interests twice before they are accepted. Long-established friendships in *Emma* and *Mansfield Park* become de facto second relationships when they take a romantic turn. Catherine Morland of *Northanger Abbey* must embark upon a second courtship with the same man when the terms upon which they can marry suddenly change (she turns out not to be the heiress her suitor's fortune-hunting father imagined her to be). And of course, Elinor and Edward in *Sense and Sensibility* are given a second chance at love when Edward's betrothed suddenly marries the second Mr. Ferrars (Edward's younger brother) instead. Finally, Marianne is given a second chance at life and love—with Colonel Brandon—after her disappointment at Willoughby leads to a near-fatal illness.

Austen's ideological point of departure from the eighteenth-century sentimental novel rests on her optimism, at play in all six of her mature works, about the potential of education to remake both self and world in ways that render happy endings near-inevitable for her heroines. Her faith in the second nature education constructs marks a departure also from her own youthful writings, in which young women are stock types and butts of satire. Marianne Dashwood is a new kind of heroine of sensibility as compared with Sophia and Laura in the wickedly funny *Love and Freindship*. Unlike Sophia, who dies of a cold after fainting in a puddle, Marianne lives to prosper in love and fortune after recovering from a cold (also contracted as a result of weeping for a lover). While Sophia claims to love a man who sports a heavenly blue satin waistcoat, Marianne learns to love a man who resorts to a flannel waistcoat—appropriately enough, to keep influenza at bay. In making her debut on the literary marketplace, Austen does not leave behind the satire of the juvenilia but the satire is directed less at young women and more at their elders, at such pillars of society and "instructors" of the young as Sir John Middleton in *Sense and Sensibility*, Lady Catherine de Bourgh in *Pride and Prejudice*, General Tilney in *Northanger Abbey*, Mrs. Norris in *Mansfield Park*, Mr. Woodhouse in *Emma*, and Sir Walter Elliot in *Persuasion*.

Austen's persistent infantilizing of potential mentors makes it hard to agree with critics like Butler and Mudrick that this novelist places her trust in society over the individual. "Society" is typically represented in *Sense and Sensibility* as a rather dull set of people belonging to the gentry and as forms of sociability, revolving around the formal drawing room, in which rational conversation is replaced by gossip and noisy games. In the London drawing room of the John Dashwoods, for example, "no poverty of any kind, except of conversation, appeared—but there, the deficiency was considerable" (175). Things are no better in the Middletons' country drawing room, where, as Elinor observes, "they could not be supposed to meet for the sake of conversation. Such a thought would never enter either Sir John or Lady Middleton's head, and therefore very little leisure was ever given for general chat, and none at all for particular discourse. They met for the sake of eating, drinking, and laughing together, playing at cards, or consequences, or any other game that was sufficiently noisy" (106). Conversation has disintegrated here into noise, associated in the novel's opening pages with the boisterous little boy who unknowingly deprives the Dashwood women of a fair share of their inheritance when his great-grandfather's judgment becomes clouded by his partiality to "such attractions as are by no means unusual in children of two or three years old; an imperfect articulation, an earnest desire of having his own way, many cunning tricks, and a great deal of noise" (4). The world of children, as represented here, is a Hobbesian universe of unabashed self-interest and cunning tricks. It is not, however, children but childlike adults whom the narrator satirizes: adults like the vacuous Sir John and Lady Middleton, their raucous guests, and the ungrateful Dashwood patriarch, who lets a momentary partiality override an impartial assessment of what he owes to his daughter-in-law and granddaughters, women who have been consistently "attentive" (4) to his needs over a long period of cohabitation.

Notwithstanding her clear perception of the limits of drawing-room society, as experienced by the Dashwood women, Austen is by no means only a critic of the drawing room. As the room of the house most open to the wider world, the drawing room also emerges in her fiction as a symbolically significant space for middle-class women, like her heroines, whose access to the public sphere remains highly circumscribed. If, on the one hand, the drawing room is the site of banal social visits, Austen also figures it as the venue for another kind of "visiting," the kind that Arendt invokes when, in the *Lectures on Kant's Political Philosophy*, she describes the judge's enlarged perspective as a species of the itinerant imagination: "To think with an enlarged mentality means that one trains one's imagination to go visiting" (43). Austen's conjoining of the vocabularies of civility and judgment in *Sense and Sensibility* has yet another dimension that deserves unpacking and that bears on our understanding not only of the politics of her fiction but of "the political" as such.

THE IMAGINATION GOES VISITING

One of the most intriguing bits of biographical information we have about Jane Austen is that she wrote much of her fiction in the family living room. In his *Memoir of Jane Austen*, Austen's nephew, James Edward Austen-Leigh, indicates that when Austen, her mother, and her older sister Cassandra moved to their final home at Chawton, the novelist did not have a study of her own. Austen-Leigh remarks how remarkable this was given that the years at Chawton were a period of intense productivity. In her first year of residence, Austen revised and published *Sense and Sensibility* and *Pride and Prejudice.* Then, between 1811 and 1816, she wrote *Mansfield Park*, *Emma*, and *Persuasion*. Her reverent nephew writes:

> How she able to effect all this is surprising, for she had no separate study to retire to, and most of her work must have been done in the general sitting-room, subject to all kinds of casual interruptions. She was careful that her occupation should not be suspected by servants, visitors, or any other persons beyond her own family party. She wrote upon small sheets of paper which could easily be put away, or covered with a piece of blotting paper. There was, between the front door and the offices, a swing door which creaked when it was opened; but she objected to having this little inconvenience remedied, because it gave her notice when anyone was coming . . . In that well occupied female party there must have been many precious hours of silence during which the pen was busy at the little mahogany writing-desk, while Fanny Price, or Emma Woodhouse, or Anne Elliot was growing into beauty and interest. I have no doubt that I and my sisters and cousins, in our visits to Chawton, frequently disturbed this mystic process, without having any idea of the mischief that we were doing; certainly we never should have guessed it by any signs of impatience or irritability in the writer.[36]

This information about the novelist, who calls to mind the civil person of Smith's anecdote in the *Theory of Moral Sentiments*, has powerfully shaped the modern reception of her work. Henry James damns with faint praise when he lauds Austen's artistry as a kind of "unconsciousness, as if, at the most, for difficulty, for embarrassment, she sometimes, over her work-basket, her tapestry flowers, in the spare, cool drawing-room of other days, fell a-musing, lapsed too metaphorically, as one might say, into wool-gathering."[37] Modern critics like Sandra Gilbert and Susan Gubar are also skeptical, and their powerful psychoanalytic reading of the female literary tradition in *The Madwoman in the Attic* identifies Austen's writing habits as symbolic of a ladylike propriety and general social conformism. Charlotte Brontë is the braver novelist on their interpretation: She gives female individualism freer expression in *Jane Eyre*, even as she (realistically) restricts this expression to isolated spaces like the attic, the room of the house furthest from its entrance and hence most removed from the outside world.

In *A Room of One's Own*, Virginia Woolf is more sympathetic, even as Austen appears to overturn Woolf's own thesis about the woman writer's need for a room of her own. Austen, Woolf suggests, might not have had a room of her own but she did have a sentence of her own, a woman's sentence, one that made clear that the woman artist's "sensibility was shaped for centuries by the influences of the common sitting-room" (116). Even as Woolf looks forward to a future for women's fiction in which "we escape a little from the influence of the common sitting room" she opens up a feminist reading of Austen's fiction that is not too dismissive of the culture of the drawing room. This culture, as depicted in *Sense and Sensibility*, encompasses not only the constraints of politeness, or the boredom of enforced sociability with dull people, but also exposure to standpoints other than one's own, a quintessential requirement of judgment as interpreted by eighteenth-century sentimentalism and Kantian aesthetics.

In this context, it is worth attending to a striking passage in *Sense and Sensibility*, which Austen's nephew must have had in mind as he recounted (truthfully or not) his aunt's writing habits, in which Austen represents a woman deep in thought in the drawing room (looking forward, interestingly, to James's own Isabel Archer in *The Portrait of a Lady*). The scene in question belongs to a sequence of explicitly coupled scenes early on in *Sense and Sensibility*, in which the narrator establishes a contrast between the Dashwood sisters by showing them responding in different ways to similar circumstances. The circumstance in question in the episode at hand is the departure of a suitor. When Willoughby leaves Barton, Marianne is prostrated by grief and avoids family and friends. In doing so, she causes much pain to those who love her and it is in part to avoid similarly grieving her mother and sisters that Elinor chooses to remain in their midst after Edward's oddly abrupt visit to Barton:

> Without shutting herself up from her family, or leaving the house
> in determined solitude to avoid them, or lying awake the whole

night to indulge meditation, Elinor found every day afforded her leisure enough to think of Edward . . . There were moments in abundance, when, if not by the absence of her mother and sisters, at least by the nature of their employments, conversation was forbidden among them, and *every effect of solitude was produced*. Her mind was inevitably at liberty; her thoughts could not be chained elsewhere; and the past and the future, on a subject so interesting, must be before her, must force her attention, and engross her memory, her reflection, and her fancy.

From a reverie of this kind . . . she was roused one morning . . . by the arrival of company. She happened to be quite alone. (79; my emphasis)

Rather than interpreting this passage as illustrative of a pious ethics of care, or simply of Elinor's selflessness, I would like to direct attention to the curious "liberty" Austen invokes, a liberty of mind or thought that is operative even in the presence of others and that encompasses "meditation," "attention," "memory," "reflection," "fancy," and "reverie." Austen's reference to "reverie" is especially noteworthy and calls to mind Rousseau's *Reveries of the Solitary Walker* (1782), a critical influence upon the late-century culture of sensibility. Nature is the favorite haunt of Rousseau's thinker or natural man, as of Godwin's young Fleetwood, who, we will recall, is brought up on Rousseauvian principles. In both *Julie* and *Emile*, as in the later *Reveries*, Rousseau's philosopher shuns the city and finds his true vocation instead in relative isolation from others. Cities, Rousseau expostulates in *Emile*, "are the abyss of the human species" (59). "The more [men] come together, the more they are corrupted." Wordsworth makes a related claim in the 1802 preface to *Lyrical Ballads* when he indicates that he chose "low and rustic life" as the subject of his poetry because "in that condition, the essential passions of the heart find a better soil in which they can attain their maturity, are less under restraint."

Not unlike Wordsworth's poet, and Rousseau's and Godwin's natural men, Marianne Dashwood feels most herself when she is by herself, when the only other present to her is nature. London, for instance, oppresses her, not only because it is the scene of her romantic disappointments but also because it precludes the liberating solitude of long country walks. But the walks that Marianne takes at the Palmers' country estate, on her return from London to the country, lead to a near-fatal illness. Many readers have interpreted this illness as a harsh plot device through which Austen brings her errant heroine of sensibility back into the folds of civilized society. But the narrator *of Sense and Sensibility* foregrounds another cause for the illness: Marianne's solicitation not of solitude as such but of spaces "where the trees were the oldest, and the grass was the longest and wettest" (231). That is, the desirability of escape to places where there is no sign of human interference, in the shape of landscaping or paved walks, becomes undercut by Marianne's need, as a human animal, for dry paths. Marianne, it would appear, is not wrong to seek solitude as such but she is wrong to imagine that nature is somehow attuned to her needs, that it is *the* friend she needs after Willoughby's betrayal.

In moving reverie out of the woods or the shrubbery and into the drawing room Austen questions an established representation of mental life as a solitary one, a questioning that is reinforced by her use of the word "meditation" in the passage above. This term recalls, of course, a seminal text of Enlightenment rationalism, Descartes's *Meditations on First Philosophy* (1641). For Descartes, even more emphatically than for Rousseau, the vita contemplativa is a solitary life, in which the thinker must withdraw not only from society, but even, to the extent possible, from the evidence of his senses. At the beginning of the Third Meditation, for example, Descartes indicates: "I will now shut my eyes, stop my ears, and withdraw all my senses. I will eliminate from my thoughts all images of bodily things, or rather, since this is hardly possible, I will regard all such images as vacuous, false and worthless."[38]

Descartes's and Rousseau's understandings of mental life distance the self from the world, and especially from the world of other people, in ways that Austen challenges. Unlike Rousseau's solitary walker or Descartes's meditator, Elinor does not need to be alone in order to think. While actual solitude is welcome to her, she can also think when "the effect of solitude" is created by the silence and employment of those around her. The outer dialogue must cease for the inner one to gather steam. But the two dialogues develop a vital connection through Austen's depiction of a woman who can be alone in the presence of others, whose liberty of thought is not diminished by her placement in

a shared social space. Challenging metaphysical conceptions of thinking as an activity that wholly transcends the world, Austen can be
interpreted as a peer of the Kant Arendt reconstructs in the *Lectures
on Kant's Political Philosophy*. As noted earlier in this study, a principal
claim of Arendt's work is that Kant restores a critical connection
between the public and the private domains by foregrounding the
"basic other-directedness of taste and judgment" (68) in the *Critique of
Judgment*; this begins to heal the age-old rift between the philosopher
and the city that was instituted by Plato's philosophy after the Athenians
put his beloved teacher, Socrates, to death. According to Arendt, Kant
reinstates the Socratic paradigm of the critical thinker or judge as a
public persona, even a citizen, by representing thinking as an activity
that gains its critical edge through the public use of one's reason.
Arendt explains: "Thinking, as Kant agreed with Plato, is the silent
dialogue of myself with myself (*das Reden mit sich selbst*). . . yet, unless
you can somehow communicate and expose to the test of others. . .
whatever you may have found out when you were alone, this faculty
exerted in solitude will disappear" (40).

Moving thinking into the drawing room, Austen highlights the
domestic woman's fitness for critical thinking and public participation,
a participation for which Elinor is well equipped as a consequence of
her civility, which connotes an at least formal openness toward standpoints other than her own. Linking the private and public domains,
Austen also challenges one of political theory's most cherished binary
oppositions, one that Arendt herself, oddly, upholds. In *The Human
Condition* (1958), for example, Arendt makes a sharp distinction
between the polis and the household, identifying the latter as the realm
of nurture and necessity only. And she laments the blurring of the
boundaries between the household and the public realm in modern
times. Describing this development as "the rise of the social" Arendt
suggests: "The emergence of society—the rise of housekeeping, its
activities, problems, and organizational devices—from the shadowy
interior of the household into the light of the public sphere, has not
only blurred the old borderline between private and political, it has also
changed almost beyond recognition the meaning of the two terms."[39]

This statement is striking for its gender politics: The household
emerges here as a dark and concave place, like the mother's womb,

which contrasts with the brightly lit world of politics. As Seyla Benhabib has argued, Arendt's opposition of public and private spheres, which contrasts sharply with modern feminism's interpretation of the personal as the political, has the elitist effect of restricting politics to the political elite and cannot account for more informal modes of participation that bear upon progressive political goals.[40] Benhabib herself understands the public domain less as "a space of competition for acclaim and immortality among a political elite" than as "the creation of procedures whereby those affected by general social norms and by collective political decisions can have a say in their formulation, stipulation, and adoption."[41]

Benhabib suggests, however, that a more capacious sense of the public and the political can be found in Arendt's biography, written early in her career, of the late-Enlightenment Jewish salonniére, Rahel Varnhagen.[42] Against her denigration of the social as a development of the household's encroachment upon the polis, the social, as it emerges in Arendt's account of one of Berlin's most cosmopolitan society hostesses, is "sociability, patterns of human interaction, modalities of taste in dress, eating, leisure, and life-styles generally, differences in aesthetic, religious, and civic manners and outlooks, patterns of socializing, and forming marriages, friendships, acquaintanceships, and commercial exchanges."[43] Here Arendt complicates her binary opposition of public and private spheres since the salon, Benhabib observes, is "a curious space that is of the home yet public, that is dominated by women yet visited and frequented by men, that is highly mannered yet egalitarian."[44] Salons like Varnhagen's, Benhabib suggests, become "fascinating precursors of a certain transgression of the boundaries between the public and the private" that has proven historically enabling to women.[45]

Certainly, Austen's English drawings are not the continental salons that Arendt and Benhabib describe. They are spaces in which people of a certain class gather rather than a locus for the emergence and consolidation of the intelligentsia. Yet Austen's representation of the drawing room in *Sense and Sensibility* as a space for thinking and judging, and her critique of the conversationally impoverished gatherings at the Middletons' and the John Dashwoods', suggest a future for the English drawing room in which it more clearly approximates the salon and the public sphere. Given Elinor's conversational skills and Marianne's growth into these skills, the drawing rooms of the married Dashwood sisters are likely to be, like Varnhagen's, social spaces in which conversation rather than noise is the rule and in which the most welcome guests are those able to join the conversation.

The drawing room is the place where middle-class women like Austen's heroines and Jane Austen herself stepped into a larger world. And in *Sense and Sensibility* Austen suggests that Elinor Dashwood's plan of general civility is better suited to navigating this world than the culture of sensibility's valorization of affective kinship. The drawing room is not the public sphere but it creates "a certain transgression," as Benhabib puts it, of public and private spaces that opens the doors of the home for women. While the screens of civility can be used to close the self off from strangers, they can also be deployed as a first step toward drawing others into "unreserved conversation." Possible consensus is the unspoken regulative ideal at work in the drawing room, just as civility is the practical law that seeks to further this ideal. Illuminating the shadowy interior of the household by casting her light on the drawing room, Austen places the norm of a common point of view at the center of a nineteenth-century tradition of fiction that builds on eighteenth-century sentimentalism and aesthetics. Her intervention on the literary scene speaks to sentimentalism's importance beyond the Enlightenment as a shaper of a (still unfolding) modern ethos in which appearances are valued over truths, second chances are given, and respect for one's own judgment becomes coupled with a willingness to see things from other points of view.

NOTES

INTRODUCTION

1. See especially Amanda Anderson, *The Way We Argue Now: A Study in the Cultures of Theory* (Princeton, N.J.: Princeton University Press, 2006); *The Powers of Distance: Cosmopolitanism and the Cultivation of Detachment* (Princeton, N.J.: Princeton University Press, 2001); and "Cryptonormativism and Double Gestures: The Politics of Poststructuralism," *Cultural Critique* 21 (spring 1992): 63–95; Andrew H. Miller, *The Burdens of Perfection: On Ethics and Reading in Nineteenth-Century British Literature* (Ithaca, N.Y.: Cornell University Press, 2008); and David Wayne Thomas, *Cultivating Victorians: Liberal Culture and the Aesthetic* (Philadelphia: University of Pennsylvania Press, 2004).

2. See, for example, Carla Hesse, *The Other Enlightenment: How French Women Became Modern* (Princeton, N.J.: Princeton University Press, 2004); Jonathan Israel, *Radical Enlightenment: Philosophy and the Making of Modernity, 1650–1750* (Oxford: Oxford University Press, 2001); James Schmidt, ed., *What is Enlightenment? Eighteenth-Century Answers and Twentieth-Century Questions* (Berkeley: University of California Press, 1996); and Roy S. Porter and Mikulas Teich, *The Enlightenment in National Context* (Cambridge: Cambridge University Press, 1981).

3. Harry E. Shaw trenchantly makes this point in relation to recent readings of realist fiction. See *Narrating Reality: Austen, Scott, Eliot* (Ithaca, N.Y.: Cornell University Press, 1999).

4. Notable examples of the ethical turn include Judith Butler, *Precarious Life: The Powers of Mourning and Violence* (London: Verso, 2004) and *Giving an Account of Oneself* (New York: Fordham University Press, 2005). The turn to aesthetics has as particularly engaging representatives Jonathan Loesberg's *A Return to Aesthetics: Autonomy, Indifference, and Postmodernism* (Stanford, Calif.: Stanford University Press, 2005) and Elaine Scarry's *On Beauty and Being Just* (Princeton, N.J.: Princeton University Press, 2001), while the turn to affect is influentially instantiated by Eve Kosofsky Sedgwick's *Touching Feeling: Affect, Pedagogy, Performativity* (Durham, N.C.: Duke University Press, 2001).

5. Notable exceptions to this neglect include the work of cultural historians such as Lynn Hunt and William Reddy. See Lynn Hunt, *Inventing Human Rights: A History* (New York: Norton, 2008) and William M. Reddy, *Navigating*

Feeling: A Framework for the History of Emotions (Cambridge: Cambridge University Press, 2001).

6. In his magisterial history of the concept of autonomy, Jerome B. Schneewind describes this shift as one from "morality as obedience" to "morality as self-governance." He observes, "During the seventeenth and eighteenth centuries established conceptions of morality as obedience came increasingly to be contested by emerging conceptions of morality as self-governance. On the older conception, morality is to be understood most deeply as one aspect of the obedience we owe to God. . . . Even if everyone has the most fundamental laws of morality written in their hearts or consciences, most people need to be instructed by some appropriate authority about what is morally required in particular cases." By contrast, on the new understanding of morality as self-governance, "All of us . . . have an equal ability to see for ourselves what morality calls for and are in principle able to move ourselves to act accordingly, regardless of threats or rewards from others. . . . We assume, in short, that people are equally competent as moral agents unless shown to be otherwise." *The Invention of Autonomy: A History of Modern Moral Philosophy* (Cambridge: Cambridge University Press, 1998), 4. Helpful discussions of autonomy as a concept in moral philosophy include, in addition to Schneewind's book, his essay "The Use of Autonomy in Ethical Theory," in *Reconstructing Individualism: Autonomy, Individuality, and the Self in Western Thought*, ed. Thomas C. Heller, Morton Sosna, and David E. Wellbery (Stanford, Calif.: Stanford University Press, 1986); Catriona Mackenzie and Natalie Stoljar, eds., *Relational Autonomy: Feminist Perspectives on Autonomy, Agency, and the Social Self* (Oxford: Oxford University Press, 2003), 64–75; Marilyn Friedman, *Autonomy, Gender, Politics* (Oxford: Oxford University Press, 2003); and John Christman and Joel Anderson, eds., *Autonomy and the Challenges to Liberalism: New Essays* (Cambridge: Cambridge University Press, 2009). Nancy Yousef insightfully interprets autonomy in psychoanalytic terms and describes it as a development of both the literature and philosophy of the long eighteenth century. *Isolated Cases: The Anxieties of Autonomy in Enlightenment Philosophy and Romantic Literature* (Ithaca, N.Y.: Cornell University Press, 2004).

7. On the fluidity of the word sentiment, see R. F. Brissenden, *Virtue in Distress: Studies in the Novel of Sentiment from Richardson to Sade* (New York: Barnes and Noble Press, 1974); Erik Erametsa, *A Study of the Word "Sentimental" and of Other Linguistic Characteristics of Eighteenth-Century Sentimentalism in England* (Helsinki: Helsingen Liike Kinjapaino Oy, 1950); and Edith Birkhead, "Sentiment and Sensibility in the Eighteenth-Century Novel," in *Essays and Studies of the English Association*, vol. 11 (Oxford: Clarendon, 1925). As Brissenden indicates, in the middle of the eighteenth century, sentiment signified "opinion, thought, judgement, mind" (99). By the end of the century it came to approximate feeling or sensibility. He also observes that we can usefully distinguish between an earlier novel of sentiment and a later novel of sensibility. I agree with Brissenden that the decades from the 1770s to 1790s were dominated by the novel of sensibility. However, throughout the eighteenth century we have literary and philosophical works that endorse an understanding of sentiment as at once judgment and feeling. These are the works I focus on in this study.

8. David Hume, *A Treatise of Human Nature*, 2nd ed., ed. L. A. Selby-Bigge (1888; Oxford: Clarendon, 1978).

9. David Hume, "Of the Standard of Taste" in *Essays: Moral, Political, and Literary*, ed. Eugene F. Miller (Indianapolis: Liberty Classics, 1985), 234.

10. Samuel Richardson, *Clarissa; or, The History of a Young Lady*, ed. Angus Ross (Harmondsworth, U.K.: Penguin, 1985), 134.

11. Michael Frazer, "John Rawls: Between the Two Enlightenments," *Political Theory* 35, no. 6 (December 2007): 756–80.

12. As I explain in chapter 2, sentimentalism is productively brought into dialogue not only with Kantian aesthetics but also with late-twentieth-century rehabilitations of Kant's moral theory such as Jürgen Habermas's communicative ethics and John Rawls's and Christine Korsgaard's Kantian constructivism.

13. Hannah Arendt, "The Crisis in Culture," in *Between Past and Future* (New York, N.Y.: Viking, 1961), 221.

14. Hannah Arendt, *Lectures on Kant's Political Philosophy*, ed. Ronald Beiner (Chicago, Ill.: University of Chicago Press, 1992), 67.

15. Butler makes this argument in a wide-ranging theoretical project extending from *Gender Trouble* to her recent writings on ethics such as *Precarious Life* and *Giving an Account of Oneself*. See especially Judith Butler, *Gender Trouble: Feminism and the Subversion of Identity* (New York: 1990) and Seyla Benhabib, Judith Butler, Drucilla Cornell, and Nancy Fraser, *Feminist Contentions: A Philosophical Exchange*, ed. Linda Nicholson (New York: Routledge, 1995). For readings of Butler's social constructionism that emphasize its determinism, see Amanda Anderson, "Debatable Performances: Restaging Contentious Feminisms," *Social Text* 54 (1998): 1–24; Allison Weir, *Sacrificial Logics: Feminist Theory and the Critique of Identity* (New York: Routledge, 1996); and Seyla Benhabib, *Feminist Contentions* and *Situating the Self: Gender, Community, and Postmodernism in Contemporary Ethics* (New York: Routledge, 1992).

16. See, for example, Lynn Festa, *Sentimental Figures of Empire in Eighteenth-Century Britain and France* (Baltimore: Johns Hopkins University Press, 2006); Anne C. Vila, *Enlightenment and Pathology: Sensibility in the Literature and Medicine of Eighteenth-Century France* (Baltimore: Johns Hopkins University Press, 1997); Markman Ellis, *The Politics of Sensibility: Race, Gender, and Commerce in the Sentimental Novel* (Cambridge: Cambridge University Press, 1996); Anne Jesse Van Sant, *Eighteenth-Century Sensibility and the Novel: The Senses in Social Context* (Cambridge: Cambridge University Press, 1993); G. J. Barker-Benfield, *The Culture of Sensibility: Sex and Society in Eighteenth-Century Britain* (Chicago: University of Chicago Press, 1992); John Mullan, *Sentiment and Sociability: The Language of Feeling in the Eighteenth Century* (Oxford: Clarendon, 1988); and Janet Todd, *Sensibility: An Introduction* (London: Methuen, 1986).

17. Important texts by Foucault include "On the Genealogy of Ethics: An Overview of Work in Progress" and "The Ethics of the Concern for the Self as a Practice of Freedom" in *Essential Works of Foucault, 1954–1984*, vol. 1, ed. Paul Rabinow (New York: New Press, 1997); "Truth and Power" and "The Subject and

Power" in *Essential Works of Foucault*, vol. 2; *The History of Sexuality, Volume I: An Introduction*, trans. Robert Hurley (New York: Random House, 1978); *Discipline and Punish: The Birth of the Prison*, trans. Alan Sheridan (New York: Pantheon, 1977); *The Birth of the Clinic: An Archaeology of Medical Perception* (New York: Pantheon, 1973; and *Madness and Civilization: A History of Insanity in the Age of Reason*, trans. Richard Howard (New York: Random House, 1965).

18. Michel Foucault, "Nietzsche, Genealogy, History," in *Language, Counter-Memory, Practice*, ed. Donald F. Bouchard (Ithaca, N.Y.: Cornell University Press, 1980), 155–56.

1. RECONSTRUCTING SENTIMENTALISM

1. Henry Mackenzie, *Julia de Roubigné*, ed. Susan Manning (East Linton, Scotland: Tuckwell, 1999), 67.

2. Cato, in a famous exemplification of Stoic principles, cries at the death of the republic rather than the death of his son. For a discussion of Cato's symbolic significance within sentimentalism, see Julie Ellison, *Cato's Tears and the Making of Anglo-American Emotion* (Chicago: University of Chicago Press, 1999).

3. As is well known, the sentimentalists, beginning with Shaftesbury, identified enthusiasm as a species of religious fanaticism. See Anthony Ashley Cooper, third Earl of Shaftesbury, "A Letter Concerning Enthusiasm," in *Characteristics of Men, Manners, Opinions, Times*, ed. Lawrence E. Klein (1711; Cambridge: Cambridge University Press, 1999).

4. I take the phrase "the feelings of spectators" from D. D. Raphael, "The Impartial Spectator," in *Essays on Adam Smith*, ed. Andrew S. Skinner and Thomas Wilson (Oxford: Clarendon, 1975), 85.

5. Foucault, *Discipline and Punish*, 23.

6. Pierre Bourdieu, *Distinction: A Social Critique of the Judgment of Taste*, trans. Richard Nice (Cambridge, Mass.: Harvard University Press, 1984).

7. Foucault, "The Subject and Power," in *Essential Works of Foucault*, 3:331.

8. Butler, *Gender Trouble*, 2.

9. For an extended reading of Butler's recent writings on ethics, see my "Facing Ethics: Narrative and Recognition from George Eliot to Judith Butler," *Nineteenth-Century Contexts* 33, no. 5 (December 2011): 437–50.

10. Butler, *Giving an Account* (New York: Fordham University Press, 2005), 20.

11. Christman and Anderson, *Autonomy*, 4.

12. Benhabib et al., *Feminist Contentions*.

13. Ibid., 21.

14. Christman and Anderson, *Autonomy*, 3. Moral philosophers tend to distinguish between a narrower "moral autonomy," pivoting around the Kantian idea of self-legislation, and a broader "personal autonomy" that encompasses the reflective endorsement of choices beyond the moral domain. See also Nancy Yousef, *Isolated Cases*, for a discussion of the term's various significations.

15. Alisa L. Carse, "The Liberal Individual: A Metaphysical or Moral Embarrassment?," *NOÛS* 28, no. 2 (1994): 184–209.

16. Ibid., 191.

17. Frazer, "John Rawls."

18. Festa, *Sentimental Figures of Empire*, 4; and Ellis, *Politics of Sensibility*, 7.

19. Janet Todd, *Sensibility: An Introduction* (London: Methuen, 1986), 7. Following earlier critics such as R. F. Brissenden, Erik Erametsa, and Edith Birkhead, Todd acknowledges that the words *sentiment* and *sensibility* are productively distinguished. A sentiment, she notes, "is a moral reflection, a rational opinion usually about the rights and wrongs of human conduct." It also signifies "a thought, often an elevated one, influenced by emotion, a combining of heart with head or an emotional impulse leading to an opinion or a principle." Sensibility, on the other hand, came "to denote the faculty of feeling, the capacity for extremely refined emotion and a quickness to display compassion for suffering" (7). On Todd's account, "The novel of sentiment of the 1740s and 1750s praises a generous heart and often delays the narrative to philosophize about benevolence; the novel of sensibility, increasingly written from the 1760s onwards, differs slightly in emphasis since it honours above all the capacity for refined feeling. It stops the story to display this feeling in the characters and elicits it in the reader in its physical manifestations of tears and trembling" (8). Todd's readings of particular texts, however, downplay the difference between sentiment and sensibility, a difference that, I suggest, is important to maintain. More sympathetic histories of the sentimental novel include Brissenden, *Virtue in Distress*, and John K. Sheriff, *The Good-Natured Man: The Evolution of a Moral Ideal, 1660–1800* (University: University of Alabama Press, 1982).

20. Mullan, *Sentiment and Sociability*, 63, 68.

21. The relevant works by Hobbes and Mandeville, respectively, are Thomas Hobbes, *The Leviathan*, ed. Richard Tuck (1651; Cambridge: Cambridge University Press, 1996), and Bernard de Mandeville, *The Fable of the Bees; or, Private Vices, Public Benefits*, ed. Phillip Harth (1714, 1724; Harmondsworth, U.K.: Penguin, 1989).

22. Hobbes, *Leviathan*, chapter 12.

23. Mandeville, *Fable*, 81.

24. This trend begins with R. S. Crane, "Suggestions toward a Genealogy of the 'Man of Feeling,'" *ELH* 1 (December 1934): 205–30. For an important challenge to Crane's seminal essay, see Donald Greene, "Latitudinarianism and Sensibility: The Genealogy of the 'Man of Feeling' Reconsidered," *Modern Philology* 75, no. 2 (November 1977): 159–83.

25. In *Strange Fits of Passion: Epistemologies of the Emotions from Hume to Austen* (Stanford, Calif.: Stanford University Press, 1996), Adela Pinch also describes Hume as a theorist of sympathy rather than judgment, whose account of the passions in Book II of the *Treatise* jars with that of the moral agent of Book III. On Pinch's reading, the *Treatise* splits into two fundamentally different narratives about feelings: "On the one hand, it asserts that feelings are individual, and that philosophy itself as well as social and aesthetic experience depends on individuals who can rely on the

individual authenticity of their own emotional responsiveness. On the other hand, it also contends that feelings are transsubjective entities that pass between persons; that our feelings are always really someone else's; that it is passion that allows us to be persons, rather than the other way around" (19).

26. See also David Hume, *Enquiry Concerning the Principles of Morals* in *Enquiries Concerning Human Understanding and Concerning the Principles of Morals*, 3rd ed., ed. L. A. Selby-Bigge (Oxford: Clarendon, 1975).

27. D. D. Raphael, "The Impartial Spectator," 85.

28. As William Godwin puts it, "the most essential of those rights which constitute the peculiar sphere appropriate to each individual, and the right upon which every other depends as its basis, is the right of private judgement." *Enquiry Concerning Political Justice and Its Influence on Modern Morals and Happiness*, ed. Isaac Kramnick (1793–98; Harmondsworth, U.K.: Penguin, 1985), 200.

29. Michael Bell, *Sentimentalism, Ethics, and the Culture of Feeling* (Basingstoke, U.K.: Palgrave, 2000); Chris Jones, *Radical Sensibility: Literature and Ideas in the 1790s* (London, U.K.: Routledge, 1993); Patricia Meyer Spacks, *Desire and Truth: Functions of Plot in Eighteenth-Century English Novels* (Chicago: University of Chicago Press, 1990), and "Oscillations of Sensibility," *New Literary History* 25, no. 3 (Summer 1994): 505–20.

30. David Marshall, *The Frame of Art: Fictions of Aesthetic Experience, 1750–1815* (Baltimore: Johns Hopkins University Press, 2005), 6.

31. Ibid., 8. Marshall's treatment of the spectator is very different from Janet Todd's and Barbara Benedict's, two critics who accord great significance to spectatorial figures in sentimental writing. In *Sensibility*, for example, Todd describes the work of the sentimental novel as a "kind of pedagogy of seeing" (4). But "seeing," as Todd describes it, is important only as a register of the emotions or of the sympathetic spectator's capacity to feel for suffering humanity. Hence, the education in vision enabled by sentimental fiction has as its goal "clarifying when uncontrolled sobs or a single tear should be the rule, or when the inexpressible nature of the feeling should be stressed" (4). While Benedict, unlike Todd, attributes to sentimentalism an extensive interest in detachment—notably, aesthetic detachment—she interprets such detachment as jarring and problematic owing to sentimentalism's affective investments. "Literary sentimentalism," she suggests, "neutralizes it own philosophical premise of the virtue of individual response through the persistent retention of stylistic and structural conventions that induce and endorse readerly detachment." See Barbara Benedict, *Framing Feeling: Sentiment and Style in English Prose Fiction, 1745–1800* (New York: AMS, 1994), 9.

32. G. W. F. Hegel, *Elements of the Philosophy of Right*, ed. Allen H. Wood, trans. H. B. Nisbet, Cambridge Texts in the History of Political Thought, (Cambridge: Cambridge University Press, 1991), 24.

33. The relevant quote from Pythagoras, which Arendt cites in many of her writings, runs as follows: "Life . . . is like a festival; just as some come to the festival to compete, some to ply their trade, but the best people come as spectators [*theatai*],

so in life the slavish men go hunting for fame [*doxa*] or gain, the philosophers for truth." Quoted in *Lectures on Kant,* 55.

34. See, for example, Jürgen Habermas, *The Structural Transformation of the Public Sphere,* trans. Thomas Burger and Frederick Lawrence (Cambridge, Mass.: MIT Press, 1989), and Scott Black, "Social and Literary Form in the Spectator," *Eighteenth-Century Studies* 33 (1999): 21–42.

35. Influential exponents of ideal observer theory include Roderick Firth, "Ethical Absolutism and the Ideal Observer," *Philosophy and Phenomenological Research,* vol. 12, no. 3 (1952): 333–44, and Richard Brandt, "The Definition of 'Ideal Observer' Theory in Ethics," *Philosophy and Phenomenological Research* 15, no. 3 (1955): 407–13.

36. Joseph Addison and Richard Steele, *The Commerce of Everyday Life: Selections from* The Tatler *and* The Spectator, ed. Erin Mackie (Boston: Bedford, 1998), 89.

37. On this point, see Anthony Pollock, "Neutering Addison and Steele: Aesthetic Failure and the Spectatorial Public Sphere," *ELH* 74 (2007): 707–34.

38. Foucault, *Discipline and Punish,* 200.

39. Michel Foucault, "On the Genealogy of Ethics: An Overview of Work in Progress" and "The Ethics of the Concern for the Self as a Practice of Freedom" in *Essential Works of Foucault, 1954–1984,* vol. 1, ed. Paul Rabinow (New York: New Press, 1997). Foucault's move to articulate a more open-ended and neutral conception of power raises the question, however, of the critical import of power. As Peter Dews has argued, "A purely positive account of power would no longer be an account of power at all, but simply of the constitutive operation of social systems." Peter Dews, "Power and Subjectivity in Foucault," *New Left Review* I, 144 (March–April 19884): 72-95, 88.

40. One terminus of this suspicion of subject-centered perspectives is what Foucault himself called his "positivism." In *The Archaeology of Knowledge,* he observes, "To describe a group of statements not as the closed, plethoric totality of a meaning, but as an incomplete, fragmented figure; to describe a group of statements not with reference to the interiority of an intention, a thought, or a subject, but in accordance with the dispersion of an exteriority . . . is certainly not to uncover an interpretation, to discover a foundation, or to free constituent acts; nor is it to decide on a rationality, or to embrace a teleology. It is to establish what I am quite willing to call a positivity . . . If, by substituting the analysis of rarity for the search for totalities, the description of relations of exteriority for the theme of the transcendental foundation, the analysis of accumulations for the quest of the origin, one is a positivist, then I am quite happy to be one" (124).

41. Foucault, "Concern for the Self," 291.

42. Martin Jay, *Downcast Eyes: The Denigration of Vision in Twentieth-Century French Thought* (Berkeley: University of California Press, 1993).

43. Emanuel Levinas, *Ethics and Infinity: An Essay on Exteriority,* trans. Alphonso Lingis (Pittsburgh: Duquesne University Press, 1969), 86.

44. Hannah Arendt, *The Life of the Mind* (New York: Harcourt Brace Jovanovich, 1978), 15.

45. Christine M. Korsgaard, *The Sources of Normativity* (Cambridge: Cambridge University Press, 1996), 47.

2. SENTIMENTALISM AND THE DISCOURSES OF FREEDOM: THE AESTHETIC ANALOGY FROM HUME TO ARENDT

1. See, for example, Schneewind, *Invention of Autonomy*; and John Rawls, *Lectures on the History of Moral Philosophy*, ed. Barbara Herman (Cambridge, Mass.: Harvard University Press, 2000).

2. Korsgaard, *Sources of Normativity*, 2.

3. Frazer, "John Rawls."

4. Samuel Fleischacker, *A Third Concept of Liberty: Judgment and Freedom in Kant and Adam Smith* (Princeton, N.J.: Princeton University Press, 1999).

5. In an essay on Kant and Smith, Fleischacker notes, in passing, the interest of the connection to Arendt. See Samuel Fleischacker, "Philosophy in Moral Practice: Kant and Adam Smith," *Kant-Studien* 82, no. 3 (1991): 249–69. A comparison of Smith and Arendt is offered by Mitchell Aboulafia in *The Cosmopolitan Self: George Herbert Mead and Continental Philosophy* (Urbana: University of Illinois Press, 2001).

6. Highly theorized renunciations of theory, as in Terry Eagleton's recent *After Theory* (New York: Basic Books, 2003), bespeak the continued investment in theory.

7. See Amanda Anderson, *The Way We Argue Now*, and David Wayne Thomas, *Cultivating Victorians*.

8. To reconstruct her thoughts on judgment, commentators have relied on remarks scattered throughout her oeuvre and developed most fully in two essays from *Between Past and Future* (1968), "The Crisis in Culture" and "Truth and Politics," and in the posthumously published *Lectures on Kant's Political Philosophy* (delivered at the New School for Social Research in the Fall of 1970). Beiner's "Interpretive Essay" in the *Lectures* offers an extensive overview of the development of Arendt's thoughts on judgment and has functioned as the basis of all subsequent scholarly discussions of judgment in Arendt's work. Further complicating attempts to reconstruct Arendt's theory of judgment is the contention of scholars like Beiner and Richard Bernstein that Arendt's writings proffer two competing accounts, rather than one consistent understanding, of judgment. The first, found in her writings of the 1950s and 1960s, is described by Beiner and Bernstein as practice oriented—judgment from the standpoint of the *vita activa*. The later account, developed in the Kant lectures, and in the 1971 essay "Thinking and Moral Considerations" (a revised version of which is included in *The Life of the Mind*), delineates, by contrast, judgment from the standpoint of the *vita contemplativa*. While, as Bernstein and Beiner suggest, Arendt confusingly dissociates judgment from action in her later writings, she does

not move from an understanding of judgment *itself* as a kind of action, as Bernstein suggests when he describes judgment in the early writings as "a form of action—debate—which Arendt takes to be the essence of politics" (21). I argue that from her earliest to her last writings on judgment, Arendt consistently identifies judgment not as action but as a certain kind of spectatorship, closely paralleling Kant's claims on behalf of a judge-spectator in the third critique. See Hannah Arendt, *Between Past and Future: Eight Exercises in Political Thought* (1968; Harmondsworth, U.K.: Penguin, 1978). See also Beiner, "Interpretive Essay," *Lectures on Kant*; and *Political Judgment* (Chicago: University of Chicago Press, 1983); and Richard Bernstein, "Judging—The Actor and the Spectator," chap. 8 in *Philosophical Profiles: Essays in a Pragmatic Mode* (Cambridge: Polity, 1986).

9. See also Jennifer Nedelsky, "Judgment, Diversity, and Relational Autonomy," in *Judgment, Imagination, and Politics*; and Linda M. G. Zerilli, "We Feel Our Freedom: Imagination and Judgment in the Thought of Hannah Arendt," *Political Theory* 33, no. 2 (April 2005): 158–88, and *Feminism and the Abyss of Freedom* (Chicago: University of Chicago Press, 2005).

10. For Benhabib on Arendt, see *Situating the Self: Gender, Community, and Postmodernism in Contemporary Ethics* (New York: Routledge, 1992), and also the essays collected in *The Reluctant Modernism of Hannah Arendt* (Lanham: Rowman & Littlefield, 2003). Habermas has publicly acknowledged his indebtedness to Arendt and G. H. Mead as forerunners of his communicative ethics. He suggests that Arendt's writings on judgment constitute "a first approach to a concept of communicative rationality which is built into speech and action itself. From this point of view, Hannah Arendt's interpretation of Kant's *Kritik der Urteilskraft* reminds us of the interpretation which George Herbert Mead has offered for Kant's *Kritik der Praktischen Vernunft*. Both converge in the project of an ethics of communication which connects practical reason to the idea of a universal discourse." See Jürgen Habermas, "On the German-Jewish Heritage," *Telos* 44 (1980): 127–31. Elsewhere, however, Habermas is highly critical of several aspects of Arendt's reading of Kant, especially of the "classical distinction [she maintains] between theory and practice" and of her refusal to grant the status of "rational discourse" to "the process of reaching agreement about practical questions." "Hannah Arendt's Communications Concept of Power," *Social Research* 44 (1977): 3–24, 22–23. For a thoughtful defense of Arendt's position, see Dana R. Villa, "Thinking and Judging," in *The Judge and the Spectator: Hannah Arendt's Political Philosophy*, ed. J. J. Hermsen and Dana R. Villa (Leuven: Peeters, 1999).

11. Benhabib, *Situating the Self*, 134.

12. Arendt's work has not attracted the same kind of attention amongst literary scholars as it has in other humanistic disciplines, though this neglect may be short-lived. Her reading of Kant is cited approvingly by Gayatri Spivak in "Terror: A Speech After 9-11," *boundary* 2 31, no. 2 (2004): 81–111. Rei Terada has recently reconstructed a proto-deconstructive Arendt in "Thinking for Oneself: Realism and Defiance in Arendt," *ELH* 71 (2004): 839–65. Further, Judith Butler's

recent writings on ethics, including *Precarious Life* and *Giving An Account of Oneself*, take their inspiration in part from the work of the Arendtian feminist philosopher, Adriana Cavarero, and especially her *Relating Narratives: Storytelling and Selfhood*, trans. Paul A. Kottman (New York and London: Routlege, 2000). John McGowan, a literary critic, is an influential Arendt scholar but he has not explored the implications of her work for literary studies. For a reception history of Arendt's work in political and social theory, see McGowan and Calhoun's introduction to *Hannah Arendt and the Meaning of Politics*. As they indicate, "Much of the response to Arendt's work during her lifetime (if we exclude the Eichmann controversy) focused on her strict distinction between the political and the social, the public and the private. Since her death, commentators have been most fascinated . . . with her attempt to fashion a theory of political judgment." Craig Calhoun and John McGowan, *Hannah Arendt and The Meaning of Politics* (Minneapolis: University of Minnesota Press, 1997), 11.

13. See *Judgment, Imagination, and Politics: Themes from Kant and Arendt*, ed. Ronald Beiner and Jennifer Nedelsky (Lanham and Oxford: Rowman & Littlefield, 2001), vii.

14. Immanuel Kant, *Critique of the Power of Judgment*, trans. Paul Guyer and Eric Matthew, ed. Paul Guyer (Cambridge: Cambridge University Press, 2000), 66. Since the third critique is cited as the *Critique of Judgment* in much of the scholarship, including Arendt's writings, I will refer to it as such.

15. Immanuel Kant, *Groundwork of the Metaphysics of Morals*, trans. and ed. Mary Gregor, with an introduction by Christine M. Korsgaard (Cambridge: Cambridge University Press, 1997), 31.

16. Schneewind, *Invention of Autonomy*, 3.

17. Kant, *Critique of the Power of Judgment*, 122.

18. The singularity of the third critique has been interpreted by many Kant scholars as a virtue, since in this work Kant attempts to resolve the antinomy of nature and freedom produced by the first two critiques. See, for example, Luc Ferry, *Homo Aestheticus: The Invention of Taste in the Democratic Age*, trans. Robert Loaiza (Chicago: University of Chicago Press, 1993); and Anthony J. Cascardi, *Consequences of Enlightenment* (Cambridge: Cambridge University Press, 1999).

19. Cited in Beiner, "Interpretive Essay," *Lectures on Kant*, 141.

20. Hannah Arendt, "Truth and Politics," in *Between Past and Future: Eight Exercises in Political Thought* (1968; Harmondsworth, U.K.: Penguin, 1978), 241.

21. Arendt, "Understanding and Politics," *Partisan Review* 20 (1953): 377–92; 310. This essay is reprinted in *Essays in Understanding: 1930–1954 / Hannah Arendt*, ed. Jerome Kohn (New York: Harcourt, Brace, & Company, 1994). In her postscript to *Eichmann in Jerusalem* she notes how "troubled men of our time are by this question of judgment," and suggests that "the nature and function of human judgment" is "one of the central moral questions of all time." See Hannah Arendt, *Eichmann in Jerusalem: A Report on the Banality of Evil* (1963; Harmondswoth, U.K.: Penguin, 1994), 295, 294.

22. In his "Interpretive Essay," Beiner indicates that, according to Arendt's friend J. Glenn Gray, she understood the concept of judgment to be a special strength of her work. Gray had observed that "she regarded judging to be her particular strength and in a real sense a hoped-for resolution of the impasse to which reflections on willing seemed to lead her. As Kant's *Critique of Judgment* enabled him to break through some of the antinomies of the earlier critiques, so she hoped to resolve the perplexities of thinking and willing by pondering the nature of our capacity for judging." *Lectures on Kant*, 117.

23. In "Understanding and Politics," she observes that "Understanding, as distinguished from having correct information and scientific knowledge, is a complicated process which never produces unequivocal results. It is an unending activity by which, in constant change and variation, we come to terms with and reconcile ourselves to reality, that is, try to be at home in the world" (307–8). In *The Life of the Mind*, Arendt reformulates the distinction between understanding and knowledge as Kant's distinction between *Verstand* and *Vernunft*, or intellect and reason. The first enables a quest for truth, the second a quest for meaning (53–65).

24. Arendt's former student and best biographer, Elizabeth Young-Bruehl, characterizes the commitment to appearances as a form of *amor mundi*, or love of the world, to be contrasted with the *amor fati* of the philosophers. See Elizabeth Young-Bruehl, *Hannah Arendt: For Love of the World* (1982; New Haven, Conn.: Yale University Press, 2004).

25. Arendt, *Life of the Mind*, 215.

26. Philosophers like Charles Larmore, Martha Nussbaum, and Alasdair MacIntyre, who are sometimes grouped as theorists of virtue ethics, have argued that moral judgment is a characteristic motif not of modern but of ancient philosophy, and especially of Aristotle's ethics, which takes context-sensitive judgments to be an integral component of *phronesis* or practical wisdom. Larmore contends that judgment does not lend itself to the system building encouraged by the moderns, for which the natural sciences provide the requisite paradigm. Judgment, as he describes it, is the "faculty concerned with the appropriate application of general rules (which may be more or less schematic) to particular situations." Charles E. Larmore, *Patterns of Moral Complexity* (Cambridge: Cambridge University Press, 1987), 21. See also Alasdair MacIntyre, *After Virtue: A Study in Moral Theory* (Notre Dame, Indiana: University of Notre Dame Press, 1981); and Martha C. Nussbaum, *Love's Knowledge: Essays on Philosophy and Literature* (Oxford: Oxford University Press, 1990), and *The Fragility of Goodness: Luck and Ethics in Greek Tragedy and Philosophy* (Cambridge: Cambridge University Press, 1986). Nussbaum's more recent work, however, is more hospitable to Kant's moral philosophy than these earlier writings and she has recently questioned the interest of "virtue ethics" as a separable tradition of ethics. See Martha C. Nussbaum, "Virtue Ethics: A Misleading Category," *Journal of Ethics* 3 (1999): 163–201.

27. "Philosophy and Politics" was delivered as a lecture at Notre Dame in 1954; it was published posthumously in 1990. See Hannah Arendt, "Philosophy and

Politics," *Social Research* 57 (1990): 73–103. A helpful discussion of this essay is given in Frederick Dolan, "Arendt on Philosophy and Politics," in *The Cambridge Companion to Hannah Arendt*, ed. Dana Villa (Cambridge: Cambridge University Press, 2002), 261–76.

28. Arendt writes: "Plato clearly wrote the *Republic* to justify the notion that philosophers should become kings, not because they would enjoy politics, but because, first, this would mean that they would not be ruled by people worse than they were themselves and second, it would bring about in the commonwealth that absolute peace, that certainly constitutes the best condition for the life of the philosopher. Aristotle did not follow Plato, but even he held that the *bios politikos* in the last analysis was there for the sake of the *bios theoretikos*." *Lectures on Kant*, 21. Citing the Platonic tradition's denigration of politics, which is linked in turn to its hostility to the senses—that which binds the philosopher to the realm of human affairs—she observes: "This, of course, cannot be Kant's position, for his theoretical philosophy holds that all cognition depends on the interplay of sensibility and intellect, and his *Critique of Pure Reason* has rightly been called a justification, if not a glorification, of human sensibility." *Lectures on Kant*, 27.

29. Arendt, *Lectures on Kant*, 42. Arendt's argument about critical thinking lessens the force of Nancy Fraser's critique of the enlarged mentality as a kind of solipsistic thinking. In her contribution to the essays collected in *Hannah Arendt and the Meaning of Politics*, Fraser takes issue with the "representativeness" Arendt claims for judgment. Arendtian judgment, she argues, remains "a monological process wherein one goes visiting in imagination, as opposed to in reality. One imagines oneself judging from various different perspectives instead of going out and talking and listening to other people. One elaborates an interior, not an exterior, dialogue. In this way, one avoids the risk of hearing others judge in ways that one could not imagine oneself judging in their situation. As a result, one insulates oneself from the sort of provocation that could actually lead one to change one's perspective." Fraser, "Communication, Transformation, and Consciousness-Raising," in *Hannah Arendt and the Meaning of Politics*, ed. Craig Calhoun and John McGowan (Minneapolis: University of Minnesota Press, 1997), 171–72. Surely, making up one's mind for oneself requires, in the last instance, an "interior" rather than an exterior dialogue. At the same time, it seems to me that Arendt importantly links the two kinds of dialogue in her delineation of the impartial standpoint, the characteristic posture of the judge. For a more optimistic reading of the enlarged mentality in the same collection, see Lisa Disch's essay, "'Please Sit Down, but Don't Make Yourself at Home': Arendtian 'Visiting' and the Prefigurative Politics of Consciousness-Raising."

30. Anthony Cascardi seems to me to misinterpret Kant's "enlarged mentality" when he characterizes it as "feeling with" (36). From a perspective shaped by Derrida's reading of Kant in *The Truth in Painting*, Carcardi suggests that the postmodernist critique of the Enlightenment project is misplaced not because it is wrong but because "the Enlightenment" that emerges from Kant's third critique

fully anticipates the postmodernist critique of reason in the form of an "'aesthetic' critique of reason" (18). It does so by affirming aesthetic "indeterminacy" and "the validity of affective modes of apprehension" (3). Cascardi's reading of Kant's aesthetics contrasts with Arendt's. Arendt's Kant is interesting not because he affirms the validity of purely affective modes of apprehension but because he makes *judgment* important and judgment is not the same as empathy. According to Arendt, we cannot posit an aesthetic modernity over and against a political modernity. Anthony J. Cascardi, *Consequences of Enlightenment* (Cambridge: Cambridge University Press, 1999).

31. John Rawls, *Political Liberalism* (New York: Columbia University Press, 1993).

32. John Rawls, "Kantian Constructivism in Moral Theory," *Journal of Philosophy* 77, no. 9 (1980): 519.

33. Korsgaard, *Sources of Normativity*, 51. See also "The General Point of View: Love and Moral Approval in Hume's Ethics," in Christine M. Korsgaard, *The Constitution of Agency: Essays in Practical Reason and Moral Psychology* (Oxford: Oxford University Press, 2008).

34. Korsgaard, *Sources of Normativity*, 138.

35. Helpful accounts of moral sense theory include Thomas Fowler, *Shaftesbury and Hutcheson* (London: Sampson Low, Marston, Searle, and Livingston, 1882); D. D. Raphael, *The Moral Sense* (Oxford: Oxford University Press, 1947); Ernest Tuveson, "The Origins of the Moral Sense," *Huntington Library Quarterly* 11 (1947–48): 241–59; and Peter Kivy, *The Seventh Sense: A Study of Francis Hutcheson's Aesthetics and Its Influence in Eighteenth-Century Britain* (New York: Franklin, 1976).

36. Francis Hutcheson, *An Inquiry into the Original of Our Ideas of Beauty and Virtue*, ed. Wolgang Leidhold, *Collected Works of Francis Hutcheson* vol. 2 (Indianapolis, IN: Liberty Fund, 2004), 25. In *The Moralists*, Shaftesbury's Theocles also forwards an aesthetic analogy in order to assert the will-independence of moral judgments: "Is there then . . . a natural beauty of figures and is there not as natural a one of actions? No sooner the eye opens upon figures, the ear to sounds, than straight the beautiful results and grace and harmony are known and acknowledged. No sooner are actions viewed, no sooner the human affections and passions discerned (and they are most of them as soon discerned as felt) than straight away an inward eye distinguishes and see the fair and the shapely, the amiable and admirable, apart from the deformed, the foul, the odious or the despicable." Shaftesbury, *Characteristics*, 326.

37. My reading of Smith draws upon D. D. Raphael, "The Impartial Spectator," *Essays on Adam Smith*, ed. Andrew S. Skinner and Thomas Wilson (Oxford: Clarendon, 1975), and *The Impartial Spectator: Adam Smith's Moral Philosophy*; Knud Haakonssen, *The Science of a Legislator: The Natural Jurisprudence of David Hume and Adam Smith* (Cambridge: Cambridge University Press, 1989); Charles L. Griswold Jr., *Adam Smith and the Virtues of Enlightenment* (Cambridge: Cambridge University Press, 1999); and Fleischacker, *Third Concept of Liberty*.

38. For Hume on Hutcheson, see *Enquiry*, 201; for Smith, see *Theory*, 322–23.

39. For excellent surveys of the moral thought of the period, see Schneewind, *The Invention of Autonomy*, and Stephen Darwall, *The British Moralists and The Internal 'Ought': 1640–1740* (Cambridge: Cambridge University Press, 1995).

40. Frazer, "John Rawls," 758.

41. Ibid., 761.

42. Smith, *The Theory of Moral Sentiments*, ed. D. D. Raphael and A. L. Macfie, *The Glasgow Edition of the Works and Correspondence of Adam Smith* (Indianapolis: Liberty Fund, 1982), 110.

43. Charles Griswold suggests that *The Theory of Moral Sentiments* often reads like a novel: "narrative and analysis are interwoven throughout" (*Adam Smith and the Virtues of Enlightenment*, 59–60).

44. Smith's nuanced account of interpersonal dynamics serves to challenge criticisms of his work like Audrey Jaffe's in *Scenes of Sympathy: Identity and Representation in Victorian Fiction* (Ithaca, N.Y.: Cornell University Press, 2000). Jaffe finds not only the impartial standpoint but also spectatorship per se inherently problematic aspects of what she describes as Smith's "bourgeois liberalism." On Jaffe's interpretation, the Smithian subject claims to be a product of social influence but finds its identity through processes of spectatorship and representation that seek to displace the social: "Smith, imagining sympathy as a scene, tells us that self-construction is social: sympathy is always embodied. But in his illustrations, sympathy 'does away' with bodies in order to produce representations, replacing persons with mental pictures, generalized images of ease and of suffering" (11). Highlighting "the close relationship between identification and violent appropriation" (5), Jaffe identifies attempts to sympathize with others as always and only a form of domination. However, if, as Jaffe suggests, mental pictures violate the integrity of real bodies then it is unclear how social and moral life is at all possible. Also, her argument that representations fail to do justice to the reality of others mobilizes a problematic requirement of perfect correspondence, or an endorsement of transparent representations: the assumption here seems to be that if representations could perfectly correspond to their objects then they would lose their pernicious character (by being truthful to the objects of representation).

45. Sentimentalism's social theory of selfhood constitutes one of its most influential legacies to the human sciences. We can see the connections, for example, to such classics of modern sociology as Erving Goffman's *The Presentation of Self in Everyday Life*. In *The Cosmopolitan Self*, Mitchell Aboulafia makes a compelling case for Smith as a precursor of American pragmatists such as G. H. Mead.

46. Hume makes a similar argument in his discussion of reputation and the "love of fame." In the *Enquiry*, he writes: "By our continual and earnest pursuit of a character, a name, a reputation in the world, we bring our own deportment and conduct frequently in review, and consider how they appear in the eyes of those who approach and regard us. This constant habit of surveying ourselves, as it were,

in reflection, keeps alive all the sentiments of right and wrong, and begets, in noble natures, a certain reverence for themselves as well as others, which is the surest guardian of every virtue" (276).

47. Elliot's letter to Smith has not survived but the editors of the *Theory* reconstruct its gist as follows: "if conscience is a reflection of social attitudes, how can it ever differ from, or be thought superior to, popular opinion?" Editor's introduction, *Theory*, 16.

48. Hume, as Samuel Fleischacker suggests, may have been the most challenging of the British sentimentalists for Kant, waking him from his dogmatic slumbers (as Kant himself put it), but Smith was probably his favorite, as is suggested by Markus Herz's description of Smith as Kant's "Liebling" in a letter to Kant. Fleischacker, "Philosophy in Moral Practice."

49. See Immanuel Kant, *Critique of Practical Reason*, ed. and trans. Mary Gregor, Cambridge Texts in the History of Philosophy (Cambridge: Cambridge University Press, 1997), 133.

50. Marilyn Friedman, *Autonomy, Gender, Politics* (Oxford: Oxford University Press, 2003), 17.

51. Judith Butler, *The Psychic Life of Power: Theories in Subjection* (Stanford, Calif.: Stanford University Press, 1997), 15.

3. JUDGING CLARISSA'S HEART

1. Jean-Jacques Rousseau, *Politics and the Arts: Letter to M. D'Alembert on the Theatre*, trans. Allan Bloom (Ithaca, N.Y.: Cornell University Press, 1960), 51.

2. For Clarissa's reception in France, see Rita Goldberg, *Sex and Enlightenment: Women in Richardson and Diderot* (Cambridge: Cambridge University Press, 1984). For its reception in Germany, see David C. Hensley, "*Clarissa*, Coleridge, Kant, and Klopstock: Emotionalism as Pietistic Intertext in Anglo-German Romanticism," *Studies in the Literary Imagination* 28, no. 1 (1995): 125–47; and "Richardson, Rousseau, Kant: 'Mystics of Taste and Sentiment' and the Critical Philosophy," in *Cultural Interactions in the Romantic Age: Essays in Comparative Literature*, ed. Gregory Maertz (Albany: State University of New York Press, 1998).

3. Tom Keymer offers an insightful reading of the place of filial obedience in the conduct-book culture of the first half of the eighteenth century, a culture that Richardson himself did much to promote as a practitioner of the genre (in the early *Apprentice's Vade Mecum*) and as a publisher of conduct books. Drawing on manuals like William Fleetwood's *Relative Duties of Parents and Children, Husbands and Wives, Masters and Servants* (1705) and the *Fifteen Sermons upon Social Duties* (1744) by Richardson's friend, Patrick Delany, Keymer notes that "in the hierarchy they describe the father both maintains familial order and symbolises the political and divine authorities of the world beyond." *Richardson's* Clarissa *and the Eighteenth-Century Reader* (Cambridge: Cambridge University Press, 2004), 100.

4. Helpful studies exploring the religious contexts of Richardson's fiction include Leopold Damrosch, *God's Plots and Man's Stories: Studies in the Fictional Imagination from Milton to Fielding* (Chicago: University of Chicago Press, 1985); Cynthia Griffin Wolff, *Samuel Richardson and the Eighteenth-Century Puritan Character* (Hamden: Archon Books, 1972); and John A. Dussinger, "Conscience and the Pattern of Christian Perfection in *Clarissa*," *PMLA* (1966): 236–45. On the concept of a "dei-form" nature, see especially Michael B. Gill, *The British Moralists on Human Nature and the Birth of Secular Ethics* (Cambridge: Cambridge University Press, 2006). Gill argues that English belief of the early modern period can be divided into roughly two camps—on the one hand, Calvinist and Puritan skeptics of human motivation (who upheld the doctrine of universal sinfulness) and, on the other hand, Anglicans like the Cambridge Platonists and their heirs, the Latitudinarians. The two camps, Gill suggested, are differentiated by how they envision the relationship between God and the individual: "The Calvinists had drawn an ironclad distinction between wretched humanity and perfect God. God could not be found within the human soul because the human soul was wholly corrupt. God, therefore, had to come from without; He had to be external to the sinful human soul. Whichcote and Cudworth [the Cambridge Platonists], in contrast, brought God into every human soul. They believed that there was a sense in which God is present within each of us, a sense in which reconciliation with God is equivalent to a reconciliation with oneself. That is why we should look within—because within each of us is present God Himself" (29). Clarissa's figure of the judging heart looks to the writings, for example, of Benjamin Whichcote, who, as Gill notes, transforms God into a presence within the individual: "Reverence God in thyself: for God is more in the Mind of Man, than in any part of this world besides; for we (and we only here) are made after the image of God" (18).

5. The heart is one of the most complex figures in the Bible, as is noted by the editors of the *Dictionary of Biblical Imagery*: It denotes "such things as personality and the intellect, memory, emotion, desires, and will." It is variously the seat of desire, a synonym for mind, and symbolic of all "the intangibles that constitute what it means to be human." Leland Ryken, James C. Wilhoit, and Tremper Longman III, eds., *Dictionary of Biblical Imagery* (New York: IVP Academic, 1998). Richardson's language of the heart and its scriptural sources are the focus of chapter 5 of Robert A. Erickson's *The Language of the Heart, 1600–1750* (Philadelphia: University of Pennsylvania Press, 1997).

6. Dussinger, "Conscience," 238.

7. In *The Power of the Passive Self*, Scott Paul Gordon identifies Richardson as one of several writers who responded to Hobbes and Mandeville's selfishness thesis by representing agency through a "trope of passivity." On this trope, self-interested calculation is denied by figuring action as "effectively *un*motivated." For the proponents of passivity, according to Gordon, the "source of crucial behaviors" lies "not in the individual will but elsewhere—sometimes in another individual, usually in external nature or in God." As such, they construct a self "whose disinterestedness

is guaranteed by forces outside conscious control," a self that is "more formed than forming," "more passively prompted than actively choosing." *The Power of the Passive Self in English Literature, 1660–1740* (Cambridge: Cambridge University Press, 2002), 5.

8. The Book of Job, as many of Richardson's twentieth-century readers have observed, is the single most important biblical allusion in a novel replete with biblical allusions. It is summoned not only by implication, through the novel's metaphor of trials, but also more directly, by both Clarissa and Lovelace. Clarissa, for example, looks to Job's story for comfort in the meditations she composes after the rape, meditations that are meant to give her earthly fortunes meaning, shape, and closure. And it is as a female Job that Lovelace figures Clarissa when he justifies, to Belford, his role in her sufferings: "Satan, whom thou mayest, if thou wilt, in this case call my instigator, put the good man of old upon the severest trials. To his behaviour under these trials, that good man owed his honour and his future rewards. An innocent person, if doubted, must wish to be brought to a fair and candid trial" (430). Helpful commentaries on the role of the Book of Job in *Clarissa* include Tom Keymer, "Richardson's Meditations: Clarissa's *Clarissa*," in *Samuel Richardson: Tercentenary Essays*, ed. Margaret Anne Doody and Peter Sabor (Cambridge: Cambridge University Press, 1989), 89–109; and Jonathan Lamb, *The Rhetoric of Suffering: Reading the Book of Job in the Eighteenth Century* (Oxford: Clarendon, 1995). For a reading of *Clarissa* that describes it as a rewriting not of Job but of the Bible as a whole, see Erickson, *Language of the Heart*.

9. Writing to Belford about one of his and Clarissa's many altercations, he describes Clarissa's triumph over him as follows: "Her whole person was informed by her sentiments. She seemed taller than before. How the God within her exalted her, not only above me, but above herself" (853).

10. Many readers, from close personal friends like Lady Dorothy Bradshaigh and her sister, Lady Elizabeth Echlin, to the wider readership that waited breathlessly for the final installment of *Clarissa*, pleaded for a happy ending to its heroine's post-rape narrative. Some suggested marriage to a reformed Lovelace, others recommended the single life. Richardson chose death—or, as he put it in the postscript, the "triumphant death" of the Christian martyr or saint. Justifying his choice, Richardson wrote to Lady Bradshaigh that *Clarissa* was not meant to be read as a novel but that if his friends chose to read it as such, they must treat it as a "Religious Novel." In response to his friend's lament that Clarissa's death would "hurt my heart, and *durably*," Richardson argued that death represented the highest fate available to his heroine under the Christian dispensation. Her early death was "her consummating Perfection"; it signaled that this "Woman of Virtue, of Christian Virtue" had perfected her soul *in imitatio Christi* to the fullest point any Christian could. *Selected Letters of Samuel Richardson*, ed. John Carroll (Oxford: Clarendon, 1964), 96, 94.

11. Richardson's impatience with his readers in the postscript to *Clarissa* contrasts with his collaborative writing practices, with his habit of actively soliciting his friends' opinions on what he wrote as he wrote. In his letters he describes his readers

as the "Sovereign Judges" of his characters, and observes, with regard to *Sir Charles Grandison*, that "Many things are thrown out in the several Characters, on purpose to provoke friendly Debate; and perhaps as Trials of the Readers' Judgment, Manners, Taste, Capacity." Carroll, *Selected Letters*, 280, 315.

12. John Dussinger suggests that Richardson takes the *contemptus mundi* motif—at play in the postscript, for example—from ascetic Christianity, which had been revived in his own day by Puritan theologians like William Law. The motif was perhaps especially attractive to Richardson by the time he wrote his second novel because of the satire to which the eponymous heroine of his first novel, *Pamela*, was subjected—for example, by Fielding, who reprised her in *Shamela* as a heroine of calculating and manipulative worldliness. Readers have long argued, however, that *Clarissa's* privileging of the afterlife over this life jars with Richardson's commitment to a worldly education in virtue. As Cynthia Griffin Wolff suggests, the dying Clarissa "may well have found the key to her own individual identity . . . but she has hardly offered a solution to the problem of defining identity which would help anyone who wanted to remain in the world." *Samuel Richardson*, 168. Likewise, Carol Houlihan Flynn contends that "although Richardson presents Clarissa as a useful moral exemplar, the ultimate self-improver, he is really presenting his reader with an anguished saint, who lives and dies for herself alone, not for the good of others. *Samuel Richardson: A Man of Letters* (Princeton: Princeton University Press, 1982), 21.

13. Clearly one reason for stressing Clarissa's meekness and piety was Richardson's anxiety about the example his heroine offered to his female audience. This surfaces tellingly in his letters, especially to his neighbor's daughter, Frances Grainger. To the latter's suggestion that "at the Age of Twenty-one . . . a young Woman must know when she is in the Right, or she never will" Richardson counters "Wrong! Wrong! Egregiously wrong . . . ." Parental demands on filial obedience, he observes, should always be reasonable but it is ultimately parents rather than children who are the better judges of the reasonable: "I would have them [children] complied with in every reasonable request, only that parents should be the judges, not the children, of the fit and reasonable." Carroll, *Selected Letters*, 153.

14. Reporting on a letter she has written to Lovelace, in which she rejects his offer of protection on the grounds that he is a man who doesn't respect a woman's judgment, Clarissa indicates to Anna: "I have written; and to this effect: 'That I had never intended to write another line to a man who could take upon himself to reflect upon my sex and myself, for having thought fit to make use of my own judgement . . . [That] I value my freedom and independency too much, if my friends will but leave me to my own judgement, to give them up to a man so uncontrollable, and who shows me beforehand, what I have to expect from him were I in his power'" (289–90).

15. Important studies exploring gender and epistolarity include Mary Favret, *Romantic Correspondence: Women, Politics, and the Fiction of Letters* (Cambridge: Cambridge University Press, 2005); April Alliston, *Virtue's Faults: Correspondences*

in Eighteenth-Century British and French Women's Fiction (Stanford, Calif.: Stanford University Press, 1996); and Ruth Perry, *Women, Letters, and the Novel* (New York: AMS, 1980).

16. The "world's opinion," as Clarissa puts it elsewhere, can have only a secondary role to play in the drama of the individual conscience: "As to the *world*, and its *censures*, you know, my dear, that, however desirous I always was of a fair fame, yet I never thought it right to give more than a *second place* to the world's opinion" (1139).

17. Scott Paul Gordon argues that Clarissa is presented to us as a responsive rather than a responsible being, whose tears, like the tears with which we sympathetically respond to her plight, vindicate her (and us) as uncalculating or disinterested moral agents: "Richardson recognizes but avoids the threat of . . . Mandevillian (mis)reading by appealing to readers' *feelings* rather than their *judgment*. It is these tears, which readers sympathetically catch from Clarissa's, that testify to her disinterestedness and sincerity." *Power of the Passive Self*, 20.

18. Mullan, *Sentiment and Sociability*.

19. Puritanism, which encouraged such introspective written forms as the diary and the autobiography, is widely recognized to have exercised a formative influence on the early novel. See, for example, Leopold Damrosch, *God's Plots and Man's Stories*.

20. Wolff, *Samuel Richardson*, 21.

21. Mark Kinkead-Weekes, *Samuel Richardson: Dramatic Novelist* (Ithaca, N.Y.: Cornell University Press, 1973), 161.

22. Kinkead-Weekes, *Samuel Richardson*, 459. Clarissa seeks to be part of a moral community. To quote Kinkead-Weekes again: "In a situation where nearly all the other characters behave like blind engines roaring along the mono-rails of self-interest, we experience an awareness of the heart's disguises and self-partiality, and the need for a felt sense of moral community, the importance of relationship in Richardson's world" (162).

23. Formal realism, as Ian Watt describes it, is "the narrative embodiment of a premise that Defoe and Richardson accepted very literally, but which is implicit in the novel in general: the premise or primary convention, that the novel is a full and authentic report of human experience, and is therefore under an obligation to satisfy its reader with such details of the story as the individuality of the actors concerned, the particulars of the times and places of their action, details which are presented through a more largely referential use of language than is common in other literary forms." *Rise of the Novel*, 32. For a critique of the idea that realism is committed to representing detail for its own sake, see Shaw, *Narrating Reality*.

24. The fullest accounts of Richardson's earliest readers' responses to the novel's ending, including accounts of the alternative endings envisioned by Lady Bradshaigh and written by her sister, Lady Echlin, are given in Keymer, *Richardson's* Clarissa *and the Eighteenth-Century Reader*, and William Warner, *Reading Clarissa: The Struggles of Interpretation* (New Haven, Conn.: Yale University Press, 1979).

25. Lois E. Bueler's insightful reading of the iconography of Clarissa's coffin underscores its connections to the virtue ethics tradition. Lois E. Bueler, *Clarissa's Plots* (New York: Associated University Presses, 1994), 44–52.

26. Conscience, Arendt elaborates, is a product of consciousness, as is implied by the very word "con-science," which means "to know with and by myself." *Life of the Mind*, 418.

27. As Richardson's biographers have noted, he took his role as publisher very seriously, and invested enormous energy in the selection of material that he thought would be morally educative. See William M. Sale, Jr., *Samuel Richardson: Master Printer* (Ithaca, N.Y.: Cornell University Press, 1950); and T. C. Duncan Eaves and Ben D. Kimpel, *Samuel Richardson: A Biography* (Oxford: Oxford University Press, 1971).

28. A similar belief is attributed to the moralizing and unsympathetic Miss Rawlins, one of the women with whom Clarissa takes refuge at Hampstead.

29. Warner's study was the first of a cluster of theoretically informed studies of Richardson's novel to appear in the early eighties. Others included Terry Castle, *Clarissa's Ciphers: Meaning and Disruption in Richardson's* Clarissa (Ithaca, N.Y.: Cornell University Press, 1982); and Terry Eagleton, *The Rape of Clarissa: Writing, Sexuality and Class Struggle in Samuel Richardson* (Minneapolis: University of Minnesota Press, 1982).

30. Nancy Armstrong, *How Novels Think: The Limits of Individualism from 1710-1900* (New York: Columbia University Press, 2005) and *Desire and Domestic Fiction: A Political History of the Novel* (Oxford: Oxford University Press, 1987); and Deidre Shauna Lynch, *The Economy of Character: Novels, Market Culture, and the Business of Inner Meaning* (Chicago: University of Chicago Press, 1998).

31. Warner is not alone in viewing Clarissa as a moralistic and judgmental heroine. Kinkead-Weekes, for example, describes Clarissa as an "absolutist," and contrasts her idealism with Anna's more flexible "human norm" (163). Similarly, Flynn suggests that Clarissa lives "not in the world of appearances but in the world of eternal truths." By contrast, Anna inhabits "the real world where one marries or prosecutes her seducer" (24).

32. In "Rape and the Rise of the Novel," Frances Ferguson provocatively argues that what is "psychological" about the psychological novel, as begun by *Clarissa*, rests not in its ascription of psychological depth to its characters but in its delineation of an inevitable conflict between intention and reception: "The novel is psychological . . . not because it is about the plausibility of its characters but because it insists upon the importance of psychology as the ongoing possibility of the contradiction between what one must mean and what one wants to mean." "Rape and the Rise of the Novel," *Representations* 20 (Autumn 1987): 109.

33. Building on Samuel Johnson's argument that one reads *Clarissa* for the sentiment and not the story, Dorothy Van Ghent contends that Richardson's novel is more reactive than active. Indeed, it transforms plot into a multiplicity of reactions: "what happens in *Clarissa* lies not in the objective event but in a multitude

of subjective reactions. *The English Novel: Form and Function* (New York: Holt, Rinehart, and Winston, 1953), 43.

34. Keymer, *Richardson's* Clarissa, 88. On Keymer's reading, Richardson's novel exemplifies Bakhtin's concept of heteroglossia because "the single authorial voice is dissolved into a multitude of autonomous and coequal voices and consciousnesses, each marked by its own idiolect and informed by its own world view" (46). Keymer's study highlights the importance of the word "judgment" in Richardson's oeuvre, even describing Richardson's realism as "forensic" rather than "circumstantial" realism, more concerned with the hermeneutics of the courtroom than with "writing to the minute." Keymer, however, is primarily interested in judgment as the work of *Clarissa's* reader rather than its heroine.

35. Keymer, *Richardson's* Clarissa, xvii. In *Clarissa's Plots*, Lois Bueler also highlights the interest of casuistry as a context for Richardson's fiction. *Clarissa*, Bueler argues, should be read not through the controlling lens of the courtship plot of Restoration comedy but as a casuistical rewriting of such archetypal plots as the "tested woman" plot of Genesis, the obedience narrative of the Book of Job, and the prudence plot of Aristotelian virtue ethics. Casuistry, she explains, enjoins attention at once to "the energies, idiosyncrasies and complications of the lives of particular agents" and the rules "provided by well-enunciated ethical systems." *Clarissa's Plots* (London and Toronto: Associated University Presses, 1994), 17.

36. Amit Yahav-Brown, "Reasonableness and Domestic Fiction," *ELH* 73 (2006): 805–30. As Yahav-Brown indicates, Rawlsian constructivism privileges "criteria that agents construct through their preferences and actions, rather than ones that inhere objectively in the world." Richardson's Clarissa functions as a paradigm of reasonableness owing to her "predisposition not only to reason but also to include others' reasons in her deliberations—to present her preferences to the scrutiny of others and, often, to revise her choices in light of such engagement" (816).

37. Yahav-Brown locates Richardson's novel in broadly the same trajectory of Enlightenment thought as I do: As Michael Frazer has recently argued, Rawls's work owes more to the British sentimentalists, and especially to Hume and Smith, than he acknowledged in the *Theory of Justice*. Onora O' Neill makes another connection between Rawls and the philosophers and novelists of judgment I am considering in this study when she suggests that Rawls's quest for a postmetaphysical ethical understanding in *A Theory of Justice* and *Political Liberalism* builds on Arendt's interpretation of Kantian judgment in the *Lectures on Kant's Political Philosophy* (it is Arendt who, before Rawls and Habermas, explores the implications of Kant's understanding of Enlightenment as the "public use of one's reason"). Frazer, "John Rawls"; and Onora O' Neill, "The Public Use of Reason," in *Judgment, Imagination, and Politics: Themes from Kant and Arendt*, ed. Ronald Beiner and Jennifer Nedelsky (London: Rowman & Littlefield, 2001), 65–90.

38. Hannah Arendt, *Eichmann in Jerusalem: A Report on the Banality of Evil* (New York: Viking, 1963; Harmondsworth, U.K.: Penguin, 1977), 294, 295.

4. A SENTIMENTAL EDUCATION: ROUSSEAU TO GODWIN

1. Jean-Jacques Rousseau, *Julie; or, The New Heloise: Letters of Two Lovers Who Live in a Small Town at the Foot of the Alps*, trans. Philip Steward and Jean Vaché, *Collected Writings of Rousseau* vol. 6 (Hanover, N.H.: Dartmouth University Press, 1997).

2. Feminist political theorists have led the way in rehabilitating *Julie* as a central work of Rousseau's oeuvre. They include Susan Moller Okin, *Women in Western Political Thought* (Princeton, N.J.: Princeton University Press, 1979); Lisa Disch, "Claire Loves Julie: Reading the Story of Women's Friendship in *La Nouvelle Héloïse*," *Hypatia* 9, no. 3 (Summer 1994): 19–45; and Linda M. G. Zerilli, *Signifying Woman: Culture and Chaos in Rousseau, Burke, and Mill* (Ithaca, N.Y.: Cornell University Press, 1994). For *Julie*'s significance within British Romantic culture, see especially Nicola J. Watson, *Revolution and the Form of the British Novel 1790–1825: Intercepted Letters, Interrupted Seductions* (Oxford: Oxford University Press, 1994); and Peter Mortensen, "Rousseau's English Daughters: Female Desire and Male Guardianship in British Romantic Fiction," *English Studies* 4 (2002): 356–70.

3. Indeed, Kant's famous motto of Enlightenment appears to have been borrowed from *Julie*. It echoes Edward Bomston's injunction to St. Preux that he awaken from childhood: "Put an end to your childhood, friend, awaken. Do not turn your entire life over to a long slumber of reason" (429). Kant indicates: "Enlightenment is man's release from his self-incurred tutelage. Tutelage is man's inability to make use of his understanding without direction from another. Self-incurred is this tutelage when its cause lies not in lack of reason but in lack of resolution and courage to use it without direction from another. *Sapere aude!* 'Have courage to use your own reason!'—that is the motto of enlightenment." "What is Enlightenment?," in *Immanuel Kant: On History*, ed. and trans. Lewis White Beck (New York: Prentice Hall, 1963).

4. For comparisons of *Julie* and *Clarissa*, see Benjamin W. Wells, "Richardson and Rousseau," *Modern Language Notes* 11, no. 8 (December 1896): 225–32; Byron R. Wells, *Clarissa and La Nouvelle Héloïse: Dialectics of Struggle with Self and Others* (Ravenna: Longo Editore, 1985); and Marshall, *Frame of Art*, chap. 4.

5. He is, as many commentators have noted, clearly modeled upon his author, the philosopher who sought to educate man out of the corruptions of civilization and into true moral and political freedom. As such, he is distinguished from the historical Abelard, the other prototype summoned by the novel's title of *Julie; or, The New Heloise*, who became known to posterity for his unhappy love more than for his scholarship.

6. For a reception history of *Julie* in Britain, see James H. Warner, "Eighteenth-Century English Reactions to the *Nouvelle Héloïse*, *PMLA* 52, no. 3 (September 1937): 803–19.

7. Mary Wollstonecraft, *A Vindication of the Rights of Woman* in *A Vindication of the Rights of Men and A Vindication of the Rights of Woman*, ed. Sylvana Tomaselli,

Cambridge Texts in the History of Political Thought (Cambridge: Cambridge University Press, 2005), 144.

8. William Godwin, *Fleetwood; or, the New Man of Feeling*, ed. Gary Handwerk and A. A. Markley (Peterborough, Ontario: Broadview, 2001).

9. On Hume and Rousseau's relationship, see, for example, Robert Zaretsky and John T. Scott, *The Philosophers' Quarrel: Rousseau, Hume, and the Limits of Human Understanding* (New Haven, Conn.: Yale University Press, 2010).

10. Wollstonecraft also criticizes Rousseau's norm of nature in *Vindication of the Rights of Woman*: "Rousseau declares that a woman should never, for a moment, feel herself independent, that she should be governed by fear to exercise her natural cunning, and made a coquettish slave in order to render her a more alluring object of desire, a sweeter companion to man, whenever he chooses to relax himself. He carries the arguments, which he pretends to draw from the indications of nature, still further, and insinuates that truth and fortitude, the cornerstones of all human virtue, should be cultivated with certain restrictions, because, with respect to the female character, obedience is the grand lesson which ought to be impressed with unrelenting rigour" (94–95).

11. Hume's suggestion comes in the midst of his defense of the "artificial" sense of justice, which he takes to be the product of custom and education rather than innate.

12. Mary Wollstonecraft, *Mary: A Fiction*, in *Mary; and, The Wrongs of Woman*, ed. Gary Kelly (Oxford: Oxford University Press, 2007).

13. Susan Manning, introduction to *Julia de Roubigné*, xix.

14. See, for example, Maurice Cranston, *The Noble Savage: Jean-Jacques Rousseau, 1754–1762* (Chicago: University of Chicago Press, 1999).

15. On this point, see Okin, *Women in Western Political Thought*; and Disch, "Claire Loves Julie."

16. For an account of Plato's importance to Rousseau's mature political thought, see Allan Bloom's introduction to *Emile*.

17. For a reading of *Julia* as a revision of *Julie*, see Kim Ian Michasiw, "Imitation and Ideology: Henry Mackenzie's Rousseau," *Eighteenth-Century Fiction* 5, no. 2 (January 1993): 1–24.

18. This parallel is explored in Ellis, *The Politics of Sensibility*.

19. Henry Mackenzie, *Lounger* 20, in *The Works of Henry Mackenzie*, vol. 5 (Edinburgh: J. Ballantyne; London: T. Cadell and W. Davies, 1808). Likewise, in his "Account of the German Theatre," a paper presented to the Royal Society of Edinburgh, Mackenzie worries about the potentially dangerous effects of Schiller's much-loved play *The Robbers*: "The energy of this tragedy's effect is not to be wondered at, especially on young minds, whose imaginations are readily inflamed by the enthusiasm of gigantic enterprise and desperate valour, whose sensibility is easily excited by the sufferings of a great unhappy mind, and who feel a sort of dignity and pride in leaving the beaten road of worldly prudence, though the path by which they leave it may sometimes deviate from moral rectitude." Indeed, upon reading

his enthusiastic reconstruction of the plot, one gets the impression that the Scottish Addison has half a mind to reactivate the failed coup of the scholars at "Fribourg" who wanted to imitate Schiller's characters but were stopped, tragicomically, from doing so. Henry Mackenzie, "Account of German Theatre," *Transactions of the Royal Society of Edinburgh*, vol. 2 (1790): 154–92.

20. Samuel Johnson, *Rambler* 4 (1750), in *The Collected Works of Samuel Johnson*, vol. 1, *The Rambler* (Troy, N.Y.: Pafraets, 1903).

21. Wollstonecraft's stance toward the eighteenth century's culture of sentiment has been the subject of much recent discussion, with a new generation of feminist critics complicating an earlier feminism's puzzlement at the harsh rhetoric that sometimes attends Wollstonecraft's discussion of sensibility. It is certainly the case that feeling appears subordinated to reason in the ideal of marriage Wollstonecraft develops in *Vindication of the Rights of Woman* (100)—which sounds a great deal like Julie and Wolmar's passionless union in *Julie*. More ambiguous is Wollstonecraft's developmental account of selfhood in both *Vindications*, which suggests, at times, that fancy, imagination, and feeling should give way to reason and judgment in a unilateral development. Several scholars have argued, however, that sense and sensibility are carefully interwoven by Wollstonecraft at various points in her non-fictional prose, and more consistently still, in her novels. On Wollstonecraft's treatment of sensibility, see especially Barbara Taylor, *Mary Wollstonecraft and the Feminist Imagination* (Cambridge: Cambridge University Press, 2003); Catriona Mackenzie, "Reason and Sensibility: The Ideal of Women's Self-Governance in the Writings of Mary Wollstonecraft," *Hypatia* 8, no. 4 (fall 1993): 35–55; Virginia Sapiro, *A Vindication of Political Virtue: The Political Theory of Mary Wollstonecraft* (Chicago: University of Chicago Press, 1992); and Mary Poovey, *The Proper Lady and the Woman Writer: Ideology as Style in the Writings of Mary Wollstonecraft, Mary Shelley, and Jane Austen* (Chicago: University of Chicago Press, 1985).

22. Walter Scott, "Henry Mackenzie," in *Lives of the British Novelists*, vol. 1, in Iaon Williams, *Sir Walter Scott on Novelists and Fiction* (London: Routledge & Kegan Paul, 1968), 77.

23. These changes are indicated in the editor's notes to William Godwin, *Enquiry Concerning Political Justice and Its Influence on Modern Morals and Happiness*, 57–58.

24. Pamela Clemit, Maurice Hindle, and Mark Philp, eds. *The Collected Novels and Memoirs of William Godwin* (London: Pickering and Chatto, 1992), 1:54.

25. See Mark Philp, "Rational Religion and Political Radicalism in the 1790s," *Enlightenment and Dissent* 4 (1985): 35–46, and *Godwin's Political Justice* (Ithaca, N.Y.: Cornell University Press, 1986); Ralph Bellamy, "Godwin and the Development of 'The New Man of Feeling,'" *History of Political Thought* 6, no. 3 (Winter 1985): 411–32; Gary Handwerk, "Mapping Misogyny: Godwin's *Fleetwood* and the Staging of Rousseauvian Education," *Studies in Romanticism* 41 (Fall 2002): 375–98; Rowland Weston, "Politics, Passion, and the 'Puritan Temper': Godwin's Critique of Enlightened Modernity," *Studies in Romanticism* 41 (Fall 2002): 445–70; Louise Joy, "St. Leon and the Culture of the Heart," *History of European Ideas* 33 (2007):

40–53. An early argument about the importance of sentimentalism to Godwin's thought is made by B. Sprague Allen, "William Godwin as Sentimentalist," *PMLA* 33, no. 1 (1918): 1–29.

26. Wollstonecraft, *Mary*, 62.

27. William Godwin, *The Enquirer: Reflections on Education, Manners, and Literature* (New York: G. G. and J. Robinson, 1797).

28. Godwin, *Fleetwood*, 232. Smith's influence is also palpable in Godwin's *Enquirer*, in passages such as the following: "One of the best practical rules of morality that ever was delivered, is that of putting ourselves in the place of another, before we act or decide any thing respecting him. The first impulse of every human being, is, to regard a different conduct with impatience and resentment, and to ascribe it, when pursued by our neighbour, to a willful perverseness, choosing, with open eyes and an enlightened judgment, the proceeding least compatible with reason. The most effectual method for avoiding this misinterpretation of our neighbour's conduct, is to put ourselves in his place, to recollect his former habits and prejudices, and to conjure up in our minds the allurements, the impulses and the difficulties to which he was subject" (436).

5. JUDGMENT, PROPRIETY, AND THE CRITIQUE OF SENSIBILITY: THE "SENTIMENTAL" JANE AUSTEN

1. Henry Austen, "Biographical Notice of the Author," appended to the posthumously published *Persuasion* and *Northanger Abbey*, and reprinted in Jane Austen, *Persuasion*, ed. James Kinsley (Oxford: Oxford University Press, 2004), 6–7.

2. James Edward Austen-Leigh, *Memoir of Jane Austen*, ed. R. W. Chapman (Oxford: Clarendon, 1926), 89.

3. B. C. Southam credits Austen also with a dramatic spoof of *Grandison*, attributed by the Austen family records to Jane Austen's niece.

4. Jane Austen, *Northanger Abbey, Lady Susan, The Watsons, and Sanditon*, ed. James Kinsley and John Davie (Oxford: Oxford University Press, 2003), 327.

5. In his well-known review of *Emma*, Scott described Austen's novels as a new kind of fiction representing "the art of copying from nature as she really exists in the common walks of life." He contrasts it with "those pictures of romantic affection and sensibility, which were formerly as certain attributes of fictitious characters as they are of rare occurrence among those who actually live and die." *Sir Walter Scott on Novelists and Fiction*, ed. Ioan Williams (London: Routledge, 2010), 230.

6. Watt, *Rise of the Novel*, 290. Watt accords Austen a very prominent place in his history of the novel. On his reading, she reconciles Richardson's "subjectivism" and Fielding's "objectivism"—the former's focus on the individual and subjective perception with the latter's on society and its rules. Austen, he argues, preserves "much of Defoe's and Richardson's psychological closeness to the subjective world of characters" but follows Fielding "in adopting a more detached attitude to [her] narrative material, and in evaluating it from a comic and objective point of view.

It is here that Jane Austen's technical genius manifests itself. She dispensed with the participating narrator, whether as author of a memoir as in Defoe, or as letter-writer as in Richardson, probably because both of these roles make freedom to comment and evaluate more difficult to arrange; instead she told her stories after Fielding's manner, as a confessed author" (296–7).

7. Marilyn Butler, *Jane Austen and the War of Ideas* (Oxford: Clarendon, 1975).

8. Jane Austen, *Selected Letters*, ed. Vivien Jones (Oxford: Oxford University Press, 2004), 176.

9. Margaret Kirkham, for example, reads Austen's politics in the context of the progressive rational feminism of her time, as developed especially by Mary Wollstonecraft. Claudia Johnson is primarily interested in linking Austen's novels with the writings of noncanonical women writers of her time, though Johnson does observe that "sensibility" is far more unstable an ideological register than Butler allows: the discourse of sensibility had itself become conservative in the 1790s, owing above all to Burke's instantiation of it in *Reflections on the Revolution in France*. Claudia L. Johnson, *Jane Austen: Women, Politics, and the Novel* (Chicago: University of Chicago Press, 1988); Margaret Kirkham, *Jane Austen, Feminism, and Fiction* (Brighton, U.K.: Harvester, 1983); Susan Morgan, *In the Meantime: Character and Perception in Jane Austen's Fiction* (Chicago: University of Chicago Press, 1980); and Julia Prewitt Brown, *Jane Austen's Novels: Social Change and Literary Form* (Cambridge, Mass.: Harvard University Press, 1979).

10. Austen, Knox-Shaw argues, was a direct heir of a British Enlightenment dominated by Scottish philosophers who were by no means the starry-eyed adherents to sensibility that Butler takes them to be. Against Butler's understanding of senti-mental culture as predominantly affective, Knox-Shaw reminds us that "Hobbes and Mandeville, though spurned by Rousseau and his followers, were an important presence in this latter-day phase of the British Enlightenment, which was, in effect, an inspired synthesis of the old empirically derived philosophies of self-interest with the social ethics of sympathy that succeeded them." *Jane Austen and the Enlightenment* (Cambridge: Cambridge University Press, 2004), 48. Austen's satire of sensibility, on this account, must be read against the backdrop of the later British Enlightenment's skepticism regarding "the intuitive morality of the Shaftesbury school" (47) and its commitment to debunking "that form of moral heroism known as enthusiasm" (48). Like Hume and Smith, Austen—on Knox-Shaw's wide-ranging revaluation of the intellectual history of the period—was an empirically minded observer of human nature, who laughed at human limitations not because she was a conservative but in order to warn against moral certitudes and closed-mindedness.

11. Further, only Hume's epistemology fits under the rubric of philosophical skepticism. His moral and political theory, like that of other sentimentalists such as Adam Smith, Francis Hutcheson, and Shaftesbury, is not a variant of skepticism since it makes a distinction between moral principles (the concern of sentimentalists) and moral facts (the focus of skeptics). On this point, see, for example, Korsgaard, *Sources of Normativity*, 13–14.

12. Clara Tuite, *Romantic Austen: Sexual Politics and the Literary Canon* (Cambridge: Cambridge University Press, 2002), 85.

13. *Julia de Roubigné*, Butler argues, owes its tragic denouement to the main characters' undue reliance "on conventions, or their own rationalizations, rather than upon the truth of instinct" (27); "they allow sophisticated, 'unnatural' ideas like gratitude or duty or honour to prevail over the truth of their sensations" (28).

14. Butler, *Jane Austen*, 196. In her reading of *Sense and Sensibility*, Butler suggests that "Marianne, and to some extent also Elinor, are drawn with strong feelings which the reader is accustomed to sympathize with, and to value for their own sake. But it is the argument of the novel that such feelings, like the individuals who experience them, are not innately good." *Jane Austen and the War of Ideas*, 196. In *Romantics, Rebels, and Reactionaries*, she argues that Austen is fearful of the doctrine of sensibility because of its radical individualism, because it implies a commitment to one's own instincts, feelings, and intuitions: "To trust as she does in her own heart is too individualistic a philosophy for society, and too individualistic even for Marianne's own good, for she cannot really depend upon her intuitions. Sensibility, one of the typically human-centered concerns of the previous expansive era, is now in the reactionary period identified as egotistical, solipsistic and potentially anarchic" (103–4).

15. Mary Poovey, *The Proper Lady and the Woman Writer* (Chicago: University of Chicago Press, 1984).

16. David Kaufmann, "Law and Propriety, *Sense and Sensibility*: Austen on the Cusp of Modernity," *ELH* 2 (summer 1992): 385–408.

17. Knox-Shaw, *Jane Austen and the Enlightenment*, 48.

18. Claudia L. Johnson, "The 'Twilight of Probability': Uncertainty and Hope in *Sense and Sensibility*," *Philological Quarterly* 62 (1983): 171–86.

19. See also Gilbert Ryle's reading of Austen's "vintner's" worldview and technique. Connecting it with Shaftesbury's ethics and aesthetics, Ryle argues that in the world of a Jane Austen novel there are no absolutes, only variations on a theme. "Jane Austen and the Moralists," in *Critical Essays on Jane Austen*, ed. B. C. Southam (London: Routledge & Kegan Paul, 1970).

20. Jane Austen, *Persuasion*, ed. James Kinsley (Oxford: Oxford University Press, 2004), 189.

21. Jane Austen, *Sense and Sensibility*, ed. James Kinsley (Oxford: Oxford University Press, 2004).

22. Marvin Mudrick, *Jane Austen: Irony as Defense and Discovery* (Berkeley: University of California Press, 1974), 91.

23. Marilyn Butler, *Romantics, Rebels, and Reactionaries: English Literature and Its Background, 1760–1830* (Oxford: Oxford University Press, 1981), 100, 99.

24. Marianne, according to Gilbert and Gubar, is the first of Austen's "lively heroines"—the precursor of Catherine Morland, Elizabeth Bennet, and Emma Woodhouse—who must learn to renounce such "tempting forms of self-definition" as "assertion, imagination and wit" and to subscribe instead to the

properly feminine lessons of "modesty, reticence, and patience." Sandra Gilbert and Susan Gubar, *The Madwoman in the Attic* (New Haven, Conn.: Yale University Press, 1979), 162. Through Marianne's narrative, Mary Poovey argues, Austen subscribes to conventional wisdom regarding disruptive female desire and the belief that "propriety must restrain this natural, amoral force." *The Proper Lady and the Woman Writer*, 190. She also suggests that for Austen, "to take Marianne's passions and longings seriously on their own terms would be to call into question the basis of Christian moral authority, the social order that ideally institutionalizes that authority, and, finally, the capacity of orthodox religion or society to gratify imaginative desires" (188).

25. Eve Kosofsky Sedgwick, "Jane Austen and the Masturbating Girl," *Critical Inquiry* 17, no. 4 (summer 1991): 818–37.

26. Edmund Burke, *Reflections on the Revolution in France*, ed. J. C. D. Clark (Stanford, Calif.: Stanford University Press, 2001), 241. All page numbers refer to this edition and are indicated parenthetically.

27. Claudia L. Johnson, *Equivocal Beings: Gender, Politics, and Sentimentality in the 1790s* (Chicago: University of Chicago Press, 1995).

28. Even *The Anti-Jacobin*, the periodical that, according to Butler, significantly framed the terms of the debate in "the war of ideas" of the 1790s, defends an "old-fashioned" morality defined by its opposition to judgment; its prospectus condemns "the modern refinement of referring in all considerations upon human conduct, not to any settled and preconceived principles of right and wrong, not to any general and fundamental rules which experience, and wisdom, and justice, and the common consent of mankind have established, but to the internal admonitions of every man's judgment or conscience in his own particular instance" (qtd. in *Jane Austen and the War of Ideas*, 159).

29. In *Vindication of the Rights of Woman*, Wollstonecraft challenges the male pedagogues who enjoin women to cultivate sensibility at the expense of sense: "Their senses are inflamed, and their understandings neglected, consequently they become the prey of their senses, delicately termed sensibility, and are blown about by every momentary gust of feeling" (136).

30. Kaufmann, "Law and Propriety," 399.

31. Several scholars have recently argued that Austen resembles the ancients more than the moderns and have turned especially to the Aristotelian virtue ethics tradition as a context for her ethical understanding. See, for example, Sarah Baxter Emsley, *Jane Austen's Philosophy of the Virtues* (New York: Palgrave, 2005); and David Gallop, "Jane Austen and the Aristotelian Ethic," *Philosophy and Literature* 23, no. 1 (1999): 96–109.

32. The sentimentalists' concern with civility predates Hume's and can be traced back to seminal figures like Shaftesbury. See, for example, Lawrence E. Klein, *Shaftesbury and the Culture of Politeness: Moral Discourse and Cultural Politics in Early Eighteenth-Century England* (Cambridge: Cambridge University Press, 1994).

33 Morgan, *In the Meantime*, 119.

34. Tony Tanner, *Jane Austen* (Cambridge, Mass.: Harvard University Press, 1981), 95.

35. Arendt, *Lectures on Kant's Political Philosophy*, 67.

36. Austen-Leigh, *Memoir of Jane Austen*, 101–2.

37. Henry James, *French Writers, Other European Writers, the Prefaces to the New York Editions*, ed. Leon Edel and Mark Wilson (New York: Library of America, 1984), 118.

38. René Descartes, *Meditations on First Philosophy, with Selections from the Objections and Replies*, ed. and trans. John Cottingham, rev. ed. (Cambridge: Cambridge University Press, 1996), 24.

39. Hannah Arendt, *The Human Condition* (Chicago: University of Chicago Press, 1958), 38.

40. Seyla Benhabib, *The Reluctant Modernism of Hannah Arendt* (Thousand Oaks, Calif.: Sage Publications, 1996). On Arendt's concept of the social, see also Hannah Fenichal Pitkin, "Conformism, Housekeeping, and the Attack of the Blob: The Origins of Hannah Arendt's Concept of the Social," in *Feminist Interpretations of Hannah Arendt*, ed. Bonnie Honig (University Park: Pennsylvania State University Press, 1995).

41. Benhabib, *Situating the Self*, 105.

42. Hannah Arendt, *Rahel Varnhagen: The Life of a Jewish Woman*, trans. Richard and Clara Winston, rev. ed. (New York: Harcourt Brace Jovanovich, 1974).

43. Seyla Benhabib, "The Pariah and her Shadow: Hannah Arendt's Biography of Rahel Varnhagen," in *Feminist Interpretations of Hannah Arendt*, 96.

44. Ibid., 94.

45. Ibid., 100.

INDEX

aesthetic judgment, 2–3, 5–6, 31–32.
  See also reflective judgment
Arendt, Hannah, on, 3–6, 30–32,
    38–39, 41–48, 79–80, 136
Austen, Jane, 122, 134–36
Hume, David, on, 2–3, 5–6, 22–23,
    29–30, 48–52
Kant, Immanuel, on, 3, 13, 30–32,
    40–42, 80
objectivity of, 2, 30, 41, 46, 49–51
aesthetics, politics and, 42–43
Arendt, Hannah
  aesthetic judgment (reflective
    judgment), 3–6, 30–32, 38–39,
    41–48, 79–80, 136
  Arendtian judgment, 3–6, 30–32,
    38–39, 41–48, 79–80, 136
  Aristotle and, 31, 43
  Benhabib, Seyla, and, 39, 47–48, 145
  conscience, 71
  critical thinking, 44–45, 144
  determinant judgment, 41
  empathy, 46
  enlarged mentality, 16, 30–32,
    46, 144
  on evil, 79–80
  Habermas, Jürgen, on, 155
  The Human Condition, 144–45
  impartiality, 4, 30, 45–46
  intersubjectivity, 4, 30, 45
  Lectures on Kant's Political Philosophy,
    5, 30–32, 42–46
  The Life of the Mind, 35, 43
  modernity and, 39

on Plato and Socrates, 32, 43–44, 46,
    71, 144
  rise of the social, 144–45
Aristotle
  Arendt, Hannah, and, 31, 43
  Austen, Jane, and, 174
  judgment and, 43, 157
Austen, Jane, 2. See also *Sense and
    Sensibility* (Austen)
  Arendt, Hannah, and, 122, 134–36,
    144–46
  Burke, Edmund, and, 120, 124–27
  Descartes, René, and, 143–44
  drawing-room symbolism of, 4, 138–46
  education and, 9, 124, 138
  judgment, 9, 119–22, 125, 129–37
  manners, 120–21, 123–32
  Richardson and, 116–19, 122–23
  as satirist, 116–17, 135, 138–39
  Scott, Sir Walter, on, 116
  sensibility, treatment of, 8–9, 116, 119,
    121–23, 131–38, 142–43
  sentimentalism and, 8–9, 116–46
  Watt, Ian, on, 117
autonomy, 1–2, 4–7, 9, 13–17, 34–38,
    47–48, 54–58, 80, 82, 96,
    128–29, 136
  Benhabib, Seyla, on, 15–16, 39, 47–48
  Butler, Judith, on, 14–15
  feminism and, 15–16, 39, 47–48, 56–57
  Foucault, Michel, on, 13–15, 33–35
  heteronomy and, 16, 56–57
  Kant, Immanuel, on, 2, 5–6, 37, 40–41,
    55–56